THE REMINISCENCES

of

ADMIRAL ROBERT LEE DENNISON

U. S. Navy (Retired)

U. S. Naval Institute
Annapolis, Maryland

August, 1975

Preface

This volume contains the transcript of eleven taped interviews with Admiral Robert Lee Dennison, USN (ret.). They were obtained by John T. Mason, Jr. for the U. S. Naval Institute and all were held in the Washington Offices of the Copley Newspapers, beginning in November, 1972 and running through July, 1973.

Some corrections were made to the original transcript by Admiral Dennison. The entire MS has been re-typed and an index has been added for convenience.

The scholar and researcher will find here the record of a truly great naval career, a career that was always dedicated to the objective of command. Even so, some unusual variants along the way color the story. Rather early in his career, the Admiral seized an opportunity to earn a PhD in Engineering from Johns Hopkins University; while working with the Joint War Plans Committee of the Joint Chiefs of Staff in World War II he specialized in Politico-Military Affairs and these interests bore fruit in the creation of a special office, Assistant Chief of Naval Operations for Politico-Military Affairs; he served for five years as Naval Aide (and friend) to President Harry S. Truman; and finally we see the full exercise of command as it reached an apotheosis in the Cuban Missile Crisis.

John T. Mason
Director of Oral History
U. S. Naval Institute.

BRIEF BIOGRAPHICAL SKETCH
ON
ADMIRAL ROBERT LEE DENNISON, U. S. NAVY, RETIRED

FAMILY

Admiral Robert Lee Dennison was born in Warren, Pennsylvania, on 13 April 1901, son of Ludo W. and Florence (Lee) Dennison. In 1937 he married Mildred Fenton Mooney Neely of Washington, D.C. They have two children, a daughter, Lee, and a son, Robert Lee Dennison, Jr. His official address is Warren, Pennsylvania.

EDUCATION

He attended Kiskiminetas School, in Saltsburg, Pennsylvania, and was graduated from the U. S. Naval Academy with the Class of 1923. He completed the postgraduate course in diesel engineering at the Naval Postgraduate School, Annapolis, Maryland, in 1929 and in 1930 received the degree of Master of Science from Pennsylvania State College. The degree of Doctor of Engineering was awarded him by the Johns Hopkins University, Baltimore, Maryland, in 1935.

NAVAL CAREER

His first duty after graduation was as a junior officer on the battleship ARKANSAS. In 1925 he qualified as a submariner following submarine training at New London, Connecticut, and then joined the sub-marine S-8. From 1930 to 1941 he had duty afloat on the cruiser CHESTER, commanded the rescue vessel ORTOLAN, was Commanding Officer of the submarine CUTTLEFISH, and also commanded the destroyer JOHN D. FORD. This extended sea service was interrupted with two assignments ashore, one between 1933 and 1935 at the Engineering Experiment Station, Annapolis, Maryland, the second during 1938 and 1939, as Assistant Naval Inspector of Machinery at the Electric Boat Company, New London Ship and Engine Works, Groton, Connecticut.

Prior to and after the outbreak of World War II, he served on the staff of the Commander in Chief, Asiatic Fleet, and in this assignment took part in the early war against the Japanese during the campaigns in the Philippines and East Indies. In the winter of 1942 he became Chief of Staff to Commander Allied Naval Forces, East Australia, with similar duty on the staff of Commander Submarines, East Australia. Detached in August 1942, he became Chief of Staff to Commander Amphibious Force, Pacific Fleet (later NINTH Amphibious Force), participating in the seizure and occupation of Attu and Kiska in the Aleutians.

In these responsible duties he was in charge of the planning and execution of assigned missions, working tirelessly handling the various tactical problems with great skill. During the Attu assault, he supervised the successful execution of the plan which enabled our forces to carry out the attacks without loss of any naval ships or personnel. For exceptional conduct while in Australia, and later at sea in the Aleutians Area, he was awarded the Legion of Merit.

Later in 1943 he returned to shore duty, and in the rank of Captain was assigned to the Joint War Plans Committee for the Joint Chiefs of Staff, also serving with distinction as Special Advisor to the Under Secretary of the Navy. During 1946 and 1947 he had duty as Assistant Chief of Naval Operations for Politico Military Affairs, where his services in connection with the coordination of foreign policy and naval policy prior to and subsequent to the end of hostilities were performed in such a manner as to reflect great credit upon himself and the Naval Service. He was awarded a Gold Star in lieu of a Second Legion of Merit for outstanding service in this field.

He had command of the USS MISSOURI during the period March 1947 until February 1948, when he reported in the highly responsible and distinguished assignment of Naval Aide to the President of the United States, and was so serving when promoted to the rank of Rear Admiral. In February 1953 he became Commander Cruiser Division FOUR, operating in the Atlantic, and in January 1954 he was detached for duty as Director of the Strategic Plans Division, Office of the Chief of Naval Operations, Navy Department. There he had additional duty from November 14, 1955 until June 1956 as Assistant Chief of Naval Operations (Plans and Policy).

From June 18, 1956 to July 21, 1958, in the rank of Vice Admiral he was in command of the FIRST FLEET. Upon relinquishing that command, he returned to the Navy Department, where he served as Deputy Chief of Naval Operations (Plans and Policy). On March 31, 1959 he reported, in the rank of Admiral, as Commander in Chief Naval Forces, Eastern Atlantic and Mediterranean and in February 1960 became Commander in Chief, Atlantic and U.S. Atlantic Fleet and Supreme Allied Commander, Atlantic. "For exceptionally meritorious conduct..." in that capacity, he was awarded the Distinguished Service Medal. On May 1, 1963 he was transferred to the Retired List of the U. S. Navy.

DECORATIONS AND MEDALS

Distinguished Service Medal; Legion of Merit with Gold Star; Army Distinguished Unite Emblem (defense of Philippines in December 1941); Navy Unit Commendation Ribbon (USS PENNSYLVANIA, Aleutians Campaign); Order of Naval Merit (Commander) by Government of Brazil; Order of Crown (Cross of Commander) by Belgium; Honorary Officer in the Order of the British Empire, by Great Britain. He has also been recommended for the following decorations:

R. L. Dennison, USN, Ret.

Order of Naval Merit (Grand Officer) by Brazil; Legion of Honor (Commander) by the Republic of France; Order of Military Merit, First Class, by the Government of Cuba; and the Order of Orange-Nassau (Grand Officer) by the Government of the Netherlands.

American Defense Service Medal, Fleet Clasp; American Campaign Medal; Asiatic-Pacific Campaign Medal, with two operation stars; World War II Victory Medal; National Defense Service Medal; and the Philippine Defense Ribbon with one bronze star.

CLUBS AND SOCIETIES

Admiral Dennison is a member of the Army-Navy Club of Washington, D.C.; New York Yacht Club; and the Society of Sigma Xi.

- Office of Information
Beographies Branch
21 May 1963

DECLARATION OF TRUST

The undersigned does hereby appoint and designate as his (her) Trustee herein, the Secretary-Treasurer and Publisher of the United States Naval Institute to perform and discharge the following duties, powers, and privileges in connection with the possession and use of a certain taped interview between the undersigned and the Oral History Department of the United States Naval Institute.

1. In my opinion the material contained in the transcript(s) is unclassified. The transcript(s) may be read or the recording(s) audited by the qualified personnel upon presentation of proper credentials, as determined by the Secretary-Treasurer of the U.S. Naval Institute. However, the user will be required to obtain permission in writing from the interviewee prior to quoting or citing from either the transcript(s) or the recording(s).

2. It is expressly understood that in giving this authorization, I am in no way precluded from placing such restrictions as I may desire upon use of the interview at any time during my lifetime, nor does this authorization in any way affect my rights, or the rights of my heirs, to the copyright of my literary expressions which may be contained in the interview.

Witness my hand and seal this 22nd day of August, 1974.

John H Dennison
Adm U.S.N. (Ret)

I hereby accept and consent to the foregoing Declaration of Trust and the powers therein conferred upon me as Trustee:

Dennison #1 - 1

Interview No. 1 with Admiral Robert L. Dennison, U.S. Navy (Ret.)
Place: His office in Washington, D.C.
Date: Wednesday afternoon, 8 November 1972
Subject: Biography
By: John T. Mason, Jr.

Q: Admiral, I'm delighted that you will do this for the Oral History Project of the Naval Institute and the Naval History Division. I wonder if you would begin by talking a little about your educational background, which is most exceptional for a naval officer, it is tremendously broad, and it was very enterprising of you to have achieved it in the way in which you did. You graduated from the Academy in 1923. Will you pick it up from there?

Adm. D.: When I graduated from the Academy, I was assigned to the USS Arkansas and soon discovered that one of the opportunities a young naval officer had for an early command was to go into the submarine service. In those days, without exception, all the officers assigned to submarines had requested such duty, and also in those days there was no increase in pay for hazardous duty or the equivalent of aviation pay for an aviator. So it truly was a volunteer service. When I found out that there was an opportunity for an early command in that service, I consulted with a couple of officers whose views I respected and got their advice that if I really was sure I wanted to go into that kind of duty, it was quite true that my chances for an early command were greatly enhanced as compared to going to a destroyer or a cruiser or battleship or a ship of that sort.

Q: And that would be a great boost to a young man's career?

Adm. D.: I looked at it more as an opportunity to practice my profession which I believe is command, not specialization in submarines or anything else. In any event, having made the decision, I applied for submarine school and was accepted. I attended the school at New London and the boats that we used for training in those days were the old N and O classes. They were quite primitive. Of course, none of our submarines had air-conditioning or any capacity really to carry very many supplies.

Q: It was pretty rugged service, wasn't it?

Adm. D.: Yes, it was, but we were young, remember, and it was a great adventure, and I soon found that there was real fellowship among the crew and the officers. There had to be. We lived right close together. It wasn't any buddy-buddy arrangement at all, but it was founded on mutual respect and a recognition of ability. I knew that the chief petty officers, for example, knew more about submarines than I could learn in years. In any event, I did graduate from submarine school and was assigned to an S boat, the S-8.

I believe I started out as an engineer officer and then, I believe, I became executive officer.

Dennison #1 - 3

Q: There were only two or three officers on board, were there?

Adm. D.: I think we had four. The quarters were cramped and there just wasn't room for any large group of officers, not that they were needed either. It was a great experience and during my period of service at the submarine school I was brought up short by recognition of the hazards of this duty when the S-51 was sunk off New London. Students were assigned to the two submarines the S-50 and S-51 for the purpose of witnessing what was called an "availability trial." "Availability trials" were made periodically by submarines in those days and they consisted of a set of trials, both surfaced and submerged, going over a period of, I believe, about eighteen hours. I was officer of the deck on the first watch, 8:00 p.m. to midnight, just before the S-51 was in collision with the SS *City of Rome*. It was a beautiful night, completely clear. The sea was calm. We were in signal communication by blinking light until shortly before I went off watch.

The next morning when we surfaced off New London to go up the river to the base, we were met by a large group of small craft, tugs and one thing and another, going out to find the submarine that was sunk. They didn't know until they saw us whether it was the S-50 or the S-51. As everybody knows, it turned into a salvage operation. The people were lost although the water was really quite shallow.

Then, later, I was involved in the incident with the

S-4, which probably I'll get to a little later, when she was sunk off Providence.

In any event, I thoroughly enjoyed my experience at the submarine school and then in the S boat and when it came my time to be transferred I went to the Navy postgraduate school in 1928 and then on to Pennsylvania State University, or State College, as it was called in those days.

Q: What were you specializing in in postgraduate at Annapolis?

Adm. D.: They called it diesel engineering. It really was mechanical engineering with a strong flavor of diesel engines in it. It was a fairly sophisticated course. Of course, we studied mathematics and related subjects along with the engineering subjects, such as thermodynamics. I found it a worthwhile two years, mostly from the standpoint of mental stimulation, rather than learning something that somebody had to teach me in a classroom, and as everybody knows, it was leading to a master's degree. They were still talking about credits and hours and a sort of check-off list of things that you were supposed to do, such as writing a thesis. I think, as I remember it now, my thesis dealt with a determination of a laboratory method to predict engine knocking tendencies in gasoline. I used an underwater spark as a light source. This emits a continuous light spectrum which I applied to various gasoline samples to produce a spectrogram. Gasoline is made up of many different hydrocarbon components. Some of these groups, such as pentane, can be considered knock inducers and others, such as some of the octane family, as knock suppressors. I had hoped to determine the types of hydrocarbons present with the hope of being able to predict a knock rating. The standard means for determining knock rating was to use a standard one-cylinder test engine to determine the point at which the various gasolines would produce a knock.

Q: What led you to that research?

Adm. D.: Well, I really don't know, it's so long ago. I came from the oil country in Pennsylvania and had an interest in petroleum and refining and associated things. And this had to do with petroleum, vaguely related to it, anyway. So that's why I did that—

Q: And why Penn State? How did that happen to be on the list for graduate work?

Adm. D.: In those days various specialists went to various universities. For example, a naval constructor went to MIT, and, as I remember it, communications people went to Harvard. The engineering people went to Penn State or Columbia. All of these, of course, after the Naval Academy postgraduate school, which in those days was in Annapolis and not out in Monterey.

While we're on the subject of education, later, in 1934, I was on duty at the experimental station in Annapolis, which had a very understanding commanding officer, Captain Cox, and

Dennison #1 - 6

I found out that it was possible for me, if I would give it enough time, to study for a doctorate in engineering at Johns Hopkins. So I talked it over with my commanding officer and he thought it was a great idea. At that time I was superintendent of the mechanical engineering laboratory, and he very kindly gave me enough time - I didn't need very much because I did a lot of studying at night - and as it turned out when I was accepted for study by one of the professors up there, Dr. Christie, I was the only one in the so-called class. So our schedules were very flexible and in the late afternoon or early evening or whenever I would go up there if I had the time. I was accepted in a resident status because Annapolis was in the geographical limits of the university.

Q: Were there any other naval officers involved at Johns Hopkins?

Adm. D.: No. I was a unique animal and, believe me, they looked at me with sort of a pale view for quite a long time.

Q: And you were unique also in the sense that you did this on your own initiative, didn't you, and your own money?

Adm. D.: Well, I did that because I wanted an education and I enquired at the Bureau of Naval Personnel if there were any funds available for this sort of thing and was told no. I was talking to a captain at some desk in the Bureau and that was all I wanted to find out, so I just got up and thanked him

Dennison #1 - 7

and started out and he called me back and wanted to know more about this. I told him what I told you and he said he regretted very much that they didn't have any such money, so I said, "That's all I wanted to find out. I think I can afford it, so that's it. My commanding officer thinks it's a good idea and I think I can handle it."

I wasn't too sure as time went on because before I was really accepted for study I had to attend the university for a year and during that time I had to qualify in French and German. My German was nonexistent. My French went back to very early school days. I studied Spanish at the Academy and didn't do very well at that either. So I was tutored. My German tutor was a RealSilk hosiery salesman! I tutored for French with a Naval Academy professor, and at the end of my period with the French professor, I asked him him how much I owed him - I'd been taking up quite a bit of his time - and he said, nothing. I said, "Nonsense. I insist on it. I've taken up all this time of yours in the evening when you might have been doing something else besides tutoring me." And he said, "Well, I don't want anything and the reason I don't is because I learned as much from you as you learned from me, because technical French is something different than just ordinary French." I could understand the scientific or technical meaning of words or phrases, and he couldn't. He could read them literally, but exactly what they meant was something else again.

Q: And actually it was a reading knowledge of these two

languages?

Adm. D.: Yes, and I needed it because a good many articles I had to use in my research were not translated into English from the French and German. So it wasn't just an academic requirement. It was a tool that you had to have.

Then, at the end of the year when I got the stamp of approval to continue with my studies, I went through with it, and at the end of that year I took my written examinations, which took me a week, and this was the type of examination where you're given problems that have no answer really, except the ones that you give them, and then the professor can find out what your thinking was and whether it was plausible or reasonable or satisfactory. And then the oral examination -

Q: Which is usually rather formidable!

Adm. D.: Well, at Hopkins they gave you a break because the chairman of the committee that gave you the oral is the professor under whom you studied, and you were allowed twenty minutes to discuss your dissertation, which had been circulated to the entire faculty. And, of course, the field for these examinations, both written and oral, went back, for example to my studies for a master's degree for certain subjects that I didn't study at Hopkins but I had studied back in those days, were part of my qualifications for a doctorate and I was thoroughly examined in these fields, believe me. The practice at Hopkins was for the president to appoint a chairman as chairman of the committee and then he designated,

I believe, four doctors to be members of the committee. But they also sent an invitation to all doctors at the university, in any field. So when my examination came around there were thirty.

Q: Oh, my!

Adm. D.: It quite stumped the chairman and not only me.

Q: What was your subject then? This must have had some bearing on this great —

Adm. D.: My dissertation?

Q: Yes.

Adm. D.: It was stress analysis and I had to do the research work at the Experiment Station and the application for it was increased. There was a need in those days for some way to use high temperature/high pressure steam in a rather confined boiler and engine room space. In order to do that you had to have some pipes that could go around a rather sharp bend. So the Navy needed the results of this research. This was my topic. Well, if a candidate for a doctorate doesn't know more about his field of research than anybody else, he shouldn't be a doctor. So I had the advantage of knowing more about my subject, than the professors.

At the end of twenty minutes they cut me off and then I was examined on almost anything you can think of, early English literature, mathematics, archeology, science, everything.

Fortunately, I'd done a great deal of reading in my life and at least had in some cases a superficial and in other cases a little bit more than that knowledge of what these fellows were talking about.

I remember one of the early questioners was a very famous mathematician who'd written several books on advanced mathematics and he'd written a very famous book on calculus. He asked me to write a differential equation, so I wrote a second-degree, second order, differential equation, and then he said, let me have a solution. Well, I could have written a simpler one than that. I didn't know he was going to ask me for a solution, so I gave him three. I put them all up. I happened to think when I was studying for my examination that they'd have a mathematician on this board that's going to examine me. I'd better brush up on something, and I just happened to think well, maybe I'd better look into some differential equations and really memorize what the answers were! Apparently this impressed the hell out of everybody.

Q: Just like that!

Adm. D.: He wanted to pursue the questioning. All these fellows did. What they try to do, of course, is to carry it on just as far as your knowledge will let you go. They'll keep probing and probing and probing. He started in on this and I was getting a little over my head when the chairman spoke up and said, "Well, Doctor, you've had some time. I'm sorry but we have to move on."

Dennison #1 - 11

This thing was supposed to last for some time. I think it was an hour and fifteen minutes, but with thirty people they could not possibly handle it. I'd already taken plenty, but this thing went on something like two hours and a half with me at the blackboard.

Q: What an ordeal!

Adm. D.: I was absolutely saturated with perspiration, and they finally excused me and I left the room and waited in the office next door. Pretty soon the chairman, my professor, came in to get me. When I came in the room he announced that - he said, "Congratulations, you've passed," and all these doctors got up and applauded.

Q: Great.

Adm. D.: They never could understand, or didn't up to that point, why in the world a naval officer would want to get into a field of advanced learning. For example, when I presented my qualifications, they didn't accept any Naval Academy credit. They picked it up with Pennsylvania State College. That record may have had some reference to the postgraduate school where I'd studied and perhaps they looked on the Naval Academy as a trade school.

Q: It wasn't accredited in the eyes of the university?

Adm. D.: It didn't make any difference in the end.

Q: Well, that's a unique experience indeed for a naval

Dennison #1 - 12

officer, even today.

Adm. D.: Well, I think they must have some more enlightened programs today. I think that now it isn't unusual to find doctors in the field of political science, which is another field that certainly has great importance for the armed services, and of law. But in those days it wasn't usual at all. I don't know whether there were any doctors in the Navy then or not. I sort of doubt it.

Q: Tell me, Sir, were you a family man at that time?

Adm. D.: Yes.

I might go back, if you'll allow me, to the submarine service in those early days. I think I mentioned that I experienced the incident of the sinking of the S-4 by the Coast Guard destroyer Paulding off Provincetown. The S-8 and S-4 were in Portsmouth Navy Yard for certain modifications to their torpedo shutters, and after this overhaul we were to go down south of Provincetown for certain trials, including submerged runs over a measured mile. I forget the number of days that were allotted for this. This was around Christmas time 1927, I believe. The S-8 finished her trials earlier than had been scheduled, so we turned the range over to the S-4 and she started on her trials and we started on around the cape to go back to New London. The Navy in those days didn't have enough money to let us go through the ship canal, we had to go all the way around in the rough and cold weather. Our radio transmitter went out, our receiver didn't, and after a few hours out we heard our call on the radio and then the S-4's call. We couldn't reply and, of course, the S-4 was on the bottom. So we turned around immediately because something had happened.

On the way back we picked up more information and we got back off Provincetown, as I recall, around midnight, perhaps a little bit before and were the only ones there and we were able to locate the S-4 and anchored quite close to her. We found her by our sonar. We heard pounding on the hull. Again, the water was relatively shallow but the weather was terrible. It was so bad the divers had an almost impossible job. So that, too, turned into a tragedy. They couldn't talk to us except by a prearranged code of signals. We sent them down instructions, we were going to have a lot of questions, and hammer on the hull one rap for yes, and two raps for no.

So we went all through the boat - is the engine room flooded, is the control room flooded, and so on, and are there any survivors in the various compartments. Well, it turned out there weren't any survivors except in the torpedo room. The rest of the boat was flooded and, again, this had to be a salvage operation. We didn't have the submarine rescue chamber in those days that was later developed along with the Momsen lung.

So that was very tragic and very sad, too. Two of my classmates were in the S-4. It was heart-breaking because one of the very last messages we got was "Is there any hope?"

which we'd arranged again by code, and we said, "Yes." We said everything possible was being done. But when it was clear it was a salvage operation, Congressman La Guardia, former mayor of New York and a very colorful character, came up to witness what was going on. He was a sort of fire-engine-chasing type. One time when they had a strike of newspaper distributors in New York, he would read the comic pages to the children of New York over the radio. But he was quite a man, and he came up to get in this act and came aboard the S-8. We had no place for him but I had to be up most all the time anyhow, so I gave him my bunk and, believe me, it was wet and damp and the whole boat was cold. The winter off Cape Cod is not too pleasant.

Q: No, it really isn't!

Adm. D.: Then we were ordered back to New London to try out a fitting to be used on the S-4. We were a sister ship, obviously, so we were similar. And again we went around the cape and La Guardia almost got pneumonia. He was seasick and terribly uncomfortable and wet. And as we were coming in to New London, he talked to me about submarine duty and how did we stand it. And I said because we enjoy it, we volunteered for this, it's just part of the business. He said, "Don't you get any money to take care of ruining your clothes and all the discomfort and hazardous duty?" I said, "No, we don't." The men in those days got a dollar a dive up to thirty dives a month. I forget what a "dive" was. It was of specified duration at periscope depth, or something.

Dennison #1 - 15

Q: And they usually pressured the skipper to see that the number of dives was made, didn't they?

Adm. D.: They didn't have to pressure the skipper because we were interested in having these men get as much as they could and it sure was experience, and they were dives they wouldn't ordinarily have made. But it was all a proper part of training.

La Guardia was astounded at the idea we didn't get any extra pay. So he said, "My God, when I get back to Congress I'm going to take care of it." And, unlike many promises, this one was made good, and he did get a law through —

Q: For extra pay?

Adm. D.: For extra pay for officers.

Q: That salvage job, was it a Navy salvage or was it Merritt-Chapman?

Adm. D.: Both occasions that I've mentioned were Navy salvage operations. It may be that Merritt-Chapman came in on the end of the S-51.

Q: I see that you were up at Electric Boat toward the end of the 1930s - 1938, 1939 - as assistant naval inspector of machinery. What did that entail?

Adm. D.: Well, before I went to that duty, I was assigned to command of the Cuttlefish, and I was ordered to the Electric Boat Company as assistant inspector of machinery. The inspector was Captain Claud Jones, an engineering duty only officer, and this involved inspection - of course, we had a staff - going out on trials and being sure that Navy specifications had been met in building and in performance. That was the principal duty, to be sure that the government was getting its money's worth.

Q: Were there some new submarines coming off the line at that point?

Adm. D.: We were just getting into the true fleet submarine - at least, true to the extent - we didn't have atomic power and all the things we now have, but these were submarines that could operate with the fleet, and the Cuttlefish and the Cachalot, the first was built by the Electric Boat Company and the latter by Portsmouth Navy Yard, were just about, I think they were, the first so-called fleet submarines. They were quite a different concept, because in the early days submarines operated out of bases and ports. They didn't really get out to sea. They didn't have the speed, they didn't have the endurance, and they just weren't built for the kind of duty that became commonplace later.

After the Electric Boat Co. I was offered the command of the submarine USS Nautilus and I turned it down, much to the disgust of some of my colleagues in submarine duty. It was a big submarine, one of our largest, as a matter of fact, and it was a relatively new one.

Q: What was your reasoning for rejecting it?

Dennison #1 - 17

Adm. D.: My reason was again that I felt my business was command. I'd had the training and experience of a fleet submarine command and I wanted another command of a different kind. So I asked to be given command of a destroyer. Well, the submarine detail officer was a friend of mine and he was quite disgusted with me and said all he could do was to release me to general assignment, or whatever they called it. So I went to see the detail officer for destroyers and he said that I couldn't have a destroyer command, and when I pressed him for the reason he said that I'd had too much command already. This, I thought, quite contrary to my philosophy of what the Navy's all about.

Q: In accordance with your age and rank, you'd had too much?

Adm. D.: Yes, I'd had too much. I had to move over and let somebody else have a chance. Well, I made such a nuisance out of myself that on one of my last trips down here this officer told me he was going to send me to the Asiatic Fleet, and he made it sound like a sentence to Devil's Island. But I knew that I had a chance of getting command there because in those days the commander-in-chief of the Asiatic Fleet ran his own Bureau of Personnel and when you crossed the international date line you sent a dispatch into him, his headquarters, expressing your preference for duty. I followed this routine and I got orders to command the USS <u>John D. Ford</u> with the Asiatic Fleet.

Q: I suppose you welcomed this assignment not only because

Dennison #1 - 18

you had command of a ship but also for service in the Far East?

Adm. D.: Yes, I did. It was far from the end of the line and, of course, it was in the front lines when the war broke out - World War II.

Q: And this was already apparent - that there was going to be war?

Adm. D.: Well, it was apparent except that nobody could come close to guessing when or how. There were many misconceptions about how and when, and not only in Washington and Pearl Harbor but in the Asiatic Fleet. I can get into that whenever you wish.

Q: And among our allies. I understand that they thought of the date 1946 as a possible time for readiness.

Adm. D.: Nobody can read the Japanese mind and it's always dangerous to try to second guess the enemy's intentions. All you can really go on are his capabilities. Knowing his capabilities, you could conjecture and speculate on what use he might make of his capabilities, but whether he will or not, or, if so, when is quite another matter. Admiral Hart, for example, thought that the war would break out in September of the year 1941 and, in anticipation of this, he evacuated all the Navy dependents out there a year before the war broke out. But when hostilities didn't start in September, then there was a feeling of relaxation, of well, it's not going to happen for quite a while. And there was a general feeling, too, that the Philippines would be bypassed because the Japanese objective involved Southeast Asia more than the Philippines. In other words, the oil in Southeast Asia and rice. But when the Japanese attacked Pearl Harbor and the Philippines, I think that obviously they were protecting their lines of communication by attacking the Philippines. They didn't estimate that we probably would not have interfered if we hadn't been involved in the war in some way. In other words, had they gone into Southeast Asia without Pearl Harbor, we probably would have done nothing for some period of time, until something came up that would have involved us. We were hypersensitive in those days, I thought, about, well, for example, we weren't permitted to visit the ports of Southeast Asia or Java or Australia, on the grounds that this would irritate the Japanese. Well, it became a very severe handicap when war broke out because none of us had had any experience in those harbors or those waters. The charts were no damned good in a great many cases, so we were very severely handicapped because of the attitude of super-caution.

So I don't think with that kind of an atmosphere that we would have blocked the Japanese sea lines to the south unless there had been an incident that involved us. That was why this timing was so difficult to estimate because there was no real basis on which to make an estimate. We didn't know we were going to be attacked. It was inconceivable that they would attack Pearl Harbor of all places. But this was the sort of general thought that is the usual thing in war.

Q: What was the general feeling when you arrived out there as to our ability to defend the Philippines?

Adm. D.: This again was a matter of timing. The United States was going to reinforce the ground forces and air forces in the Philippines. They had started putting in more air and a little bit of build-up in the Army, and MacArthur, if you remember, when he first went out there had the Philippine Army, not U. S. Army forces.

Q: That's right.

Adm. D.: And then he finally became commander of the whole thing. But our timing was such that we were overtaken badly overseas by the outbreak of war because none of this build-up had really been accomplished. The Navy hadn't been reinforced.

Q: The Navy had had a promise of reinforcements, a number of cruisers and so forth?

Adm. D.: Yes, that was another plan. I don't ever recall seeing the plan itself. We did have a war plan called Rainbow 5. This involved combined operations with the British naval forces and the Far East, at that time under command of Admiral Tom Phillips. Phillips came up to Manila to consult with Admiral Hart many times before the war.

But who could have guessed that Pearl Harbor was going to be struck? Of course, when we got the news it wasn't general knowledge the extent of the disaster, how many ships had been sunk and what ships, but it was a very, very severe blow. We knew when we finally got the news that there was no hope of reinforcing the Philippines. We'd have to fight with what we had there and the Navy was going to be very largely ineffective.

Q: What was your actual duty out there? You were skipper of the John D. Ford. What kind of a ship was that?

Adm. D.: The John D. Ford was destroyer No. 228 and was part of Division 12. We had a squadron out there. The Ford was the flagship division 12. I had come to the favorable attention of Admiral Hart and this involved an exercise in fueling from a tanker under way with a destroyer on either side of the tanker. My ship was on the port side and the Paulding was on the starboard side. The Paulding finished and cast off her lines. In those days we didn't have the techniques developed of fueling without any lines between the ships. In those days we rode a bow spring and a breast line. Of course, now that's old hat. There aren't any lines except the fuel lines and messenger lines.

Q: That was a technique that developed later on.

Adm. D.: Yes. But in this case the Paulding cast off with her rudder a few degrees to port. The captain didn't

Dennison #1 - 22

realize what was going to happen if he went ahead and started to cross the bow of the tanker before he could back down and get the heading adjusted. I could see what was coming. I could see her stacks and masts and everything. So I backed down full on my lines to the tanker. They didn't part until I pulled that damned tanker around I think maybe 25° or 30°, then they snapped. But it saved the Paulding because instead of heading right across the bow of the tanker and being perhaps sunk, there was a glancing blow that caused some damage to her top side and so on, but that was all.

So Hart convened a court of inquiry or a board of investigation or something. I really hadn't done anything that anybody with any sense wouldn't have done anyhow, but he wrote me a letter of commendation, which was unheard of. So, later on when we were having fleet exercises in southern waters of the Philippines and he was anchored in his flagship in some harbor there - I've forgotten which it was - and I got a message to report to the commander-in-chief. So I got permission to leave the formation and went over and made a flashy show of bringing my destroyer up and getting a lifeboat over before the wake caught up to it -

Q: Seamanship!

Adm. D.: Showing off is what I was doing! The chief of staff, Admiral Purnell, met me and said, "That was a classy job of seamanship. In any event, Admiral Hart wants to see you." I reported to Hart and he said, "I'm going to detach you and order you to duty on my staff, but your primary duty is going to be senior patrol officer in Manila because things are going badly there and we're in trouble. What do you have to say?"

Well, I told him a long story about how I got out there in the first place and how I'd struggled to get a command. Now I was coming up to promotion to commander and I said the senior patrol officer is not much of a job and I'd like to stay where I was. When I got all through, he said, "Is that all you have to say?" I said, "Yes, Sir," and he said, "You're detached.

Q: It sounds like him!

Adm. D.: Anyway, I did get his backing. I said, "If you're going to make me patrol officer, I hope I can count on you to tell the commanding officers that when I have somebody on the report that they're to pay pretty serious attention to it. If they think punishment is warranted, then the man should be punished, so we can stop some of this stuff that's going on." I got all kinds of cooperation out of the police and constabulary and really had no problem.

Q: What was this in point of time?

Adm. D.: Oh, it may have been six months before the war started. Something like that, and my title on his staff was assistant war plans officer. Well, of course, when the war broke out there wasn't any shore patrol, and what I really was was the only contact between General MacArthur casually and socially. There was a big difference in rank and age.

Dennison #1 - 24

Well, Hart made me his contact with MacArthur. After the outbreak of hostilities, I moved to Corregidor and Hart moved to the south.

Q: During the period prior to the outbreak, what sort of messages did you have to carry back and forth? What were the negotiations? Were you trying to get General MacArthur to cooperate readily with the Navy?

Adm. D.: Well, MacArthur had a very elementary understanding of the use of a navy. He, like a good many Army officers of his time, looked on a navy as a seaward extension of the army's flank and that's all. This developed very plainly later on when we moved from Australia through the islands up to the Philippines.

You must realize that there was no personal contact between Hart's staff, MacArthur's staff, or MacArthur, or Hart. MacArthur didn't know what we were up to in terms of ship movements or what our war plans were, nor did we know what his plans were. So that was the purpose of my being in this particular capacity.

Q: To keep a dialogue of some sort!

Adm. D.: Yes. It wasn't much use until the war did break out.

Q: Hart says in his official report to Secretary Forrestal that he had a lengthy conversation and meeting with MacArthur in late September of 1941, during which time he outlined the Navy war plans to MacArthur and the use of the ships and so forth, and MacArthur had no comment whatsoever on the thing. Were you present at that meeting?

Adm. D.: No, I wasn't. I'm sure it probably took place but it was not a day-by-day contact. MacArthur was completely open with me. When I first reported to him he called his staff in and instructed them in my presence that they were to show me all the dispatches that were exchanged between themselves and Washington and he intended to do the same, whether I asked for them or not, because how could I ask for something I didn't know existed? I was amazed. I didn't then know as much about army customs as I do now, so I was appalled to find Willoughby, the G-2, telling the G-2 in the War Department things that were completely different from what MacArthur was telling the chief of staff of the Army. There were no communications intra-staff worth a damn.

I had several very interesting experiences with MacArthur that throw a little light on him. One was that before Cavite was destroyed he had moved to headquarters in a wooden building on the top of a wall - it's a walled city. In the wall they had tunnels and bomb shelters. I was in his office one day in this ramshackle building when the air raid alarm went off. We didn't have any guns, the ammunition was all gone. We couldn't reach these bombers anyway at the altitude they were flying, so they could just bomb at will. Their practice was to make dummy runs to test out the wind and all that, then they'd make a firing run and let go. Well, in this particular raid we were the target. When the air raid alarm went off,

MacArthur's staff always beat it to a tunnel with their files and their gas masks and I don't know what all. I eased forward to the edge of my chair to leave, thinking, of course, that MacArthur would be going to the bomb shelter. When he saw what I was doing he said, "I'm enjoying our conversation and I'd like to continue it, if you would care to stay here with me." So I thought it he can take it, I can. How ridiculous. He's the one that ought to be in a bomb shelter. So we sat and continued our conversation with all these bombs going off all round us. Thank God, the building wasn't hit. But that was MacArthur. He was fatalistic.

Then, I went over there one morning around nine o'clock and he said, "Before I talk with you, I want you to hear what I'm going to tell my staff." So he called his staff in and he said, "Gentlemen, I'm going to declare Manila an open city as of midnight tonight." This was really an ancient concept of war, the idea being that the city would not support any military activities and therefore, the enemy would spare it, not pillage it, not knock it down, or capture it. This was the first that anybody had ever heard of it, so after he got through with this, I said, "May I go back and talk to Admiral Hart?" which I did. I told Admiral Hart that I'd just heard General MacArthur instruct his staff that he intended to declare Manila an open city as of midnight that night.

Well, Hart didn't usually show much emotion but he said, "What!" Then he got up out of his chair and said, "Come around here and sit down and write that down." So I wrote down a simple sentence, "At 9:10 this morning General MacArthur told me" and so on. He sat down again and read it and he still couldn't believe it, because he'd been making preparations to operate out of Manila. They'd moved the submarine tender Canopus in alongside the sea wall in the port district. We'd taken off warheads, torpedo exploders and distributed them all over that general area so they wouldn't be concentrated any place, and had put some camouflage over the tender. She was in shoal water so that, had she been hit, she wouldn't have submerged. We were planning on continuing submarine operations. We had barges of fuel oil all around the Manila area and all kinds of supplies which we couldn't possibly get out -

Q: You needed time, yes.

Adm. D.: Certainly more than a few hours, which meant that we couldn't back up this concept of an open city because we had to have those supplies. We couldn't get them out. But here's an example of complete lack of consultation or accord between two senior commanders - MacArthur didn't comprehend what this would mean to us. Later on, when Hart left, he polled his staff - the few of them that were left, he'd sent most of them including his chief of staff down to Java - to ask them whether we felt that he should stay. Of course, we all knew damned well that what we said didn't make any difference anyhow. We told him he wasn't serving any useful purpose there. He'd sent his flagship down and he was based ashore. We didn't have any ships except some destroyers, three I think, and some submarines and the submarine tender.

Q: You had about twenty-nine submarines, all told, did you not?

Adm. D.: We had quite a few, yes, and they were going to try to continue to cooperate out of Subic Bay. We said, "You ought to go," so he decided he's go out on the Shark submarine. He ordered me to go to Corregidor where Rockwell was, who was commandant of the naval district and who was given the job of operating the Asiatic Fleet naval forces left in the area, but Hart, typically, hadn't briefed Rockwell on what his war plans were, what his thoughts were. He told me, for example, when I put him aboard the Shark that the gates to the south were closed, the Japanese fleet is there, we can't get any more ships out. Well, we did. I mean this was just stupid. The destroyers were sitting ducks and one of the first things I told Rockwell was what Hart had told me, and No. 2 that I didn't agree with him and why. It meant that these ships would go out and, of course, they didn't have any torpedoes, they were running short of fuel oil and they had to get out, or sit there and have everybody killed.

Finally, the submarines had to go because the Canopus was hit. We were under aerial surveillance all the time. They had to sit on the bottom during daylight when they'd come off patrol and then come up at night for replenishment, and then go and sit down on the bottom again. And this was in tropical waters and not very comfortable. So, finally, we just had to get out.

Dennison #1 - 29

We didn't have the stuff to operate with. The destroyers were sent out and they all got out and got down to Java.

Q: Admiral Hart, in his report, laments the fact that if he had taken earlier action he could have ordered out and saved approximately a thousand naval personnel who eventually went to Corregidor and most of them became prisoners.

Adm. D.: Well, this was really an inexcusable thing. We'd taken over some ship - I forget now what its flag was - put a prize crew aboard it and she sailed with a naval captain and a few naval officers without anybody in her. Why? There were a lot of Navy people who had no way that they could be of assistance to the defense of Corregidor or Bataan or anything else. They were mechanics or enginemen, storekeepers, some of the personnel from Cavite and all they were doing was drinking water and eating food because their skills weren't needed, and I don't wonder that Hart laments the fine officers that were left behind, constructors, for instance, could have been of great assistance.

Q: Was it perhaps because of the uncertainty of plans?

Adm. D.: I can't explain it. I really don't know. Uncertainty, hell, we knew that we had to get out of there. We knew where our own ships were and why they were there. And, again, when I got out to Corregidor and reported to Rockwell after seeing Hart off - and, incidentally, the last thing he said to me was, "Do you have any binoculars?" I said, "I haven't got anything with me but what I've got on and a .45." So he took the binoculars off his neck and handed them to me! He said, "Now you have."

But when I reported to Rockwell I had to pick up the threads with MacArthur who had insisted on setting up headquarters for himself and his chief of staff, Sutherland - in an old wooden building on top of this rock. His staff, the rest of them, and Rockwell and his people were down in the tunnels of Corregidor. They finally had to almost carry MacArthur off the top of that rock.

Q: Were the Japanese in possession and did they use a bomb sight of any kind at that point?

Adm. D.: Bomb sight?

Q: Yes.

Adm. D.: Yes, they had bomb sights.

Q: Comparable to our Norden?

Adm. D.: No. At that time they didn't. Just what kind of bomb sights they had, I don't know, but for sure they weren't just dropping by eye - they came awful close. They weren't missing by much.

I went up to talk to MacArthur to ask him what his plans were, and he and Sutherland broke out some gasoline company's road maps - they didn't have any army maps, they'd all been lost, burned up or bombed or something, and MacArthur very painstakingly went over exactly what his troop movements were going to be. By that time the Japanese had landed south of Manila and were moving north. They were opposed by Philippine forces with some U. S. officers. He told me exactly when they were going to come through Manila, and I said, "Well, can't you just hold till we get these supplies out of there?" He said, "I can't afford to let these troops engage because I could never get them disengaged. They're not well enough trained. They'd just get in there and be absorbed and lost, but they can slow the Japanese down." Then he told me about the movement of troops through Manila and also the forces that had gone down to Bataan and at that time, which was I guess maybe January, he predicted almost to a day how long Bataan could hold out.

So, finally, Hart sent for me. At that time I was acting chief of staff to Rockwell. He wanted me to come down to Java, which I did. I went down in the submarine Permit. We did a war patrol on the way down, which lasted for something like forty days, and by the time I got there Hart had just left and turned over that command to Vice Admiral Glassford, who was commander of the Yangtze Patrol. He had not been on Hart's staff. Hart, at that time, was the ABDA Float, the American-British-Dutch-Australian forces. Wavell became the commander of the whole outfit, and when Hart was relieved he was relieved by Admiral Helfrich of the Dutch Navy on the grounds that the Dutch really ought to be in the high command -

Q: It was their home territory!

Adm. D.: It was their home territory, yes. Of course, Helfrich didn't have any concept of how to handle task forces - not that he had all that much power -

Q: The Dutch had a fair navy, too, out there didn't they?

Adm. D.: Yes, but it was a different kind of a navy - submarines. It wasn't equipped for operations like that - some destroyers, I believe. Glassford was in Soerabaya when I arrived and that is where Admiral Hart and the remainder of his staff were. He sent for Glassford to come up to Bandung, which is in the mountains above Djakarta, and the next thing any of us knew at Soerabaya - Glassford sent a dispatch down for me and two lieutenant commanders whose names I've forgotten and a group of submarine officers to report to him, and the remainder of the staff were to get aboard some tender and go to Australia.

Q: And then you were to become the immediate staff?

Adm. D.: I asked Glassford when I reported to him what I was to do and he said I was to be his chief of staff. So I said, "What did Admiral Hart tell you about his plans and what his estimate of the situation was?"

Glassford said, "You won't believe this but he never asked me to sit down and when I reported to him all he said was, 'Glassford, I'm leaving and I'm turning over to you.'" I said, "Is that all he said?" And he said, "Yes, that's every word he said."

We stayed in Java, Bandung, until almost the day the Japanese invaded in the north. They had a task force operating to the south of Java at the port of Tjilatjap, a very important one for us for evacuation purposes, but they hadn't closed it for some reason which I can't understand. I went out again by submarine and Glassford went by plane, a KLM airliner, I believe, then we met in the Fremantle area. We were the last to leave, the commands had all dissipated. Helfrich called a conference of all the senior commanders there including a Britisher and an Australian. I had learned that he had stationed a tanker about halfway between Java and Ceylon - he hadn't told anybody about it except the Dutch. Obviously, he planned to pull out and his own ships would be refueled before they went on to Ceylon. I told Glassford Helfrich didn't know we were leaving, but at this meeting the British and the Australian admirals said they were through, that they'd used up everything they had, and they were getting out. Glassford played a hell of a good game of poker. He later told me he had told Helfrich that we would stay with him to the end and he said, "I was the last to leave the meeting and Helfrich called me back and said, 'Glassford, there's one thing I want you to understand - I appreciate and I'll never forget what you told me. But I don't intend to stay here and become a prisoner of war."

Wavell had already left.

Q: It was a hopeless situation?

Adm. D.: Oh, it was from the very beginning.

Q: Would you talk a little about the formation of what was called Task Force 5, the naval ships that Hart assembled August 1941 and then he asked the Navy Department to amend the war plans to think in terms of surface defense of Manila?

Adm. D.: Well, with Task Force 5 we were wrapped up with the British and, of course, the thing that killed any such plan as that (Rainbow 5) was the loss of the Prince of Wales and the Repulse at Kuala Lumpur. But the idea of the task force was - and that's why he gave up his own flagship - to form a group of ships and get them to sea, but as far as defending the Philippines was concerned that was hopeless because they didn't have the gun power, they didn't have the antisubmarine capability, and above all no air cover.

Q: It was a fleet in name, but not actually in fact?

Adm. D.: No, that's right. The Asiatic Fleet as a whole wasn't designed as much for fighting purposes as it was for politics-military purposes. It had very little power. The submarines were by far the most powerful components. The ships were, by and large, pretty old. The Houston was a fairly modern ship in those days. The Marblehead was not one of our newest by any means, a light cruiser. The destroyers were old. So there was not much that we could have done to stop any kind of a real invasion.

Q: Hart said at one point in his report that he made efforts to get the Army to cooperate more closely in terms of the air power - airplanes - and to have a coordinated effort between the Navy and the Army in terms of air power.

Adm. D.: All we had there were patrol planes -

Q: PBYs?

Adm. D.: Yes, and they were not combat aircraft in the sense of having any fire power at all. I'm not aware of exactly what it was he was talking about, but we didn't have any air cover for our ships of any kind. He may have had that in mind, although the Army didn't have very much of that kind of air out there either. They had bombers and, as you may remember, at Clark Field MacArthur simply couldn't believe that we were being attacked or would be attacked by a force that came out of Formosa and he held those planes on the field until they were lost completely, which dismayed the Army Air Force people no end.

There just wasn't anything like the power out there that would be required for any kind of air cover or opposition to any invasion operation or air-to-air combat. Our antiaircraft guns were just pathetic. I was in Cavite just after it was hit. MacArthur sent me over there and it was completely devastated. Manila wasn't seriously damaged until much later.

Q: At that point declaring it an open city was helpful, then, was it?

Adm. D.: It wasn't helpful at all. Nothing happened. The Japanese weren't interested in destroying Manila in those days. They couldn't have cared less. They wanted the city. They didn't want a bunch of rubble. Of course, towards the end of the war it was a different matter.

Q: Would you say something about the merchant shipping that was saved for the allied cause. I saw one report, it was 200,000 tons.

Adm. D.: Out of where? Out of the Philippines?

Q: Yes, out of the Philippines.

Adm. D.: I don't have any figures and I don't remember ever seeing any. I would have to look at the source of that. It seems incredible that it would be that much.

Q: The lack of communication, the lack of cooperation, between the Navy commander and the Army, was this due to personalities or was it simply two men going their own way and two services?

Adm. D.: No, I think the same thing happened in Pearl Harbor. No, this was long ago before there was any real liaison, at the least, between the Army and the Navy. The Navy, of course, with its Marine Corps, had a built-in amphibious landing capability. These forces, however, were not intended for operations much beyond the beach line. We didn't have any plans in those days for the use of Army forces in amphibious operations. There just wasn't any understanding of the complementary role of the Army to the Navy and vice versa.

I just mentioned a while ago MacArthur's concept of the role of the Navy. Well, of course, this horrified naval officers, and we brought some of this on ourselves. I don't know what Admiral Carney, of course, had to say in his report but we never really supported MacArthur with the Seventh Fleet. We were out fighting our own war, and MacArthur's concept was based not on the use of naval forces or naval air, but his original plan was to move in 600-400-mile jumps which he considered to be the range of land-based air, objective after objective marching all the way up to the southern tip of Mindanao and moving up, so when we went into the strategy of jumping into Leyte Gulf, many of us were thinking it made a lot more sense to bypass the Philippines entirely. But it took an awful lot of doing almost over MacArthur's dead body to do that.

Q: That was a Nimitz concept, wasn't it? Or at least he spearheaded the thing?

Adm. D.: Yes, and there wasn't any naval officer I know, Halsey or anybody else, who didn't think this was the way to do it. It was the only way to do it. This step-by-step thing I just use as an illustration of the different ways of thinking between the Army and the Navy, and the Army was busy at ports all over the United States and a few outposts, while the Navy was making friends and contacts with other navies all over the world, and they just didn't move in the same environment or atmosphere.

Q: Admiral, I would think that just plain common sense would dictate that an attempt be made at a meeting of minds in a situation like Manila where they were beleaguered almost -

Adm. D.: Well, it wasn't. I think it wasn't until Admiral Nimitz and Admiral King came along that we commenced to develop an understanding of the needs and the methods for developing cooperation between the different services. Admiral Nimitz was very, very keen on this particular subject. He believed with all his heart, and quite properly so, that our security depended on some kind of a linkage, or at least understanding, between the Army and the Navy. Of course, this was before the days of the Air Force, but he would have felt the same, too, because we did in effect have an air force in World War II.

Q: Even Nimitz didn't have an easy time with MacArthur, though.

Adm. D.: Who did? Later on I can talk a little bit more about when MacArthur was relieved of command in Korea by President Truman, President Truman's views on this, and what little I know about MacArthur's views on it.

I asked General Bradley one time why it was that MacArthur with this brilliance of his just didn't seem to have some element in his character that would make him really great, because this business about telling me when Bataan was going to fall, this was not speculation, this was seasoned military judgment. Bradley, of course, had known MacArthur for many, many years, and he said, "Well, Bob, he doesn't have the instinct or touch to get people to work with him and cooperate with him and to submerge his own ideas of grandeur. And that's probably true, he just didn't have it. A pity, too, because I think he was a great man.

General MacArthur's treatment of me was quite different from his treatment of his own staff. He was very autocratic with his own people. It seemed to me that he didn't really confide or trust in anybody, with the possible exception of Sutherland. But even then I don't think there was any real understanding between them. His treatment of me I think underlines the fact that he looked upon the Navy as something entirely apart from the Army. The little example of his orders to his headquarters not applying to me when he told his staff to get under cover when an air raid -

Q: You might have been a visitor there!

Adm. D.: Well, he just wanted to talk. I'm sure he wasn't pulling my leg. He had every intention of staying there.

I heard one end of a conversation when a bishop in Manila called him up on the phone, obviously deeply distressed, and he apparently had asked MacArthur what he could do for his people. And MacArthur - completely extemporaneously, he didn't know this fellow was going to call and didn't have any idea what he was going to talk about - he gave the most moving talk to this man. He tried to explain to him what the situation was and what he could do to support the morale of his flock. He almost had me in tears. I never heard anything like it. He could do that. He did have the magic. But he had also all this bombast about "I shall return" which led us into the loss of a good many men and a hell of a lot of time and a lot of material. He was a curious man, but he was no more curious in his own way than some of our own commanders.

Admiral Hart, for example, was a fine man but completely out of focus and out of touch with the concepts of warfare that became so needed of understanding in World War II. Things moved awfully fast. Remember we just barely were getting in radar. It was kept as such a hell of a secret from our own people that practically nobody knew how to use it - the few sets that we did have. This was stupid, and of course we didn't get any help from the good old Navy Department. I remember in the very early days of the war when we were getting the hell kicked out of us the Bureau of Engineering sent out a dispatch wanting us to send in samples of fuel oil from the Japanese ships that we'd sunk!

Q: Get it off the top of the ocean!

Adm. D.: We hadn't sunk any ships, number one. There was an air of unreality. And in Java it was just the same with the Javanese as it was with us. When I got to Soerabaya which was early in the game, it was in February or March, I forget when, the people there didn't know a war was on. I mean, they - it was a long way away and they only came in contact with a few of us, and the club life and dances and pretty girls and all that, having a gay time was going on. There was no real concern. They weren't going to be invaded, ridiculous. And the same atmosphere in Australia, even worse, because there we ran into some very serious labor difficulties that interfered with the operation of our own ships. I'll tell you about that later.

Q: Business as usual!

Adm. D.: Exactly. They still had to go to the races, work only eight hours a day, and go on strike if they didn't like things.

Q: Is it possible that MacArthur, in his relationship with you - you had a good relationship with him - was based not only on the fact that you represented a different service but also your recognized intellectual attainments. Did this make any impression upon him?

Adm. D.: I have no idea because I don't believe he would care or have any way of knowing what attainments I might have had. I did have some discussions with him. But, no, I think it was just because he was being courteous to the representative of another service. It was his gentlemanly way of acting. He made it clear that I wasn't under his orders. He was a thorough gentleman. There was no question about that, and I think it was more that than anything else.

But I remember long before the war broke out my wife and

I were at a party with the MacArthurs, a very small party, and MacArthur, after dinner, he and I were the two men that were there, and MacArthur started to talk about his father and the great lesson he'd learned about war from his father, and I thought here's a priceless opportunity and I started to prick up my ears and be sure I didn't miss these words of wisdom I was about to hear. And he said, "My father told me that the great secret in battle was to fight like hell." That was the end of that!

Q: Not for self-preservation but just to fight like hell!

Dennison #2 - 42

Interview No. 2 with Admiral Robert L. Dennison, U.S. Navy (Ret.)
Place: His office in Washington, D. C.
Date: Thursday afternoon, 9 January 1973
Subject: Biography
By: John T. Mason, Jr.

Q: Good to see you this afternoon, Admiral. Last time, you broke off your story as you joined Admiral Glassford and now you want to relate something at Tjilatjap.

Adm. D.: When we arrived at Tjilatjap, having already ordered our few remaining destroyers to proceed to Australia, the port was jammed with merchant shipping.

Q: They were fugitives, weren't they?

Adm. D.: Most of them were fugitives, yes, and some of them were there legitimately at a very unfortunate time. Here again, there was a Japanese task force that we knew was operating south of Tjilatjap and really watched that port and blockaded it, which was really inexplicable. Our destroyers, three of them, I think, were briefed by me on how to go because we knew about where the force was, and one of them, the Pillsbury, instead of proceeding towards Bali and heading in towards the coast of Australia and working down the coast, started to cut across on a course direct to Fremantle and ran into this task force and was sunk.

Q: That was the skipper's decision to do that?

Adm. D.: Yes, it was not in accordance with the instructions that we'd given him.

At any rate, after seeing to it that our forces and our people were out, then it was time for us to go, that is, Glassford and myself. But before I went, as a final clean-up, I went down to the docks. At about the time I got there, a bus packed with wounded U. S. Navy sailors drove up with a chief petty officer in charge. These men were badly shot up. They were from the cruiser Marblehead which had been badly battered and later was able to escape with serious damage. These men had been taken ashore and put in a hospital somewhere near Tjilatjap, and then it became necessary to evacuate them. There was this busload of them and I presume there were other loads that had gone out previously, because I don't think that one bus contained all the wounded from the Marblehead. The ship's surgeon, Dr. Wassell did a heroic job of taking care of the wounded and was later decorated, I believe with a Navy Cross, for his effort.

But this one busload of people had had no luck in getting aboard any of the ships in the harbor. The masters of these ships claimed they didn't have any room and they didn't want any wounded people -

Q: For them, it was just a handicap!

Adm. D.: Oh, yes. One of the two petty officers told me that had happened, that he'd been rejected. I decided to take over and get them aboard a ship so that they'd have some chance of getting out of there.

I went aboard a merchantman and the captain was on deck so I started to talk to him. While he was explaining to me that he didn't have any room for this group of wounded people, I motioned for them to come aboard, which they did. He wasn't about to throw me off or throw these people off bodily.

Q: He saw them arriving then?

Adm. D.: Oh, yes, and he didn't know what to do about it except tell me that he didn't have room for them, didn't want them, and so on. When these guys got aboard in typical bluejacket fashion, they found a place on the upper deck which they staked out with their seabags and their few possessions and got the more severely wounded people bedded down - remember that the weather is warm in that part of the world at that time of year -

Q: Which can be an asset and also a detriment!

Adm. D.: In this case, it probably was an asset because these people needed some warmth in the condition they were in.

At any rate, we got them settled down and a few of them that were able to get around went into the ship's medical supplies and so on and got enough stuff together, maybe some K rations or something as well.

So after doing that particular task, Glassford either had or was about to take off. I was to go out in a submarine that night. The submarine was to enter the port and then go out, which is what happened. We had a fairly sizeable group and, of course, the submarines which were operating under extremely difficult circumstances, because they had to go all the way up beyond Australia to find any targets, and that's a long, long trip.

Q: Yes, in tropical waters. What sort of facilities did the Australian Navy have at Fremantle at that point?

Adm. D.: They didn't have much. They had a marine railway, which we could use to haul out submarines. Some of these submarines were pretty badly shot up. I remember one incident which illustrates, I think, the attitude of at least Australian labor toward the war.

This submarine came in and, as I remember, it had some bullet holes in the superstructure, around the bridge. At any rate, she had some damage, some of it electrical, which had to be repaired. Our practice was, when these boats came in, to let all the people possible go so they could get a little bit of breathing spell before having to go out as soon as the ship was ready.

Q: There wasn't much around Fremantle for them to do, was there?

Adm. D.: Well, there was fresh air and sunshine and relaxation, although there wasn't a hell of a lot to do, that's for sure. But that was something that was badly needed. I mean when you're submerged in one of these old submarines with no air-conditioning all daylights hours and a good part of the nighttime, you really need something. In my own experience, I'd had a forty-day patrol coming down to Java and we ran out of food. I think all we had left was some flour or sugar or something like that for the last two days. I remember I lost about forty pounds and I was no exception. We had these great big water blisters under our arms or on various parts of our bodies. This was an exceptional case, I think, a forty-day patrol, at least unusual, but they needed-our sailors in Australia - all the rest they could get, which was little enough.

This particular submarine was hauled out and the labor unions were not operating under any kind of wartime urgency and they threatened to march down and release the brakes on her and this sort of thing, and let her slide off the railway back down into the water.

Q: One of the operational units protecting them!

Adm. D.: That's right. We'd retained the captain and several officers and a few enlisted men. Of course, we heard the story about what these labor people intended to do in this yard, so it was perfectly evident we had to make the repairs ourselves. We couldn't afford to do that. Sure enough, at the appointed time on May Day or whenever it was, this whole group of several hundred people started into the shipyard and approached the submarine on the railway. The captain raised his megaphone and said, "Halt!" None of these stopped, so the next he said, also through the megaphone, was, "Load!" And everything was quiet even though there were numbers of people and you could hear these bolts going back, ramming the machinegun and getting it ready to go. When they heard that and they realized that the captain meant business, they stopped. Because we did mean business. They weren't about to do that to a United States ship.

After milling around for a few minutes, not advancing any, they decided that the better part of valor was to get the hell out of there, which they did, and leave us alone.

But this incident wasn't peculiar to Fremantle. We had the same sort of thing happen on the west coast of Australia. After the Battle of the Coral Sea we had some badly banged up ships that came in there, and again we wanted to get them back on the line just as fast as we could. I was sent to the yard, I think it was Cockatoo Point - maybe that's in Sydney - but at any rate within our area up there, to talk to the man, who was a former naval officer, in charge of that plant. These ships had to get into dry dock and had to be patched up and ready to go back to sea just as fast as we could get them there. Again the labor unions took the attitude that they wouldn't work overtime, wouldn't do certain jobs, and I said, to this man, "How is it possible? Have you told these workmen that we're here protecting your country. We're fighting your fight. You haven't got anything to fight with here." Most of their Army troops were over in North Africa, and they didn't have any Navy to amount to anything to begin with. This man said: "Well, obviously you won't believe this, but I've done just that, told them the consequences if they didn't help you all they can, and they told me that they would rather be taken over by Japan and not concede anything in labor relations that might adversely affect their comrades when they came back from the war and had to go back to work again."

Q: Completely unrealistic.

Adm. D.: Of course, it's a different world, but I had to believe this man because he was obviously honest. I'd never talked in any way to these people myself because that would be third-party intervention and I'm sure would have been equally ineffective.

At any rate, I just wanted to bring this in because this incident that I just recounted about Fremantle and the Marine railway was only indicative of the general attitude in certain segments of the Australian population towards the war.

Q: And yet the war had come very close to Australia with the raid on Darwin, the Jap raid on Darwin, and earlier in 1940 the German raiders in the Tasmanian Sea had sunk so much shipping?

Adm. D.: The Coral Sea wasn't exactly miles away either! But communications in Australia were incredibly bad then, and Darwin, to most Australians, was a completely unknown part of the country. It's way to hell and gone, up in the northwest corner and more or less isolated from the continent itself. Of course, the whole centre of Australia is a desert. It's a rimland.

Q: Well, Sir, I know you left Australia in short order, but do you have any knowledge, did their attitude change as the war progressed? Did they ever relent in this area?

Adm. D.: It really didn't make any difference because, as the war progressed, we started fighting our way back up through the South Pacific and the need for operating from bases as remote as Australia greatly diminished, in fact, disappeared. So I really don't know what attitude the Australians had as the war progressed. It was the same when I got to Java. The casual observer would never know that a war was going on. There were parties at night, dancing, and music, pretty girls —

Q: The Dutch inhabitants?

Adm. D.: Yes. This was Surabaya. Even the Dutch Army in Java was working on an eight-hour day. They weren't really ready to fight.

Q: How do you explain this, Sir? Does colonialism nurture this kind of thing?

Adm. D.: I don't think it had any bearing or any relationship to colonialism. I think there were probably two reasons. One, most of the things that you mention were not visible. I mean, who sees a ship being sunk at sea? Maybe nobody. So they hear about this without really knowing what the significance is. It isn't as if they looked down the street and saw some Japanese soldiers and some of their neighbors or themselves got shot. It's an unwillingness to believe that the horrors of war are really on your own doorstep.

Q: Well, we, as a people, in the United States suddenly came to life with Pearl Harbor and we didn't see it actually.

Adm. D.: That's different. We had communications that were much better than anything in Australia. We had pictures, we had visual evidence. The papers were filled with it. The press themselves got involved and wanted to talk to Congress, for example. The day of infamy. So, this was quite different. Our people are more easily involved in such a thing emotionally because many people had fathers or sons or husbands in the armed services. And, of course, the Pacific Fleet was fairly sizeable. A lot of people had a personal involvement, at least through their relatives. But here was the Australian Army out in North Africa, not involved in the direct defense of Australia, so in fact the main defense, or, in fact the only defense, was at sea.

That's my own rationalization. There may be deeper reasons, of course, going back to history, in this case labor's. I just don't know, but there was an air of unreality not only in Surabaya, for example, but also in Perth, Fremantle, Brisbane, Melbourne and Sidney.

Q: Well, we certainly can be grateful for the fact that the Australian government had a different attitude, because in 1940 they refused to send their Navy out to Singapore to join in the defensive there. They said they needed them.

Adm. D.: The government was another thing. Obviously, anybody with any sense realized the direct involvement of Australia in any war in southeast Asia. I mean it was a different type of war at least. But not the great mass of Australians. They wanted their horse racing to go on, which is good. This is a great Australian pasttime. And business as usual. Even in Melbourne, a wonderfully cosmopolitan city, there was an air of unreality. They couldn't believe what was going on.

I remember when we got to Melbourne - perhaps I'd better go back to Fremantle, then I'll get on to Melbourne.

Q: Yes. In Fremantle you were to serve as chief of staff to Glassford, who was based there?

Adm. D.: Yes, he was based there - well, he was in transit, let us say, because we weren't really based anywhere. We were sort of floating round. We were there not very long. I remember, I believe it was in Perth, we were put up at the Weld Club and they were very hospitable but the atmosphere there was completely unreal. In spite of the various shortages that existed in Australia, food and clothing and other things, it didn't make people think maybe something was going on. On the shortage of clothing, I remember Admiral Glassford invited me to have dinner with him one night - we were both staying at the Weld Club - and I went 'round to his room and he appeared in a Royal Australian Air Force sky blue uniform cut on U. S. Navy design. The Australians had run out of navy blue cloth. I must say it was quite a striking-looking thing.

Q: Pretty snappy!

Adm. D.: Theatrical! He said, "What do you think of it?", and I said, "It's certainly striking." Then he said, "Why don't you get one like it? - because I didn't have any clothes either - just khaki and not very much of that.

I said, "For two reasons. One is that I am not a vice admiral, and the second reason is I won't be working for you all the rest of my career!"

Q: You have to watch your Ps and Qs!

Adm. D.: Yes. He took it the way I meant it, I think. Our stay, in general, was brief and really uneventful because the forces had been largely redeployed and the operation of the submarines to the north was unproductive in that particular area.

Q: But Captain Wilkes continued there, did he, with the submarines?

Adm. D.: Yes, he did and I forget when he left.

Q: In May Admiral Lockwood relieved him.

Adm. D.: Yes, Lockwood came, and then they set up a command called U.S. Submarines, West Australia. I believe the full title was Commander, U. S. Naval Forces and Submarines. But at any rate, the commander was Rockwell. I had been sent for to come and join him in Melbourne to leave within a few days to go to Brisbane.

Q: This was after MacArthur had arrived in Brisbane?

Adm. D.: MacArthur and Rockwell left Corregidor at the same time, as you recall. MacArthur was there and he also later moved up to Brisbane.

So we went to Brisbane and started operating, but again the command set-up was very strange and very loose. To illustrate the confusion, a tender came in with a squadron of S boats commanded by Ralph Christie, who was a captain, and he thought that he was to relieve Rockwell, or at least to take over this command. I don't believe he really knew that Rockwell was there. I met the ship when it came in and went up to call on Ralph and I said, "What are you doing here?" He said, "I'm going to command the U. S. submarines here."

I said, "We've already got a commander," which he hadn't heard. So he didn't take over the command.

Q: Almost more commanders than ships!

Adm. D.: That's right. And that's where the submarines started to operate - the S class of submarines. I stayed in Brisbane for several months, as I remember, and the people were hospitable. They were commencing to realize that something was going on because the war was closer to Brisbane than, certainly Melbourne. Then Rockwell got orders to command the Amphibious Force, Pacific Fleet, and again asked me to go with him as Chief of Staff.

Dennison #2 - 54

The first job we had was to train Army forces to mount an invasion to recapture Attu.

Q: Because the Japs had come in there in June.

Adm. D.: The Japs had taken over and our job was to go up there and take it back.

Q: Where were you to train the amphibious forces? In Hawaii?

Adm. D.: No. We were based in San Diego and we trained the Army forces mostly at Fort Ord, up near San Francisco. The ships were trained off the coast. We used San Clemente, for example, for training in shore bombardment. In those days we were concerned mostly with armor-piercing projectiles. We never fired live ammunition in gunnery practice.

We had three battleships, the Pennsylvania, the Nevada, and the Idaho. The Pennsylvania was our flagship. The Marines were not involved in the operation except to assist Rockwell in training these Army troops. The Army division, I believe was the Seventh and the commander was Major General Brown, who was later relieved of command because of his performance.

Q: At that point did you have any difficulty in getting supplies? Did you have landing craft?

Adm. D.: We had a great deal of difficulty because a lot of things that we needed, forklift trucks, for example - we had a couple of good thieves who were able to round up some of of these supplies. We couldn't have gotten them through normal channels.

Q: They were all going toward the Mediterranean?

Adm. D.: They were all going some place else, because the war in the Pacific was a sort of secondary thing. We had amphibious ships. We had the APAs and AKAs, but again we had to use some merchant ships. LSTs were just coming in, and we had a squadron commander, a captain with three or four people on his staff, and they were the only professionals in this particular LST outfit. We were sent ROTC units from Yale and Harvard to be officers on these ships, and these were perfectly marvelous young men, but they didn't know anything about the sea and they certainly didn't know anything about LSTs.

Q: They were old landlubbers, weren't they?

Adm. D.: Yes. They were all the same rank, so when they showed up we just lined them up and went down the line and said, "You're the captain and you're the executive officer. You're the first lieutenant. You're the gunnery officer", and so on. Then we started over again with the next ship, and that was the way it was. We had no way of measuring their qualifications, so that was the only way we could do, tell one guy he was the captain. Seniority, hell, they didn't have any seniority.

Q: Did you have any schedule, any time limit, for the training?

Adm. D.: Yes, we did, and pretty damned tight. And the reason it was tight was because of oncoming amphibious operations in the South Pacific under Kelly Turner, who took over the title Commander, Amphibious Forces, Pacific, after Attu and then Rockwell became commander of the 9th Amphibious Force.

But we trained the Army troops and they had more difficulty about supplies than the Navy did, because they had been trained in desert warfare. They were more equipped for desert warfare. Nobody had ever thought about operations in a place like Attu. The question of clothing was extremely important, and the Army didn't know anything about combat loading of AKAs, and the Marines had to pitch in and teach them that. We thought we'd really taught them how to combat load a ship. Obviously, you put in last what comes out first. That's the basic principle, for an amphibious landing. Ammunition. You'd better have plenty of that where you can get at it in a hurry. That ought to be somewhere near the top of the pile. But when we got to Attu, the first thing that came out of this particular AKA was the sedan of the commanding general!

Well, there weren't any roads on Attu. It was nothing but rocky, mountainous terrain.

Q: A good target it made!

Adm. D.: Yes. I mean it was as useless a piece of equipment as you could possibly imagine, but it was in what the Army calls the table of organization and equipment. One division out there, one sedan for the commanding general, and so on down the complete list. The tables didn't have to do with where you were going to fight. This was just the way it was, or was then. I hope it's not now the Army system.

Q: Did you have any feed-in from North Africa and the experience other people had gained there?

Adm. D.: No. It wouldn't have helped very much anyhow. We hadn't had any experience really of fighting in a place like the Aleutians.

Q: No, but some of our people had experience with LSTs.

Adm. D.: Oh, yes. Maybe the squadron commander had some experience. I don't know. We had some Navy people who knew something about LSTs, obviously, and about amphibious operations. And we had a commander of transports who was very capable and had had considerable experience. But the gunfire part of it and the battleships, we had strange experiences there.

We went out for our first shore bombardment exercise at San Clemente. We had carefully laid out the range. We had all kinds of observers to spot the fall of shot and all that kind of stuff. It was very carefully planned, and we went out and started firing. None of the shells exploded. They were all duds. So we stopped it and sent a dispatch off to the Bureau of Ordnance telling them how many duds there'd been and what the range was and what the angle of elevation of the guns was, everything, and nothing happened.

Q: Did this apply to any one particular type shell?

Adm. D.: Well, these were all the same caliber, 14-inch, and they were all standard Navy shore bombardment projectiles. In other words, the idea is that when they impact the head fragments, not like armor-piercing. But they didn't work. So we waited for a reply to this dispatch. It was a cry for help, because we had to sail in a very short time. We finally got one and it was a very simple dispatch, very short. It said, "Who verified dud action?" With that, almost before anybody could pick up a pencil, out came a real blast from Admiral Nimitz to the Bureau and the Chief of Naval Operations!

I forget what he said but it was unmistakable what he meant. In other words, forget the verification. We did have duds. We want to know what to do about it right now.

What happened is something that hadn't been foreseen. We were using reduced charges because we were going to be fairly close in when we did this bombardment and the fuses in the heads were armed by what is called setback. In other words, inertia moves the firing device into position when the shell is fired. But with a reduced charge, it wasn't quite enough to do it, so the warheads were never armed. When they hit they just didn't explode. So there were two solutions. One was to increase the powder charge, which meant an increase in the angle of elevation or standing off at a greater distance, or change the setting of firing mechanism. I forget now which solution we finally adopted.

But I just point this out to show that it wasn't just entirely the Army ready to fight in the desert that had a time getting ready for this operation, but also the Navy.

Q: It wasn't too unusual. I had an account from Admiral Whiting, who was in command of the Massachusetts off North Africa and who shot some 16-inch shells at the Jean Bart and they didn't explode. They just went through, which created quite an incident in the White House.

Adm. D.: Well, think of the tragic experience we had with torpedo warheads in the Pacific. That was a real disaster.

Q: Yes, you must have had some experience of that in Australia, did you not?

Adm. D.: I certainly did. Some of the shots couldn't possibly have missed but nothing happened. Some of our skippers finally got wise, as to what was the cause. They set their fish so that they weren't depending on the influence fuse device, but on impact. Lockwood was the one who really solved it. He dropped these warheads off cliffs and God knows what all to find out what was going on. We never had fired one of these torpedoes in peacetime to test the exploding mechanism.

Q: And that has its roots in peacetime economy!

Adm. D.: That is correct, yes. There were a lot of things that we apparently didn't know about. Radar, for example. It was such a closely held secret that most of our own people didn't know about it and damned few ships were equipped with it. For example, in this operation in the Aleutians we only had a few ships with radar. Here we had this great mass of shipping - LSTs, for example, which had to be literally hurried around through incredibly bad visibility because they were just navigating blind. So you had two or three sheep dogs with a hell of a lot of sheep wandering around in all directions. It was a pretty scary experience.

But to go back to mounting this operation, there's one thing that might be of interest because it concerned Admiral Nimitz.

I hadn't known Admiral Nimitz. I'd met him, of course. Everybody had. I later got to know him very, very well. At one juncture, Admiral Rockwell gave me a letter and asked me if I would take it out to Nimitz.

Q: From San Diego to Pearl?

Adm. D.: Right. I got on a Navy flying boat. I wasn't alone. The plane was loaded. And I set out for Pearl with this letter. Well, it turned out that the letter had been inspired by General Holland Smith, who was head of the Marines that were helping us train the Army, and Rockwell had written it in his own handwriting based on either what General Smith had told him or notes that he'd given him, and this was "eyes only," "top secret," and all that.

I got to Pearl in time to attend the morning staff conference. So my friends were there, Forrest Sherman, Lynde McCormick, two of my best friends. I, of course, sat down in front of Admiral Nimitz and pretty soon he called on me to report, and I said, "I was only sent here to give you a letter," so I proceeded to march up and hand it to him. He started to read it and his face got livid. He was mad and it was one of the very few, if not the only time, I ever saw him like that, even when I got to know him better. He finally looked up at me and he said:

"Dennison, did you write this?" Well, it was in Admiral Rockwell's handwriting. I said, "No, Sir," and he said, "Well, the weight and the space that you took up in that plane coming out here could have been better taken up by mail for the Pacific Fleet."

Q: You wanted to crawl through the floor!

Adm. D.: I couldn't understand it. I didn't know what was in the letter, in the first place. Obviously, I hadn't written it. All I was doing was handing it to him. So after he let loose a couple of other blasts, I said, "Admiral, may I be excused?" He said, "With pleasure!"

I left the room and waited for my friends to come out, and pretty soon they all came out and I grabbed hold of McCormick and Sherman and said, "Damn, you fellows. You knew I didn't write that letter. Why didn't somebody speak up and keep me from being shot out of the water?"

They said it wouldn't have done any good and it was obvious I didn't know Admiral Nimitz. I said, "I certainly don't, if this is a demonstration of what he's like." They said,

"Well, he showed us that letter after you left and what

it was was a complaint about the Army in Hawaii trying to take over the amphibious role of the Marine Corps. This was what Holland Smith heard. Here was Nimitz breaking his heart to improve relations between the Army and the Navy after the Pearl Harbor debacle, and he doesn't want to hear any such stuff as that. He wouldn't believe it anyhow."

I don't believe it was true myself. So that's what hit him. This was the kind of stuff he just didn't want to hear anything about.

Q: It was a very inappropriate thing to bring up at that point.

Adm. D.: It was a hell of a thing to bring up. This was just another incident in the business of this amphibious operation into the Aleutians.

Q: Admiral, in retrospect, was that a necessary operation? Would the Japs have gone anywhere, and why not let them wither on the vine out there?

Adm. D.: The thing that really triggered off the operation was not what the Japs could do from there - I mean the weather is so terrible, there are no port facilities, nothing - but they obviously were planning on taking over the chain. They occupied Kiska as well as Attu.

It was United States territory. That's something you don't do. You don't come over and grab some of our land. So we had to take it back, regardless of strategy. We couldn't just let them sit there.

Q: It was a matter of national honor?

Adm. D.: Yes, I think that's probably reason number one, two and three.

Kiska, of course, was another matter. This was a much more strategic location, but we didn't really have time to develop any real intelligence about those places because we had to invade too early to develop sufficient intelligence in order to release these ships to go to the South Pacific. We did have some pretty spotty intelligence, a good deal of it based on aerial reconnaissance and rumors and stories and all kinds of stuff. We did know pretty much about Kiska, about the caves on the island and the beaches, not in the detail we would like to have had, but at least we knew something.

Again, our plans were bold and would have been effective. We had to make this landing, and as it turned out we didn't find any Japanese. We sent this report back immediately and nobody would believe it. We kept getting these messages, have you looked in this cave, latitude, longitude so and so, and where did they go? Why didn't you catch them? This was brought about by necessary haste to get the forces relieved.

But, to go back to Attu. As we approached Attu, after a rendezvous in Cold Bay, which is down at the other end of the chain -

Q: This brings us, in point of time, to the next year. Isn't that true?

Adm. D.: I'm talking now about the invasion of Attu.

Q: 1943?

Adm. S.: We rendezvoused with all our ships in Cold Bay, got them all together, and started out toward Attu. Not long after we got going, we got a directive from Nimitz for the heavy ships, the battleships, with a suitable escort, to break away from the formation and proceed westward to intercept and destroy a Japanese force which was supposed to be headed our way.

Well, the weather was incredible. It was cold and visibility was almost down to zero. We went out there to see if we could make contact, but we didn't. As far as we could tell, there wasn't anything around anywhere. It turned out later that there wasn't any such task force at all. Where this rumor came from I don't know.

So we came back and rejoined these slow-moving amphibious types, but we were running out of fuel. They were getting low. We found ourselves on D-day blanketed by fog, and navigation up there in those waters is not simple, I can assure you. The Japanese did have some submarines there, it developed as the operation went on, because the _Pennsylvania_ was almost hit by a torpedo. I saw the wake of it, so I know. But we had some fine people and some fine destroyer people particularly.

When D-day arrived it was perfectly clear to most of us that we had to go or withdraw, which would mean that our

Dennison #2 - 65

timetable would be way off, it would take a long time to re-fuel that task force. It was either that or forget it. So the decision was made just to land. Well, the Japs had withdrawn from their coastal positions inland because the weather was so damned bad and they couldn't believe anybody could make a landing. It was pretty hard for me to believe, too.

We landed on the north and south coasts with no opposition at the beaches. We didn't lose anybody.

Q: No opposition except the elements!

Adm. D.: No. The destroyers had to herd these landing craft and guide them in because obviously they were blind, they didn't know what they were doing, where the beach was or anything else. They could steer a very rough compass toward it but it wasn't accurate enough, but the destroyers with their radar could do it and did a magnificent job. Then, of course, we opened up with all kinds of bombardment, too, to cover the landings so that it was impossible for the Japs to come down to the beach until we were well established. It wasn't until later that they started to move inland and they ran into these suicide attacks by the Japs. We did lose some people and the Army general panicked. He asked for reinforcements which we didn't have and he didn't need, and he was relieved.

Q: Did the shells explode properly for the bombardment?

Adm. D.: Oh, yes, every one of them was fine, and, of course, we had a lot of smaller caliber fire from the destroyers in the immediate area of the beaches. In spite of the visibility, the gunfire support was fine. We had to develop our own doctrine, for example, in this gunfire support because it was pretty new stuff. Just exactly how you did it and who controlled what.

Q: Actually, it was a rather unique amphibious operation never duplicated anywhere else.

Adm. M.: No, it wasn't, and it was one of the very first, as you know. We set the pattern in our various doctrines for amphibious operations all over the place, principally in the southern Pacific. It was really quite an operation.

Q: There was a change in the over-all command, was there not, because of friction between the Army and the Navy?

Adm. D.: In this particular operation?

Q: Yes.

Adm. D.: No, it wasn't a matter of friction at all. It was a matter of inexperience or incompetence on the part of this particular general. He was actually relieved by General DeWitt, who was commander of the Army forces in the western United States. I forget what the title was, but he was the top, four-star general.

Q: Yes, and he was based at San Francisco, I think.

Adm. D.: Probably, the Presidio. He was a fine man, he really was very understanding. He was the one who relieved Brown. Nobody else really could. He was in the Army chain of command, of course, he was under our operational command. Then he was relieved by a fine general — I can't recall his name, something like Cordell.

Q: I was also thinking about the change in the over all naval command in January 1943, before the actual landings, when Admiral Nimitz relieved Admiral Theobald and sent Kinkaid up there instead.

Adm. D.: Kinkaid's job was a different thing entirely. He was in command of that area, but he really had very little to do with our particular operation. He would supervise intelligence and so forth and all that. We were the ones on the spot with operational control and command of all these forces. Kinkaid and his staff were extremely helpful, but in this kind of an operation you've got to be on the spot. I mean you've got to be out there. Nobody can tell you to land the landing force or how to do it.

Then, as I told you earlier, Kelly Turner was set up in business as Commander, Amphibious Forces, Pacific Fleet, to get into the remarkable operations in the South Pacific. Rockwell stayed on briefly. It was apparent that we had nothing further to do and certainly in the Aleutians we'd done our job, and I put in for command of a destroyer squadron, which the Chief of the Bureau told me I could have — that was Admiral Fechteler. I'd run into him and Admiral King, who came out a couple of times before and after the operation to be briefed and so on. This may have been unfortunate because Fechteler, when he got this request of mine, after having told me that I could have a squadron when I was able to leave, wrote and told me that he'd looked through my jacket to find a note in it that said when Dennison is available for transfer he is to be ordered to the Navy Department.

Q: This was King's?

Adm. D.: No, I think it was either Admiral Edwards or Admiral Cook. It turned out it was all right but when I got to Washington I was ordered to report to the Joint Chiefs of Staff on the Joint War Plans Committee and also the Combined War Plans Committee, which was a U. S.-British operation.

So I left my seagoing job for the time being and did that.

Q: You were about due to come back from combat, anyway, I would think.

Adm. D.: I didn't think so!

Q: Tell me about that very interesting assignment.

Adm. D.: Which one?

Q: When you came back to the Department to the Joint War Plans Committee.

Adm. D.: It was interesting and even more than interesting because this was where really the war plans originated. The

Joint Chiefs didn't do any operational planning, obviously. A high command doesn't do that sort of thing. What they did do was make strategic decisions.

I remember the Joint Chiefs of Staff came into being because of the British chiefs of staff organization and we needed a counterpart and a counterbalance. Very shortly after this thing came into being we made five-star officers like fleet admirals to counter British admirals of the fleet and so on and generals of the Army to counterbalance their field marshals. But the Joint Chiefs of Staff, as the Joint Chiefs, were involved in the prosecution of the war that we were fighting, and one of our problems that appeared in the Pacific was how the hell to keep the British, principally one or two of their aircraft carriers, out of it, not because they weren't great sailors and all that but because the characteristics of their ships were such that they just didn't fit in with the operations of our particular kind of task force.

Q: They'd never been trained at fueling at sea?

Adm. D.: No. They didn't have anything really, but they had to get there for prestige reasons mainly. You remember that the chairman was Admiral Leahy, who had been sent as ambassador to Vichy France by President Roosevelt and was recalled to be chief of staff to the commander in chief. There wasn't any statutory chairman then because we obviously didn't have a National Security Act. But he took that position of chairman ex officio. King, of course, was the Navy man, and George Marshall and Arnold, and they were an exceptional group of people obviously. I mean the war was pretty well fought. But Leahy was the one that could bring this group together.

Q: He being the mouthpiece of the President?

Adm. D.: Indeed he was and everybody knew it. He didn't really use any pressure, but his technique was most interesting. I attended a good many meetings and one of the things he used to do - Marshall, for example, would start discussing some plan of his, something he thought we ought to be doing next, and Leahy would say, "Well, George, I'm just a simple sailor. Would you please back up and start from the beginning and make it simple, just tell me step one, two, and three, and so on." Well, Marshall or Arnold, or whoever it was, kept falling for this thing and they would back up and explain to this simple old sailor. And as they did it - which is what Leahy knew damned well would happen - and went through these various steps, they themselves would find out the weakness or misconception or that there was something wrong with it. So he didn't have to start out by saying, "This is a stupid idea and it won't work."

Q: They tripped themselves!

Adm. D.: Yes. Of course, the president was deeply concerned and eminently concerned with a good many things at the beginning of the war and as the war went on, particularly the invasion of Japan. One of his primary concerns was the number of U. S. casualties. I can remember Leahy pressing for estimates of what U. S. Casualties might be in this invasion of Honshu and

Kyushu, and there never was an answer to it because you could go from one extreme, where the entire Japanese population were going to rise up with everything that they could lay their hands on, to a token resistance by a few of the Japanese armed forces. Nobody knew what the opposition might really be, so there never was an answer to that. But the upshot of it was that in this particular instance, the operations of the chiefs, that realizing that we had a very narrow time span in order to accomplish this invasion, either we did it in a bracket of a couple of weeks or so or we didn't do it for another year, they ordered the invasion forces mounted. They had to because there'd have to be the hell of a long lead time to get a force like that going. But there was never any automatic execution. They didn't say "prepare and then execute on such-and-such a date or on or about," as they did in a good many operations. And, thank God, it never came off. It became apparent as time went that the Japanese were beaten, and beaten really because they were completely cut off from all kinds of supplies and would starve to death, and there was no reason to invade, as it turned out.

Another example of the operations of the Joint Chiefs was trying to talk MacArthur out of this island-hopping thing from Australia up to Mindanao and working his way up in little increments, which would have taken forever. We got in the Leyte Gulf deal because the Chiefs realized that this was the thing to do and Halsey was quite vehement about what he thought about the operation. All of us thought - when I say "all of us" my contemporaries certainly - this 400-mile thing was ridiculous.

Dennison #2 - 71 -A

But MacArthur was thinking in terms of a Navy being an extension of the Army's flank. Apparently he didn't have any concept of what naval power could do, in this case, in permitting a move from where he was, to the south, into the Leyte Gulf area, then later farther north.

Q: Hadn't he been reading the battle reports?

Adm. D.: It took an awful lot of doing, but this is one example of how they operated. They sent for Sutherland to come up and brief the Chiefs on what was so great about those island-hopping things. He put up a pretty good case but it didn't wash. So this is one the Joint Chiefs of Staff resolved really by maybe 50 percent persuasion and 50 percent directive. This was sort of unusual. They didn't usually operate that way. They just figured out what the strategy was to be and depended on their commanders to carry the strategy into action. Of course, they even went further and said what the objectives ought to be and some idea of the time frame.

Another thing that they did, the operations in the Joint Chiefs, we would prepare a paper on some particular action we thought ought to be done or accomplished. The papers were in standard form, which really was taken from British practice, and the form was to state the problem and that really turned out to be the most important thing, to make up your mind what the problem was or what it was you wanted to do. Then you listed - at least the British did - factors bearing on the problem. We changed that to facts bearing on the problem, and then a discussion, and then conclusions, then a recommendation.

That was the usual form of most of the papers.

When the Joint Chiefs of Staff got it, they called a meeting, of course, they'd read it and made up their minds what ought to be done about it individually, but when they came to act on any one of these documents, they never approved a paper because they couldn't agree, and quite naturally, on a discussion or the reasons that led to these various conclusions. They might agree with the conclusion, but for different reasons, so all they ever approved was the recommendation, which was a simple one or two-paragraph thing.

But they really performed -- it's stupid to say -- an irreplaceable function because it's pretty obvious that there had to be some kind of an organization to run this war. And, thank God, we had the kind of people we did to do it.

Q: Would you talk about Admiral King's role in the Joint Chiefs?

Adm. D.: Well, King, of course, was commander in chief of the United States Fleet. He was the single naval person in the United States in a position of real power. He wasn't the chairman, of course, because Leahy was. King was a very positive individual. He had a very capable staff of his own, some of the most intelligent men we had. He had his own mechanism for making up his mind or having things brought to him or brought to his attention. He was very capable and also very, very well informed. I remember one time, to go back to Leahy's technique, I forget what the subject was but it had something to do with Japanese activities, and the way he started off was by saying, "Well, when I was a boy I was brought up with the idea that the U. S. Navy was invincible," or whatever it might have been, and after the first time, King stood up and said, "Admiral, when you were a boy who would have believed that the Japanese would have taken over the Philippines and Southeast Asia?"

King had so many things to his credit, but one of the things I'm sure he's entitled to have credit for is getting attention finally directed to the war in the Pacific and away from the British concern about the continent of Europe. And had we not got going in the Pacific when we did, and, God knows, we were operating on second or third priority for so long, the war would have been quite a different thing. It was King, and probably King alone, who finally swung it so that we did start thinking in terms of the Pacific and our interests in that area.

Q: That strategy had been developed by Churchill and Roosevelt, had it not?

Adm. D.: Which strategy?

Q: Concentrate on the Atlantic.

Adm. D.: Yes, that was agreed to at the very, very kick-off of the whole game. Churchill made his point and we agreed. But regardless of whether it was first priority or not, we had to have a second one and we had to be doing something about it, which King was responsible for. Churchill, understandably, was interested in what happened in Europe primarily,

Dennison #2 - 74

but a lot of his ideas like this "soft underbelly" business was laid in Europe and many of these things were unnecessary and even ridiculous, I thought, and so a good many others did.

Q: Another word about King's role and King's participating in the decisions of the Joint Chiefs and then journeying to California to meet with Nimitz and to pass this on. Was that the idea? He had numerous conferences out there.

Adm. D.: Oh, yes, he did indeed. He knew what was going on. As I told you, he came out to see us a couple of times. He was interested in the most minute details. He had a very keen mind. I first knew King when I went to submarine school. He was commandant, or whatever the title was, of the school in New London, so I'd bumped into him off and on through the years and I knew a little bit about him. He was a hard man to know. I can't claim I ever knew him, but I do remember one thing, if you want to hear an anecdote about him.

Toward the end, after President Truman became president, and after the war the Joint Chiefs of Staff sort of went down hill because they were no longer needed, or so it was thought then. It became having a luncheon meeting every now and then. King was relieved as Chief of Naval Operations by Admiral Nimitz.

Well, King became ill, but he lived in Bethesda at the Naval Hospital, and he had an orderly and a driver and wasn't bothering anybody. At this particular juncture he wasn't seriously ill, but this was some place for him to live and operate. He had an office in the Navy Department for quite a while.

I remember when I finally got away and Admiral Nimitz ordered me to sea - I haven't told you that story, it's an interesting one that I'll tell you later - I went in and called on King. This was when I took command of the Missouri. He had a lot of nice things to say which I didn't think he even knew about. Anyway in this hospital business, the commanding officer of the hospital is really not a very intelligent man, and I heard that he was trying to get King out of the hospital. So I told President Truman and he said, "Stop it. If Admiral King wants to live at the hospital, that's the least that we can do for a man like that. I don't want him disturbed." I said, "Aye, aye, Sir." And you'd better believe that he wasn't, either. The commanding officer was.

Q: Well, King actually was on active duty still, as a fleet admiral.

Adm. D.: Yes, of course, he was. That wasn't the point. I mean he didn't really need, at that particular time, hospital care. It wasn't that. He just didn't have any place to go. It didn't take the president long to react to that one!

Q: During the wartime period, did the Joint Chiefs meet every day?

Adm. D.: It's pretty hard to say every day, but it it wasn't every day it was exceptional when they didn't. You see there were so many intelligence reports coming in, battle reports, and all kinds of things that they had to have to keep current, even if they weren't going to make a decision and, of course, they didn't make decisions one every ten minutes. Some of these things required a good deal of discussion and consultation with some of our allies. Some of them were Combined Chiefs of Staff matters, others were strictly Joint Chiefs.

Q: But it certainly took a considerable amount of their time?

Adm. D.: Oh, yes, there's no question about that. But that was their job. King, of course, as the rest of them did, had a service job. But the services couldn't operate, or the forces in the services, without direction from the Joint Chiefs. So unless the Chiefs did something, no man like King or Marshall or Arnold could do anything except keep the things going.

Q: Well, now, you got involved with the Combined Chiefs, too?

Adm. D.: Yes. I was on the War Plans Committee for the Combined Chiefs.

Q: Would you talk about that?

Adm. D.: This was interesting because it brought on so many instances of difference between the United States and British strategy in the war. The British are great negotiators. I thoroughly admire their techniques. I did then and I do now. For example, you'd sit down in a committee and one of the Britishers would make a proposal and start a discussion on a subject, and when it became apparent that he was sort of outwearing his welcome and we were getting damned well sick of this, then one of his colleagues would pick it up, a new voice with different emphasis, but the exact same plan. I mean, he didn't disagree. They never disagreed in front of us.

Q: The old idea of repetition!

Adm. D.: Yes, and also of change of pace. It wasn't just one guy talking. Each one of them, and all of them had the same point of view. This was a useful negotiating technique. And they all knew their lessons, there's no doubt about it. I mean when they came into a meeting, they'd been thoroughly briefed. They'd gone over all the points that you might raise and had a rebuttal, or some way of evading it, and they had a few principles that they got from on high. One was, of course, a directive from Churchill. I forget now what operation it was, but I remember that we badly needed cargo shipping for some amphibious operation or support of an operation, and the British didn't have any, so they said. So we were trying to hash this out as to where the shipping was going to come from and why it was the British didn't have any.

Well, when you really pinned it all down, they fell back on the Churchillian phrase "inescapable commitments," and this was the reason why they couldn't produce something, in this case shipping. Well, when you pressed to find out what these "inescapable commitments" were, it meant that the British took off the top what they thought their requirements were for commercial shipping, and they had some pretty severe ones because they have a small island and they need shipping to live.

Q: And they were losing an awful lot!

Adm. D.: So the "inescapable commitments" came off the top. On the other hand, our approach to the problem was, let's put everything into the pot and win the damned war, and then we'll figure out what to do, and "inescapable commitments" be damned. Our idea is to get in there and fight and get the thing over with. This kind of thing when you ran into vague generalities made dealing with them a bit difficult.

I remember that one of the things that I could do that helped us, and helped them, I'm sure, was to be able to summarize exactly what the two positions were, and present theirs as fairly as I could, then I would ask, "Have I said what you mean and what you've said?"

Q: You took the factors and made a summary out of them?

Adm. D.: Yes! They ended up by decorating me with the Order of the British Empire, and one of my friends said, "I don't know whether you got this decoration because you're a patriot or a traitor."

Q: When you met with the Combined Chiefs, their concern was largely the European aspects of the war, was it?

Adm. D.: Of course, it was at first entirely. It wasn't

until this got to be in hand -

Q: No, when you first came aboard.

Adm. D.: Oh, yes, and we were bedeviled by a lot of things that were agreed to between us and the British. For example, the Atlantic Charter. We had no desire for territorial aggrandizement, and so on. But it turned around and bit us pretty badly. Not that we ever did have any desire for that, but we avoided after the war any appearance of, for example, staying in the Shantung Peninsula in China on the grounds that this could be interpreted as meaning that we intended to occupy. Remember that this particular time was the birth of the United Nations. That was one of the things that didn't have to be said. Of course, another one that can't be laid at the doorstep of the British, we did it ourselves, was the declaration of the policy of unconditional surrender, which didn't come about, never could have come about, and, at the time, my recollection is, the indications are that Roosevelt made this declaration because some of our allies felt that we might be trying to make some kind of an independent, individual deal not in the alliance, but on our own. He wanted to make it perfectly clear that we were fighting for total victory. But the thing became outmoded, of course, as time went on.

Q: Some of our allies - was it mainly the Russians who may have raised this?

Adm. D.: I don't know whether anybody actually raised it -

this issue. It would have been a pretty damned serious thing to accuse us of, being prepared to start independent negotiations. But, rightly or wrongly, at the time it might have been a good idea if we did adopt that policy, but it became badly outmoded as time went on, a few months went on. It was perfectly obvious in the case of Germany or Japan we couldn't and didn't have an unconditional surrender. It would be unthinkable to destroy a country. We would have ruined our own. It turned out in both instances that our efforts were immediately turned toward establishing government and getting it running.

Q: You said that Admiral Leahy obviously was the mouthpiece for President Roosevelt –

Adm. D.: He was more than a mouthpiece –

Q: In the Joint Chiefs, in the Combined Chiefs meetings, who spoke for Churchill in the same sense?

Adm. D.: I forget now who their chairman was, but whoever it was did.

Q: Was it Sir John Dill?

Adm. D.: Dill was for a while, but I just don't remember. They had the same kind of a set-up with one man, but you'd better believe that they all had the same point of view.

Q: You must have had to struggle with the subject of allocation of landing craft and so forth?

Adm. D.: That was one of the most troublesome ones because the one you mention, landing craft, were in very short supply for a very long time. We didn't have a priority list, but implicitly we did, as to what operation was going to get these. I just mentioned a minute ago about the Aleutians and the South Pacific. It wasn't a matter of allocating resources. We just didn't have it, and we didn't for a long, long time. You probably could say we never did. Of course, when the war in Europe started to wind down, then that released quite a few assets.

Q: But until the Normandy landing this was of paramount importance to the British and they were claiming all of them, were they not?

Adm. D.: Oh, yes, and they got most of everything, too. We weren't holding back. We didn't say we have an "inescapable commitment" below the Canal or something. We just fought with what we could scrape together. The British weren't concealing anything. They were perfectly open about it. But we were the ones, it seemed to me, that were making most of the concessions.

Q: We were manufacturing most of the material, too.

Adm. D.: Yes, and, incidentally, when you mention landing craft, had it not been for the Truman Committee - Senator Truman - we would have been in real trouble about landing craft.

Q: In what sense?

Adm. D.: Well, because he was the one who looked into the status of these various programs, contracts, and what not, and he had enough foresight to see that this was going to be a pretty crucial item, to get somebody going on the construction of a different type of ship. I can't think who it was that did so much construction of these types. Anyway, Truman had a great deal to do with the amphibious-ship program.

Q: Did you meet him at that time?

Adm. D.: No, I didn't meet him until after the war.

Q: Did the Combined Chiefs concern themselves with the lease-lend shipments to Murmansk and the Russians? Was this a problem?

Adm. D.: Not that I recall. Of course, we were deeply interested in them because we had a real interest in that project, and it cost a lot of men and a lot of ships.

Q: And one problem in dealing with the Russians, they seem to have had a penchant for asking for more than they actually needed. They were thinking in post-war terms and they wanted to build up supplies.

Adm. D.: That's true, and the British to a lesser degree were doing the same thing. We weren't. We were in there and put in everything we had to settle the war.

Interview No. 3 with Admiral Robert L. Dennison, U.S. Navy (Ret.)

Date: Wednesday afternoon, 17 January 1973

Place: His office in Washington, D. C.

Subject: Biography

By: John T. Mason, Jr.

Q: Admiral, we were talking about the role of the Joint Chiefs of Staff and the Planning Committee, of which you were a part. Now, for a moment, perhaps you'd focus on the plans which were authorized and drawn up by the Joint Chiefs for the ultimate invasion of the Japanese islands themselves. Tell me again what were your primary concerns in this proposed operation?

Adm. D.: There were a number of different points of view about, first, the necessity for an invasion. Admiral Leahy, for one, felt and quite rightly so that Japan had already been defeated by being cut off from her sources of supply, food, products, and it was only a matter of a relatively short time before the country would collapse.

Q: Was this reflecting President Roosevelt's point of view, do you suppose?

Adm. D.: It's pretty hard to say. I think probably Roosevelt felt that but couldn't afford to adopt that as a key to his strategy, because others felt that this kind of a war might drag on with no decision for a very long time and that there was a necessity for a military conquest of the Japanese islands. An additional factor, of course, beyond the necessity for an invasion was what would the casualties be - the U. S. casualties - and would they be acceptable. This was a very grave concern of the President's and was expressed to the Joint Chiefs many times by Admiral Leahy, who was trying to get a believable estimate in answer to that question.

In order to get an answer the Joint Chiefs inquired of anybody who was involved in this, all kinds of authorities, and the answers we got about what the Japanese reaction to invasion would be varied all the way from 100 percent opposition to landing, not only by the Japanese military, but by Japanese civilians, to capitulation.

Q: Kind of a national hari-kari!

Adm. D.: Correct, a national kamikaze or suicide attack or however you want to describe it - to everybody laying down his arms and folding. And there was nothing but opinion to base a judgment on. Obviously, we could never know until we tried. There never was a real determination of which was the more likely.

I think from a conservative standpoint we obviously had to plan for the worst in the form of opposition, which, of course, would be everybody fighting.

Q: What was your own personal opinion in this matter?

Adm. D.: I basically agreed with Admiral Leahy's views because we had plenty of intelligence to show what straits Japan was in. But beyond that I felt that if we could give some indication of how we were going to treat the Emperor

Dennison #3 - 85

and the Japanese governmental structure in a way that wouldn't destroy their form of government, our chances of making a successful invasion were enhanced. And of course, this was a concern of a great many people, what we were going to do about the Emperor of Japan as a person and as a chief of state. In the end, of course, as everybody knows, we put MacArthur in there and did not destroy the government or the Emperor.

Q: At what point in time was that decision made, to install MacArthur as a kind of a second emperor?

Adm. D.: I've forgotten. It may have been part of the overall planning for the invasion. If it wasn't, it followed very, very closely because this was part of the same package for the conquest of Japan.

On the invasion itself, the plan basically was to put an invasion force on Kyushu, the southernmost island, and have it move north onto Honshu. Now, anyone who wishes to look at a map will find out that this is not a very simple thing because of the bottleneck of the water and all sorts of things. Concurrently, there was to be an invasion of Honshu and the central plain, and there was considerable debate at one time about invading Hokkaido, which most people with the exception of the Army Air Force thought was ridiculous.

Q: They felt otherwise, why?

Adm. D.: This is a very personal and probably biased point of view, but they were running out of airfields to base these heavy bombers on that were running out of their ears, and with everything saturated within reach of Japan, this would give them a lot of real estate to put in more bombers to hit the islands south of Hokkaido. Of course, this is probably unfair and probably oversimplified.

In any event, the mounting of such an operation as the invasion was such a massive undertaking that some kind of a decision had to be made because of the time element. The best period of time during the year, as I remember now, was in the early fall, October, November, or some such -

Q: This would have had to be in 1945, then?

Adm. D.: Yes. Or, if we didn't do it then on account of weather factors principally, it would have to be postponed for a good many months.

Q: At one point in the Quebec Conference they had thought that it would take eighteen months after Germany surrendered. Was this the reason it was based on?

Adm. D.: Well, that was one reason. And, of course, you remember Stalin's statement that he would enter the Pacific War something like ninety days after the end of the war in Europe, which he did incidentally, which was another mistake from our viewpoint. But this is another matter which I'll go into in a minute or two.

The decision had been made at least to mount the operation, to assemble the shipping and get out the operation plan and the operation orders, and the assignment of forces, and stationing and positioning of troops. There were all kinds of matters that had to be taken care of. So the decision was made to mount the operation and withhold any decision or any indication of the decision on whether the plans would be executed. And the decision never was made because time overtook us. It became apparent long before that that the Japanese had in fact been defeated, and they can argue from now to six months from now what effect on the Japanese the decision to drop atomic bombs on Nagasaki and Hiroshima had.

Q: Did the possible use of the atomic bombs ever come up as a subject to the Joint Chiefs?

Adm. D.: Not that I recall. It was never a subject for discussion, where we would use it, or if we would use it, or when we would use it. But President Truman, of course, wouldn't act on his own. He had to be getting advice from his advisors on whether or not to drop the bomb and where. But whether that was a factor or not really is another matter because, again, it was pretty obvious that Japan was going down the drain. It was just a question of when.

So the operation was being mounted, plans were being made, and the decision to execute never was made.

On the matter I just mentioned about the Soviets coming in to the war. Stalin guaranteed that it would be ninety days after the surrender of Germany.

Q: This was a guarantee he gave at Yalta, was it not?

Adm. D.: I believe it was at Potsdam. And he kept it almost to the day. But this brought into the debate the question of whether their participation was necessary. I, for one, felt that the problem was not to get the Soviets involved in the war in the Pacific, but to keep them out of the war in the Pacific because of giving them a voice in what went on in any kind of a peace settlement, which they probably would have had anyway, but not to the extent they did have because of their participation.

Whether their participation was necessary depended in part on what would be the attitude of the Japanese forces in Manchuria. These forces at one time were crack troops of the Japanese Army, but as the war went on we had intelligence information which showed that these crack troops had been defeated by us in the South Pacific and their replacements had been untrained troops of inferior quality that never did amount to any kind of a respectable military force.

Q: Well, they were only pursuing a common-sense sort of policy, weren't they?

Adm. D.: Yes, of course, but it had a great deal to do with whether this force based on Manchuria was a respectable force that we'd have to defeat, or whether they would all lay down their arms, or what would happen there. At any rate, for whatever reason Stalin did agree to come in and he did.

Q: In the Joint Chiefs, when this whole thing was discussed, the point of view you just expressed as being yours, was this embraced by others?

Adm. D.: Yes, but not very many.

Q: Most of them felt Russia should come in?

Adm. D.: Yes. Obviously President Roosevelt did, and it would be pretty hard to change his mind that this would have been a desirable if not essential factor, had things gone differently. Indications were that they wouldn't be needed, but there again it was a matter of judgment.

Q: In that connection, were you at Yalta?

Adm. D.: No.

Q: Did you have some part in the preparation for Yalta?

Adm. D.: When was Yalta?

Q: It was in February of 1945.

You say you obviously did work on some of the plans for Yalta but you don't remember anything specific.

Adm. D.: Yes.

Q: Admiral, I know for a fact because this had appeared in a number of places that throughout the war both President Roosevelt and Mr. Churchill were coming forward with ideas which weren't in the main stream of military activity, shall we say. How did the Joint Chiefs deal with this?

Adm. D.: As tactfully as they could! The British really were the ones that came up with some of the most startling ideas. One, for example, was Churchill's idea — maybe it wasn't his idea, but he put it forward — to freeze a large mass of sea water to make a field for the operations of aircraft. They had some very elaborate plans on how this could be done. The idea was you'd end up with a great big mass of ice water around in the North Atlantic some place and this would be an ice deck for the operations of air. Of course, there were other things like training dolphins to detect submarines.

Q: They were a little bit ahead of time with that!

Adm. D.: Yes, they were. They really had some fantastic ideas and, of course, you couldn't discard these ideas out of hand, strange as they may seem, because maybe there'd be some sense in some of them. Roosevelt wasn't nearly so bad. He had some individual ideas. He fancied himself as some kind of a naval strategist. I think I told you in one of our interviews about dispatches to Admiral Hart saying about surveillance craft early in the game, telling him exactly where to station them, how many to put out, and who was to man them. He went into great detail about how to do this operation. But most of these ideas came out of the British.

Q: Somebody, in speculating on ideas of this nature expressed by Roosevelt, attributed it to the fact that he had a number of friends in yachting circles, men who had been sailing the

Dennison #3 - 91

seven seas, and had unorthodox ideas.

Adm. D.: Well, don't forget that Roosevelt himself was not only a yachtsman but he served in the Navy Department and he was deeply interested in the Navy and the sea. So he was not what you might call an amateur, he was a very well educated amateur.

Q: Well, Admiral, your role with the Joint Chiefs came to an end. Tell me what you did at that point.

Adm. D.: It came to an end rather abruptly. When it was apparent that Japan was defeated and the war was over, I was ordered back to the Navy Department to report to Admiral Cooke.

Q: Who was then deputy?

Adm. D.: Yes. Not deputy. I think he was vice chief, wasn't he? He said that he had sent for me because of a situation that had arisen in a committee called the Subcommittee of the Far East under State Department chairmanship. I've forgotten what they were a subcommittee of, but at any rate this particular group was charged with making certain arrangements and certain plans for the Japanese surrender, and what had upset Admiral Cooke was the fact that they were about to recommend that the document be signed by General MacArthur and only by General MacArthur. This upset the Navy considerably because, after all, we felt that the war in the Pacific had been won by naval ships under Admiral Nimitz.

Dennison #3 - 92

I tried to explain to Admiral Cooke from what little I knew about it that the Navy membership of this committee was really representing the Secretary of the Navy and I had no such ticket. He said, "That doesn't make any difference. Just go down and tell them that you're a member and then get in there and get this thing changed."

Q: How big a committee was this?

Adm. D.: It was quite a sizeable one. It seems to me that there were ten maybe.

Q: And the Army was there?

Adm. D.: Yes, the Army and the Navy and State and hangers-on. But I did carry out my instructions and I did step on a lot of toes in doing it.

Q: What happened when you stepped on toes?

Adm. D.: Nothing, because I had the backing of the people in the Navy and the other people couldn't care less. Nobody really knew who the hell I was and they probably didn't care.

Q: It was then something that had just not been thoroughly thought through?

Adm. D.: Well, it had been thought through, I guess, but it was going to be rammed through - I guess that's a better word. Of course, the Army was all for it and I don't know what axe State had to grind, if any. In any event, what finally happened was that the recommendation was made that Admiral

Nimitz sign on behalf of the United States when MacArthur had signed, which he did. The minute it was decided that Admiral Nimitz would sign for the United States –

Q: And MacArthur would sign for?

Adm. D.: The Supreme Commander Allied Powers, or whatever his title was. Nimitz' signing, of course, would mean that other nations would have to sign, which is exactly what happened on the deck of the <u>Missouri</u> on the 2nd of September.

Then, after that chore had been completed –

Q: How long did it take you to change this thing around?

Adm. D.: Only a matter of days because time was running out on us. I can't claim sole credit for doing it. I've just forgotten how it came about but it did. Then I stayed on for a while, making a nuisance out of myself, and finally this particular committee started to dry up and I went back to the Navy Department and about the first thing I did was try to sell my views on the need for the Navy to have participation in matters of postwar settlement.

Traditionally, the Navy was opposed to the State Department or diplomats and/it mostly was a dirty word. We wanted no part of dealings with the State Department and for years this was acceptable, but obviously at the end of this great world war there were all kinds of problems that we would have and did have with rival interests in the Pacific and in Europe. The Army had a very well-organized plan manned by a very capable group of officers to really deal with these problems. Dean Rusk, for example, was an Army colonel and was one of the participants in these activities. He was a colleague of mine in most of these activities.

It seemed to me that we should have some branch within the Navy responsible for planning in this area, representing the Navy on the joint committees that were springing up all over the place. I sold the idea to Admiral Cooke and Admiral Conolly, who —

Q: Richard Conolly?

Adm. D.: Yes, who was a very fine officer and Admiral Nimitz who told me to go ahead.

Q: Nimitz by that time had become CNO?

Adm. D.: Correct, yes. I went to work and had to overcome a great deal of resistance within the Navy because of this traditional Navy attitude.

Q: May I interrupt for just a second to ask how were these interdepartmental relationships carried on by the Navy during the war itself, with the State Department in particular.

Adm. D.: Well, you see, the liaison or consultation or whatever you want to call it was on the Secretary's level or through Leahy on the Joint Chiefs of Staff. There wasn't really any setup of interdepartmental committees, except one or two very minor entities.

Dennison #3 - 95

Q: We, in ONI, I know, had a special representative to the State Department, but it was a single person.

Adm. D.: That's right. There wasn't any such thing as far as the rest of the Navy was concerned. At least, I know that there was no CNO participation.

Q: So there was no background tradition and this is what you were dealing with?

Adm. D.: Right. We were trying to decide what we ought to have as a division of political-military affairs and Nimitz gave me his blessing so I drafted this document with the help of some warrior friends of mine, a charter which would establish the office of Assistant Chief of Naval Operations for Political and Military Affairs. Incidentally, that division under a slightly different title is still in the Navy. I had a very difficult time -

Q: On what basis were you opposed?

Adm. D.: Mostly because it was hard to sell the idea to some people that there was a need for this sort of thing. They wanted a Navy sort of isolated from participation in political affairs, even if they were international political affairs. But it was inevitable.

One of the things they did was to draft the trusteeship agreement for the ex-Japanese mandate. Now, this was a matter of very grave concern to the Navy. This is only an example of the kind of thing. And, of course, indirectly we are concerned with monetary problems. Germany, for example. As part of the government, and a very important part, we had to participate in any mechanism for doing it.

Q: It seems to me this was one of the fundamental lessons of the war itself?

Adm. D.: That's exactly what I thought. But I finally got everybody to agree to this charter. There was an outfit called Op-02 under a vice admiral that was supposed to be the liaison with the State Department only for matters of protocol and passports and administrative matters. That's all, but not for high-policy matters. So I did get the charter approved and went in and handed it to Admiral Nimitz. He looked it over and read it very carefully, and he must have talked to Forrestal about it, who was then Secretary of the Navy. In any event, I got the word that this was exactly what he wanted and he approved it. So I went in to see him and said, "Admiral, now my job is done." It took a little bit of doing, too.

Q: Why did it take a little bit of doing?

Adm. D.: Because of all the convincing and arm-twisting and maneuvering and getting people to help me. I was all alone. Anyway, somebody had to be operating in the meantime, so I was doing a lot of this stuff without any charter. It was just obvious the Navy had to be represented on some of these things. My friends in the Army and Army Air Forces used to kid me about it because they had a really well-organized team. One of them would be a member of a committee or subcommittee and who was the Navy guy but me. Then his colleague would be present at the meeting of some other committee and again I would be the Navy representative!

Anyhow, after Nimitz had approved this I went to him and said, "Admiral, now my job is done and I want to go to sea." He looked up at me and he said, "No, your job isn't done. I want you to take this job." I protested and I said, "It was written for at least a rear admiral and I'm not, I'm just a captain." He said that didn't make any difference. He said, "I want you to not mention the subject to me again for a year and get organized and get going." So I did. I started out with one secretary. Then I got some people from Forrestal, who were really cracker-jack people. Mostly Reserve lawyers. I remember John Rockefeller III was one of the people who helped me. Then there was a lawyer named Shepherd, Mike Fowle, Jack Geilfuss, another lawyer, a labor lawyer. That's about all.

Q: What problems did you have to face at that point?

Adm. D.: There were a number of problems that required some immediate solution. They had a strange organization going called the Committee of Three. This was during the formative stage of the State-War-Navy Coordinating Committee, which was the body that was supposed to handle all these interdepartmental and other problems that became national problems, or were already nation problems. And this Committee of Three were the three secretaries of War, Navy, and State. Forrestal would go up to these weekly meetings with no agenda, no notes, no advisors, and the result, of course, was chaos because I would get calls from my opposite numbers in the other services and also State, "Why hadn't the Navy done so-and-so"? I said I'd never heard of it. And they said, "Well, your Secretary is reported to have said that this is what the Navy's going to do."

Well, it turned out that Forrestal had made some commitment at this meeting. The same thing happened in the Army and also the State Department.

In the meantime I'd become Forrestal's political-military advisor and I said, "This has got to stop, Mr. Secretary. Can't you arrange to be accompanied by somebody at these meetings?" He finally made a deal that each member of the Committee of Three would have one person with him who was not supposed to participate. He wasn't supposed to keep any notes. There was no written record.

Q: Why did they want it so informal?

Adm. D.: Because there wasn't any authority for such a committee and these were pretty powerful people. This may have been one factor. And they didn't really see any need for formalize it. These three big powers would get together and decide these matters and State, War, and Navy would carry out whatever it was that they were supposed to carry out. It sounds incredible now, but this is what happened.

Q: A little cabal within the Cabinet!

Adm. D.: Right. But then what happened was just great because the Army representative was under-Secretary Howard Peterson, a lawyer from Philadelphia, a very fine man, and the State Department man was H. Freeman Matthews, called Doc Matthews, or Jack Hickerson who lives here in Washington and is a very knowledgeable man, foreign service officer and had been ambassador to several countries. We would get together after the meetings and decide what commitments had been made and maybe what commitments should have been made, and agree among ourselves who was going to do what, and then go back to our own departments and say this is what was said or what was agreed to by Secretary Forrestal at this meeting and carry it out.

Q: Did you run into any snags with the Secretary?

Adm. D.: No, because it was obvious that somebody had to carry out these instructions. They weren't making any notes. How did they think anything was going to happen? Everything got fouled up for a while until they did this. And we weren't supposed to make any notes, so we had to get together and decide what had been done or should be done. Then when these Committee of Three meetings were over, they would call in Admiral Leahy and the organization then became the National Security Agency. Admiral Sydney Souers was the first director of it and then General Vanderberg. Where they got the money to operate this agency, I don't know, but this was the forerunner of what later was a statutory agency, the Central Intelligence Agency, started by President Truman. So they were really serving two functions - the Committee of Three and the National Security Agency.

While all this was going on, the State-War-Navy Coordinating Committee was functioning with a number of subcommittees. They were dealing with all kinds of postwar problems, and this required an awful lot of staff preparation, briefings, and God knows what all. John L. Sullivan was the one who went to most of these meetings and I went with him to all of them. I was the Navy representative on practically every subcommittee that anybody ever heard of. So that was a great piece of machinery and absolutely essential.

Q: It just sort of evolved, didn't it?

Adm. D.: Yes, it did, all through necessity because no one department could handle these problems. There was no question about that. And it wouldn't do to have the President's Cabinet do it or any agency that existed in the government. At any rate, we handled a lot of problems.

Q: Would you talk about some of those problems that you had to wrestle with?

Adm. D.: Yes. One of them and perhaps one of the most significant ones - was how to handle the ex-Japanese Mandates. Here were millions of square miles with an aggregate population about the size of the State of Rhode Island with zero communications, no central government. The Navy was in Guam, which was not part of this mandated territory but was in the area. So, again, like so many problems, there were two schools of thought diametrically opposed to each other. The Navy, of course, was strongly on the side of annexing the islands to protect our interests . . .

Q: And running them the way Guam was run.

Adm. D.: Yes. And the State Department was strongly in favor of turning them back to Japan or giving them independence or some dream that you couldn't possibly accomplish. Number One, you couldn't give them back to Japan, for Heaven's sake. And how can you have a group of separate islands become independent? That was also a do-gooder dream, really.

Q: Did the United Nations as an idea enter into this? It was in existence.

Adm. D.: I was about to come to that. Some years ago, Forrestal had foreseen this kind of thing and anyone who cares to look in the Forrestal Diaries can find out what was going on before the time I'm talking about, but nothing had been decided. Forrestal felt that some kind of a trusteeship should be established. When I was wrestling with the problem, I had to draft an agreement and I discovered, of course, something that was well known but had been overlooked mostly, that the United Nations Charter contained a provision for setting up what was called a strategic trusteeship under the Security Council. General trusteeships are under the Assembly, and it required, as in all trusteeships, somebody to administer it and so on, but, under the Security trusteeship, the administrator can have rights to exclude people from the area and do all kinds of things that can't possibly be done under a general trusteeship. In other words, we had complete protection for security purposes or strategic purposes - exploding a few atomic bombs down at Bikini, for example, and we've done, I think, through the years, a fine job of bringing these people up towards self-government.

Q: And making a regular report to the United Nations?

Adm. D.: Yes, but it's sort of a pro forma thing. This developed into the hell of a debate within the government, and the Army finally sort of passed it over to us, to me, because they felt we knew more about it than they did and that we were perfectly capable of carrying out the battle.

One of the people from the State Department who was opposed to our ideas was a very capable Negro later in the United Nations Organization. Ralph Bunche. But he finally came around to our point of view and did a perfectly magnificent job. He headed up briefings of the press and all these various societies who were interested in the welfare of these islands and explained just how we were going to carry this off and what our plans were, and how it was the best, and maybe the only, solution. So I became a member of the team that was to go up to brief Warren Austin and be with him during these negotiations in the Security Council, which I did. We briefed Austin who really didn't know very much about it, and we had mistakenly thought that in the Council we would run into a Soviet veto and we were prepared for quite a debate.

As I remember there were two sessions and Austin presented the case for trusteeship very forcefully. He pointed out that it was completely within the provisions of the Charter and that as administrator, which we proposed to be, we would do certain things in the interest of the islands. Well, instead of being opposed by the Soviets, the Soviets agreed wholeheartedly. They said, in effect, the United States won that war, they defeated the Japanese forces in those islands, and we think this is a generous offer. We were opposed by the British, who were supported by Australia and I believe New Zealand, on legal grounds. These were mandates under the League of Nations and on and on, and we had no authority to set up legally.

Finally, Warren Austin got up and said just a very few words - he didn't get up, everybody was seated - and said, "Let me remind the Council that we are in these islands, our forces are there, our flag is flying, and if the Security Council does not see fit to grant this trusteeship, then we will annex those islands." With that, the chairman or whoever he was called for a vote and there was unanimous agreement!

Q: What was back of the British objection? Did they want the mandate for Australia and New Zealand?

Adm. D.: No. It could have been just British intransigence. I don't know whether they thought that one day this might properly be in the sphere of British or Australian or New Zealand influence. If so, they hadn't looked at the map. It was quite a long way away and the day, of course, will never come. I don't really know what their objections were. But we completely misread the Soviets on this issue because they had axes to grind of their own. The Kurile Islands, for example, or some other deal.

That's one example of what went on in this State-War-Navy Coordinating Committee. And another one in which the Navy was left carrying the fight was about what to do with U. S. property in the Philippines. Remember, in 1936 we promised them independence in ten years, but most people had forgotten that the grant of independence was conditional upon Philippine acceptance of certain U. S. statues, one of which was the Tydings-MacDuffie Act which had to do with U. S. coaling stations in the Philippines which under the grant of independence were supposed to remain the property of the United States. Of course, we did have a lot of property around there, bits and pieces that we really should have given back years ago. But things like Sangley Point and our need for certain airfields. We had no further need for Cavite, for example. We would never have another Asiatic Fleet. So there were certain things we could and should and did give back, but then we ran into the State Department again, "Why do you want Sangley Point? And why do you want this radio station or whatever it might be?" So at the final meeting, which was in Acheson's office - he was then Assistant Secretary and later became a dear friend of mine - the Army representative didn't say anything, Sullivan was supposed to represent us but he was ill, which left me to do it and I got some of my lawyer assistants and went up to Acheson's office with a stack of law books with little pieces of paper for place marks and put these books in front of me. Acheson recited what the case was all about and invited views.

The Army practically passed. They said they understood what the Navy position would be and that was that. Well, what was the Navy position? I told them what the facts were, as I just told you, about the legal position, but beyond that the strategic need for these things in the foreseeable future, U. S. security interests. We agreed completely that certain facilities and certain properties should be turned over to the Philippines. Well, I got through with this plea and Acheson spoke up and said, "Well, the State Department position will be to agree with the Navy position concurred in by the Army."

So, the thing was over and we got up to go, and he knew that I was associated with Sullivan and with some of his other legal friends, and he put his arm across my shoulders as we walked to the door and said, "That was a very convincing argument that you presented. Very capable," and I said, "Thank you, Sir." He said, "By the way, what was your year at Harvard Law?"! I said, "I'm sure that was meant as a compliment and I'll take it as such, but I'm just a garden variety naval officer. I'm not a lawyer." He said, "Oh," and I never knew whether he was pulling my leg or not because why he would assume I was a graduate of Harvard Law except that so many of these people that were around in those days were graduates.

There are two examples for you of the kind of things. Reparations was another one and currency problems in Germany. All kinds of things.

Q: You really covered the globe!

Adm. D.: We had to.

Q: Was there anything involving the Russians specifically?

Adm. D.: Certainly not bilaterally. Of course, indirectly they were involved in all these things, but as far as U. S.-Soviet relationships were concerned I don't remember any issue. But there were plenty of them going round, the Middle East and all round the world . . .

Q: I suppose this involved you with the Atomic Energy Commission, too, did it not?

Adm. D.: Yes, it certainly did and, of course, there was Atomic Energy Commission participation in these things and their position in international affairs became really more and more important as time went on. President Truman looked to them for advice and got all their documents. Forrestal had some, which he had no business keeping. When I stole the Forrestal papers I subtracted them and got them back into the proper files, but that's beside the point.

To answer your question, there was not any direct participation by the Commission in the State-War-Navy Coordinating Committee, nor do I know of any participation in any other intergovernmental organization.

Q: Admiral, it must have become readily apparent to you that there was a woeful lack of educational background in the Navy for matters of this sort. This, then, became one of your driving ambitions, did it not, to underscore the need for teaching?

Adm. D.: It wasn't really an ambition. I was personally involved in it and it appeared to me then as it does now and all the time between that the Navy, when you look back in naval history, Perry in Japan is one example, really has been in the forefront of formulating and carrying out United States policy and doctrine. I don't think the Navy should ever forget that. The Navy indeed does have a very vital role in not only national security but in diplomacy, the carrying out of U.S. policy as stated by the President.

I do recall something you might want to insert back where I was talking about Admiral Nimitz telling me to get out of the office and get to work.

Q: Yes, spend a year working on this project.

Adm. D.: I carried out his instructions. I didn't open my mouth. But a year to the day from when he told me that he sent for me and told me to go and pack my suitcase, that I was going to sea. I thanked him and then as I was about to leave I said, "By the way, where am I going? and he said, "You're going to command the Missouri", which was one of the best commands we had. I think I might have told you this. Is it on your record?

Q: No, it is not.

Adm. D.: So he carried out his promise. I went in to Admiral King to say goodbye to him and I had no idea that (he still had office in the Navy Department), he would know anything about what I was doing. I hadn't had any contact with him, but when I said goodbye to him, he said, "I've been watching your progress and I'm delighted with your duty assignment. I feel that you certainly rate it and should have it." So I thanked him.

Q: Before you depart for the Missouri, you did become advisor to Secretary Forrestal. Tell me about that.

Adm. D.: Yes, I think I mentioned that a while ago. When I became Assistant Chief of Naval Operations for Political-Military Affairs, I was appointed by Forrestal as a matter of formal title, but I was Political-Military advisor to him and I attended his staff meetings and he would call on me for a briefing or counsel about some problem. My office in the Navy Department was almost directly over his and we were connected by a pair of loudspeakers and I had some of the strangest experiences with him. He would buzz me on the squawk box and put some question to me. . .

Q: At any hour of the night or day, I take it?

Adm. D.: Well, I was there many hours of the night and day. For example, the one I'll use is not far-fetched at all. "What about the Kurile Islands?", then, click, everything would go off! Well, what about the Kurile Islands? So I'd have to go down and look through his appointment book and ask his secretary if he'd written any letters to anybody or gotten any letters from anybody, who he'd seen, and then I could figure out whether this man had any problem with the Kurile Islands and so figure what it might be.

Q: What a waste of effort! I mean, a few words would have saved you that.

Adm. D.: This was Forrestal's way of doing business. He did business really by asking questions. It was almost impossible to ever get an opinion out of him. In the many talks I had with him I never really was sure I understood if he had a position or, if he did, what it was. But he was extremely selfish and thoughtless. When we were trying to figure out what words to put in this draft trusteeship agreement, he invited me down for lunch and his guest was

John Foster Dulles, and after lunch he told Mr. Dulles what I was interested in and asked him if he could give me some advice. So Dulles spent quite a bit of time and said, "If you want to see an example of tough language, look up the U. S. treaty with Panama. My firm was asked by the Panamanian government to represent them in a suit against the U. S. to recompense for the change in the value of the dollar when the U. S. went off the gold standard. We did some research and, after studying that treaty, we advised them we couldn't take the case because the treaty says, in effect, that nothing the United States would do would abrogate the treaty, even if they didn't pay Panama a nickel." But this was simply an example of Forrestal. He knew that Dulles knew a whole lot about these problems and he knew I was having a hard time, so he just made sure that we got together.

Q: He basically was very much interested in all of these international problems.

Adm. D.: Oh, very, very much so. He was very internationally minded. Sullivan did a great job for him on this State-War-Navy stuff, and Forrestal was a very intelligent man, there's no question about it, and he knew so many people. He attracted a lot of extremely capable people around him on his personal staff, most of whom thought then and do now very, very highly of him. I had mixed feelings about him. My job on the State-War-Navy Committee advising him was difficult. It sounds ridiculous, but I used to be picked up in the morning on the days we were having meetings by John Sullivan's driver then go around and pick up Sullivan at his home, and I'd brief him in the car on the way into the Navy Department, and then go with him to the meeting. I got damned well fed up with this, and I said one day, "I don't think that what you're doing is fair. It's your responsibility to represent us at these meetings. It's mine to give you the best counsel I can and at least let you know what's going on and what the problems are, and I don't think you're giving me a chance to carry out my responsibilities." He got mad and said, "You must think I'm pretty stupid if I can' understand these things in the time we have."

I said, "I didn't say that." But that made him pay a little more attention and give a little more time on some of these things. Some of these problems are not simple. They're very complex.

Q: He was a pretty good Secretary though?

Adm. D.: Oh, he was a very good one, completely different from Forrestal, whom one wouldn't call unapproachable, but the difference between talking to Forrestal or with Forrestal and Sullivan was like day and night. Sullivan would tell you what he thought and you never knew what Forrestal thought, at least I never knew.

Q: Well, ultimately Forrestal's resignation as Secretary of Defense was called for by the President. Would you talk about what happened after that?

Adm. D.: Yes. Just before this happened, the President asked me one day if I knew who the Secretary of Defense was. I played along and said, "Yes, Sir. James Forrestal." He said, "You're wrong. I'm the Secretary of Defense. Jim calls me several times every day to ask me to make decisions which are completely within his competence and it's getting more burdensome all the time and it's something I shouldn't be called on to do."

Well, he finally asked for Forrestal's resignation and I was with the President on the morning of the day when Forrestal was to be relieved by Johnson. I remember the ceremonies were to be in the Pentagon at noon, and the phone rang and I could hear, of course, only the President's side of the conversation but about all he said was "Yes, Jim. That's the way I want it, Jim." He hung up and said, "That was Forrestal," which, of course, I had gathered. "He wanted me to tell him whether I really wanted him to be relieved by Louis Johnson today." But none of us, including the President, realized that Forrestal was really a very ill man. Why this escaped us, I don't know. The President must have felt and I must have felt that what he was doing was not rational, but he just couldn't make up his mind apparently, couldn't make a decision, and that's why he was leaning on the President.

He went down to Hobe Sound to stay with some friends of his and really came apart, as I understand it, because the President sent for me several days after Forrestal had been there and said, "We've just had some strange calls from Jim Forrestal. He thinks his phones are tapped. I've had the Secret Service check this out and this isn't the case. And he kept talking about his papers. Do you know anything about any papers of his?" I said, "Yes, I do", because I'd written some of them and Forrestal kept a file, a personal file, of materials that he thought was important. It was completely private. His secretary, Kate Foley, knew what was in it, but I didn't know what it was. So he said, "Will you take care of it?"

I said, "Yes, you can forget it, Mr. President, I'll take care of it.

This sounds like a dime novel, but I got the Secret Service people in the White House to get a small panel truck. We went over to the Pentagon immediately, went to Johnson's office, and took that file cabinet. I could recognize it. I knew what it looked like. I'd seen it. And we hurried back to the White House.

Q: You must have had some altercation with the security guards over there didn't you?

Adm. D.: No. I was in uniform and the Secret Service identified themselves. I must say that the guard system must have been pretty damned lax. Maybe if we'd tried to take something smaller than a file cabinet we'd have had trouble. Like stealing a grand piano, you know! But nobody foresaw that

Forrestal was going to die. We thought that he was going to get all right and go back and then we'd give him back the file cabinet.

I called up Kate Foley and asked her to come over.

Q: She was then serving with Johnson?

Adm. D.: No, she wasn't. I think she was doing nothing. At any rate, she came over and I said, "Please look through this and see if everything's intact, as far as you can remember, and lock it and seal it and give me a key and the combination or whatever it was in a sealed envelope, and you and I will sign it. I don't want to get into but we must have a key here or the combination or whatever is needed.

So, that was done and when Forrestal had this tragic death, I went with President Truman just two days before that to see him in Bethesda, but even then we didn't know and, of course, his physician didn't see this one coming either. I think on balance they thought it would be more hazardous to put him in close confinement so they gave him a certain amount of freedom.

Q: How did he act when you called on him?

Adm. D.: He seemed to be subdued and very quiet. He didn't have very much to say. He was glad to see the President but he obviously was ill. He wasn't vivacious at all. He didn't have very much to offer. But he did commit suicide and here we were with the papers in the White House.

Q: Did he know that you had his safe?

Adm. D.: Yes. Everything was in order. His phones weren't tapped and his papers were secure. Not only did I do that but I went down to his house with Kate Foley and went through his voluminous files there. These were innocuous, like "Dear Jim, I'm so glad to see you've been appointed Secretary of the Navy," and he'd write back and say, "Thank you so much, Tom," and that kind of thing. Why he kept it I'll never know, but there was an awful lot of that. We even went into his bedroom and opened up the drawer of his night table and there was a slip of paper in there which was another story. A memorandum from Franklin Roosevelt saying that when so-and-so leaves I want Ed Pauley to be appointed, and this led to a dispute about his confirmation, which Mrs. Roosevelt said Pauley was gentleman enough not to dispute, but her husband never would have appointed Ed Pauley to any job in the Navy Department.

At any rate, to get back to his papers. The problem then was what to do with them. Mrs. Helen Ogden Reid of the Herald Tribune was a dear friend of Jim's and she arranged to buy these papers to get some money into his estate. Well, of course, there was the question as to whether anybody had the authority to sell the papers. The government could have taken the position that they were the property of the U. S. Government, not Jim Forrestal's. I told the President what I planned to do. I didn't want to get him involved in any of this. I just wanted him to know what I thought ought to be done and I just was telling what I intended to do. He could stop it if he wanted to. It was a rather touchy problem.

In the first place they were called the Forrestal Diaries. Well, they weren't diaries at all. They were simply day-by-day who he'd seen and maybe a note or two. Some of them had pretty strong views about various people, but nothing very significant. So it seemed to me that the only way out of this would be to get a couple of writers, whoever Mrs. Reid wanted that we could accept, and she did, we did, we both did. She came down to see me. She suspected my motives. She didn't know me or anything about me, but I could sense that she didn't trust me. Well, we got over that one in a hurry.

Q: You were in a Democratic White House!

Adm. D.: Maybe that had something to do with it. At any rate, we got over that hurdle and we did get hold of some people. One of them was a Reserve naval officer. And we made a deal with them that they would send me a chapter or chapters of this book as they were written and then we would screen them for security and send them back. Then, when the book was finished, the papers were to be returned to me. Everybody agreed. Well, we had a hell of a time because the Defense Department - I forget who they sent over - and the State Department with Adrian Fisher, State Department counsel, and George Elsey helped me. He was on the President's staff. He's now head of the American Red Cross. We started going into this and it got kind of touchy and the Defense Department signed off, and I don't blame them but there wasn't really anything about national security in there. There was some of this atomic energy stuff which I'd taken out anyhow. They kept their part of the bargain. Fisher modified the language a little bit, but nothing substantial was done to it. The book manuscrips was prepared and the book was eventually published.

Then Mrs. Reid and I had another meeting. What to do with the papers? I said, "What do you want to do with them?" Well, she wanted them kept intact, and I said, "That's exactly what I want." The President's term was about to expire and I've still got the damned things. How about giving them to the library of Princeton University." This was completely agreeable to her and it certainly was a solution for me. I didn't want the damned papers and the President wasn't going to want them. She'd gotten some money into the estate, the book had been published. Her mission, as she saw it, had been completed. So, again, one of these last-minute deals. These were the very closing days of the President's administration. Again I got hold of a truck and, under guard, sent the stuff, after calling up Princeton and writing letters and making some kind of a deal, and got them in the Forrestal Library at Princeton University, where they still are. I did at the time, but now I don't know whether any part of them are closed or not.

At any rate, that's the story of the Forrestal diaries.

Q: What was the need for getting money into the Forrestal estate? Had it been depleted?

Adm. D.: I've no idea what his finances were, what his obligations were. Maybe Mrs. Reid did or maybe she didn't, but she just thought two things, I imagine. One was that possibly or probably they'd need more money. The other was she was so much interested in Jim Forrestal and here was a record of his term of office, so she thought, and it ought to be published in some way so that people wouldn't forget him.

Interview No. 4 with Admiral Robert Lee Dennison, U. S. Navy
(Retired)

Place: His office in Washington, D. C.

Date: Tuesday, 30 January 1973

Subject: Biography

By: John T. Mason, Jr.

Q: Once again, it's very good to see you. Before you tell me the story of your tour of duty in the battleship Missouri, which was a real assignment, would you lap back for a moment and tell me about your trip in October 1945 to the Far East, to Japan and China, in the interest of reparations - what could be paid by the defeated nations, etc.?

Adm. D.: Secretary Forrestal was ordered by President Truman to go to Japan and, en route, to pick up Edwin Pauley at Los Angeles. Pauley was to be in charge of reparations with regard to Japan, and the idea was to pick Ed Pauley up, go to Japan with him, and make an inspection of what was going on there, then leave Pauley to take care of the dealings with the Japanese.

Q: Pauley was actually a personal friend of Truman's, was he not?

Adm. D.: Yes. Pauley, of course, was an ardent member of the Democratic Party and was a friend of President Truman.

At the last instant, almost, Secretary Forrestal decided he couldn't go and assigned his Under Secretary, Artemis Gates, to go in his stead. I was to go since I was Assistant Chief of Naval Operations for Political-Military Affairs, and Forrestal had appointed me as his politico-military advisor.

Q: So you were going regardless?

Adm. D.: When Gates took off I was with him. His aide, Captain Vosler, was along, and several other people joined us from time to time.

We stopped at Pearl for a brief visit and then took off for Japan. We stayed in Tokyo for several days. We had an opportunity to overfly Nagasaki and Hiroshima, which had just been bombed recently by atomic weapons.

Q: That was an essential trip, wasn't it, to view the results there?

Adm. D.: Yes. We had to come back with some appreciation of what condition Japan was in and gauge as best we could the temper of the Japanese people. As far as the Japanese were concerned we found them to be in general friendly to the Americans, and there didn't seem to be any resentment against the United States. I think as time went on we came to learn that the Japanese couldn't understand our magnanimity. They were clearly beaten and they knew it, recognized it, and they couldn't understand kindness and sympathy on our part. I don't believe they ever did.

Q: Just an example of the great divide between the East and the West!

Adm. D.: But while we were in Japan it seemed desirable to try to talk with Chiang Kai-shek so we flew to China. I believe we landed in Shanghai first and went on up to Chungking, up the Yangtze River.

Q: Which is quite some distance!

Adm. D.: It was a long walk for Chiang Kai-shek's people. We had a small gunboat up the river - I forget the name of it - stationed of Chungking, but we had no forces there. It was an outpost and Chiang Kai-shek had gone there for obvious reasons. He had no place else to go.

Q: We had some sort of an ambassador there, did we not?

Adm. D.: Yes, we had an ambassador there. I believe his name was Robertson who in civilian life was a banker, I believe, from one of the southern states. Walter Robertson. We stayed in the palace compound. Chiang Kai-shek lived in what had been Sun Yat-sen's summer palace, but it really wasn't a very elaborate palace and it was quite small. The Generalissimo had built quarters in a compound around the palace where most of us stayed. He gave a banquet for us and invited members of his own Cabinet along, of course, with Madame Chiang Kai-shek to discuss matters in general, and it wasn't until the following day that the three of us, Pauley, Gates, and I, sat down with him and Madame Chiang kai-shek to get down to the matter of reparations.

Q: They had been forewarned of this?

Adm. D.: Oh, yes.

Q: And given some consideration to it?

Adm. D.: It must have been quite brief warning because we ourselves didn't really know we were going to Chungking until after we got out in the Far East. So it had to be a matter of a week, perhaps.

Q: This was a decision on your part?

Adm. D.: Yes. We were there and it seemed to be stupid not to take advantage of our opportunities to find out more than we could just by going to Japan. Then we felt we had some other business, which I'll get to a little later. But Chiang Kai-shek, like all the rest of us, had no idea what Japan's capacity to pay was. He didn't really know what damage China had suffered. So the discussion was more philosophical than it was practical. Chiang Kai-shek was not supposed to know English and he spoke at some length in Chinese. There was an interpreter present but he was a rather junior officer and when he started to interpret Madame Chiang Kai-shek wasn't satisfied apparently, so she took over the translation and she was most eloquent. She got into quoting some figures from the Generalissimo's speech and in the midst of this he, presumably not knowing English, broke in and corrected her.

Q: He recognized figures, perhaps.

Adm. D.: He did more than that because the figures would be meaningless without putting them in some kind of context. Nothing really substantive came out of this conversation. I do remember Madame Chiang Kai-shek making one statement to the effect that no amount of reparations could compensate China for her lost youth, but as far as material damage went or Japan's ability to pay were matters that had to be determined in the future.

Q: In general, Sir, did they more or less feel that there was an obligation to have Japan set them up in business again or what?

Adm. D.: I don't believe our conversation got really down to that kind of a point. My concern was not so much the reparation problem. I didn't keep any notes. Perhaps Pauley's papers would throw some light on that for anybody who was interested in it. But we did go to Tientsin and to the Shantung Peninsula. I must give you a bit of background on that.

The United States Marines had a rather small detachment that had been guarding the railway down from Manchuria that went through Ch'in-huang-tao, Tientsin, and I think it eventually got down to Shanghai. It was run by the Japanese before and there were Chinese renegade troops and bandits and God knows what all sniping at the railway. As I recall, we had one or two Marines wounded and there was dissatisfaction here, in our own country, about exposing our Marines to that kind of risk. In the various railway stations you'd find Japanese guards, American guards, and Chinese guards all doing the same thing and apparently getting along just great.

Q: Nobody in over-all command?

Adm. D.: No, nobody was in over-all command. Nobody seemed to be mad at anybody. But we ended up with a force of Marines in Tsingtao and the commander there was later commandant of the Marine Corps, General Lemuel Shepherd.

Q: Wasn't Krulak there also at that time?

Adm. D.: He may have been on his staff. I don't remember seeing him.

It was my job to brief General Shepherd on exactly what the situation was in Washington and to pass on information to him that I happened to have. But the problem as far as the United States was concerned was what to do with this force, and I can remember telling Forrestal on one or two occasions that I felt we should keep our forces there, that they were in a position where it would be impossible for anybody to dislodge them by force. They were at the end of a long, narrow peninsula. We had all the forces at sea. They couldn't be attacked from seaward and there didn't seem to be any requirement for us to get out of there until conditions in northern China had stabilized. Remember, at this time period, we were very much concerned with getting the United Nations a going concern and people in government kept reminding themselves what Roosevelt had said in the Atlantic Charter along with Churchill that we had no ambitions for territorial aggrandizement and we were unduly concerned that the members of the United Nations would think that we were staking out a claim to the Shantung Peninsula or North China or God knows what.

So, had we stayed it might have become a different Far East. I think we should have maintained our presence there to create some stability in China and to show the Chinese, mostly, that we did have a concern for overall stability in the Far East.

Q: Was the magic carpet concept also a part of the thinking in this area, bring the boys home?

Adm. D.: Well, yes, and the Army felt this more than anybody else. Their rundown of forces was done on a unit or individual basis, with the result that a division might lose its key people and be really ineffective. In other words, if they'd taken out a company or a battalion as a unit, that would have been one thing, but when you get down to measuring length of service and so on you end up taking one man here and another one there and so on.

Q: It tended to decimation!

Adm. D.: Yes, and in the end what you have left are people but you may have lost all the key leaders or key personnel.

Q: Like taking the skipper and the exec of a ship!

Adm. D.: Correct. This was something that really left us without any teeth out there. We made several mistakes about that time. One was to what degree should we support Chiang Kai-shek or his forces in north China, Manchuria. General Wedemeyer was out there. I forget where his headquarters were. I think it was Shanghai. The question was raised either by him or perhaps back in Washington as to how many troops we should lift - remember, we had a pretty sizeable amphibious force out there - into north China and support them.

Well, the decision was made that we should lift five Chinese Armies, which sounds like an awful lot of people, but the Chinese Army is far from being the size of a U. S. Army so we ended up by not having enough men to physically control - and I don't mean just go out and shoot, but establish a presence, set up outposts, set up people to keep that part of the country quiet. The U. S. rationale I've always thought was very, very odd. Any number beyond this magic number of five would really indicate our interfering with the Chinese civil war, as it was called by some people.

Q: Agrarian uprising!

Adm. D.: Yes. Our over-all policy was not to interfere in the internal affairs and all that stuff. But this again was an unfortunate thing. We certainly let Chiang Kai-shek down in many people's view, including mine. But that's what happened in north China.

When we left Shepherd our journey was just about completed, we'd been to Peking and we'd been to Chungking and we'd been to Shanghai and we'd been to Tientsin -

Q: This was before Admiral Settle went out there?

Adm. D.: I don't remember his being there.

Q: He was in Harbin and places like that.

Adm. D.: I didn't run into him. Ballentine was in Japan, I remember, J. J. Ballentine. I've forgotten who was the commander of the amphibious forces. I think it was Admiral Cook but I'm far from sure of that.

But we did return, leaving Pauley to carry out his mission.

Q: What sort of reaction did you get when you made your recommendations on the Shantung Peninsula to Forrestal and later to President Truman?

Adm. D.: I can't recall exactly the reaction of Forrestal. I think you'll find mention of this in his diary. He mentioned that I had told him my concern. President Truman, I don't know as a matter of policy. I was briefing him, you see. I didn't get into the matter of policy. I was explaining to him the situation of our forces there, what kind of position they held, and whether or not they were at all vulnerable and that sort of thing.

Q: With the aid of those maps that you had?

Adm. D.: Yes.

Q: Admiral, if you'd like to do that I think it would be fine to add to the record here some account of that brush with death in Japan, just to illustrate the fact that some of these trips are far more demanding than they may sound on the surface.

Adm. D.: This was rather a minor incident, but when we went to Tokyo, Captain Vossler and I were in one airplane along with a chief yeoman, I believe, and Gates and Pauley, as I remember, were in a different plane. Vossler and I landed at Atsugi, an airport just outside of Tokyo, in the dark. Practically all the lights on the field had been blown out, there were bomb craters all over the runway, so it was sort of a hairy landing operation, but Ballentine knew we were coming in and had somebody meet us and bring us in to headquarters in Tokyo. Well, the driver that he latched onto was a bluejacket who really didn't know anything about the Japanese roads and didn't know much about anything, so he promptly got lost and we found ourselves going along a narrow path with a rather sharp declivity on one side, on the right side of the car. He managed to side-swipe a two-wheeled Japanese cart, which I'm sure didn't please the poor Japanese farmer who had his stuff in it, but eventually he lost control of the car and the right front wheel slipped off the road. The car started to slew around and did a 180-degree turn which left the left side of the car abreast of the slope. When the car started into this maneuver, the forward motion was checked - I was sitting in the right rear seat - the body was sprung, the door came open, and I went out. Fortunately, I didn't hit a damned thing on my way out, but I made a somersault in the air and came down flat on my back.

I looked up and saw the sedan rolling over and coming down on top of me. I was stunned, fortunately, because I didn't react by putting up my arm, although I was conscious. So the thing rolled over and came to rest upside down with my chin sticking out just beyond the rear of the car and my arms and legs were pinned underneath. I crawled out. There was no noise inside the cab. Everybody in there had been stunned, I guess, or shaken up a little bit -

Q: That's an understatement!

Adm. D.: Yes! I told them for heaven's sake, don't move because the car was almost going to complete its turn.

Q: Sort of teetering there.

Adm. D.: Yes, and it would roll over a bit farther. There was nothing I could do to avoid being crushed. I was pinned there. Then the gasoline cap in the rear came off and gasoline started to come out. Finally, I was able to work my arms out and slither from under the thing, covered with mud, of course.

In the meantime, Vosler and the driver were able to get out, once there was no danger of my being completely crushed under the damned thing. As I was lying there and saw that car come down, I thought, what a hell of a way to finish this war after having gone through it, to be killed in an automobile accident outside of Tokyo.

Q: And that on top of the hairy landing at Atsugi! Quite a story.

Adm. D.: There we were with practically no clothes and .45s, with no idea exactly where we were. There was nothing to do but just start walking, which we did along this path and eventually came to a railway station. I forget whether we had any money left. We had some U. S. money anyhow. The station was crowded, all Japanese and some of them finally decided we must be trying to go on to Tokyo. Well, we didn't know whether they were going to knife us or shoot us or what, but they were extremely helpful.

Q: Were any of you bleeding? You must have been.

Adm. D.: No, none of us were cut. I wasn't cut and didn't have any wounds, just hurt. When the train came along they pushed us into a coach and made people get out of the way so we'd have some place to sit down, and eventually we got in to Tokyo, what there was left of it.

Q: That is indeed a story, but it does illustrate the rigors of traveling in the Far East!

Adm. D.: It wasn't easy.

Q: Well, Sir, in March of 1947 you were released from your duties in the Navy Department and you took over command of the - I guess it was the premier command in the Navy, wasn't it, for a captain - of the battleship Missouri?

Adm. D.: Yes.

Q: And you were in command of her for almost a year. Would you tell me about that, Sir? What were some of your duties in that time?

Adm. D.: My job, of course, was to command the Missouri. I had some very fine officers. I was allowed to pick some of them myself. It was an extremely rewarding experience, every minute of it.

When I reported for duty in Norfolk, I had time to take the ship out and put her through her paces so I could get the feel of just how she handled. That class of battleship was extremely easy to handle. The ships were so maneuverable and had so much power and they found out when that type joined some task forces, that their turning circle was less than a destroyer, which led to some near collisions at first because if you had a destroyer, let's say, off your starboard quarter when ships in the force tried to make a 90-degree turn to the right the destroyer couldn't turn as sharply as the battleship did, so somebody had to do something or you'd be in collision. Of course, there was a hell of a lot of weight there, so the momentum was something, and to bring one of those ships to a stop took a little distance in spite of the power.

Anyway, after getting the feel of the ship and getting my officers to know me and I to know them, we were ready for business and we did some goodwill cruising. I remember getting permission to take the ship in to New York. I remember one thing that happened there was rather amusing. I think I mentioned before that John Rockefeller had been a member of the Forrestal group and I'd gotten to know him quite well, so I sent John a telegram from Norfolk saying that I'd unexpectedly been ordered into New York and asked him if he and his wife would like to come down and have lunch with me and bring their children and anybody else that they would like to ask in my name. I did get a reply saying that they both would be delighted to come and bring their children, and they did and we had an extremely pleasant lunch. But on arrival in New York I was handed a message that said: "Dear Captain Dennison, I am the telegraph operator who handled your message to Mr. Rockefeller and I just want to tell you that if you're having trouble filling your table I would be delighted to come."

So I got a message right back to her and said, "I'm very grateful to you for your offer but my table is filled, but if you will present this letter to the officer of the deck at any time you wish to visit the ship, he will be glad to see that you're shown around."

When the Rockefellers came I told them the first part of this story and Blanchette Rockefeller said, "What did you do?" I said that first I reported it to the telegraph company. It never occurred to me that such a thing could get personal. We all feel that a telegram is pretty private, although if you stop to think you realize that somebody had to handle it, but I don't like that." And she said, "Oh, you couldn't possibly have done that." Well, as a matter of fact I didn't and I told her what I had done. Well, that's a very minor incident.

I was ordered finally on a very important mission and that was to proceed to Rio in command of a small task force, the Missouri and some destroyers and a supply ship, to pick up President Truman who was flying down to Rio to sign the Inter American Treaty of Reciprocal Assistance, and of course, signatories from all over Latin America were there. It was a big occasion. I met President Truman on his arrival and I thought I had a complete recollection of what he looked like. But I went to his quarters where he was staying and came into his office. He was alone. It may have been the lighting, but I'll never forget my first impression of looking into his eyes, they were so piercing. He wore trifocal glasses, which may have had something to do with it.

Q: Very thick lenses?

Adm. D.: Yes, very thick. It was very striking. We had a talk.

Q: You had an in with him inasmuch as you were skipper of his favorite ship!

Adm. D.: Yes, not only his favorite ship, but it was also the one that his daughter had christened. She was its sponsor. So we started off on the right footing. We had a big reception aboard ship for everybody.

Q: You mean for the delegates to this signing?

Adm. D.: Yes, and I remember President Dutra of Brazil was there. When he came out to the Missouri, the President and I stood on the quarter deck to greet him. There were all kinds of boats in the harbor bringing distinguished guests aboard and the Missouri had such a broad beam that when you were standing back where we had to stand with the guard and band and what not, you could just see the top grating and you obviously couldn't see who was coming up the ladder. My navigator who was officer of the deck was trying to get traffic arranged, got word that Dutra was on his way, so the President and I came out, and after a moment or so I could see my navigator waving boats away and one boat apparently insisted on coming alongside and Bomberger - that was the navigator's name, who later became vice admiral - was apparently trying to get this boat clear.

I thought I'd better see what was going on, so I walked over and stood beside him, and I looked over down the ladder and who should be coming up but President Dutra. What threw Bomberger was the fact that Dutra was dressed in a Brazilian Army uniform, and never having seen the President he wasn't quite prepared for that and he didn't recognize him!

Q: He tried to clear him off!

Adm. D.: His aide or coxswain or whoever he was insisted on coming alongside. I don't think President Dutra realized what the commotion was about. I got back in my place and was beside the President when we gave Dutra full honors.

Q: Dutra was the only other head of state, I take it then?

Adm. D.: Yes, he was President of the host country.

Q: How would you manage a reception for an international conference like that? The ban on serving liquor was in being wasn't it?

Adm. D.: Yes, it was, but I think most foreign nations understand that and we just served canapes and punch and soft drinks. Of course, the ship was well decorated.

Q: And Brazilian coffee, no doubt!

Adm. D.: Yes, we had Brazilian coffee. My cabin was loaded with Brazilian coffee. And I suppose for people who aren't used to that kind of a setting it was a real experience. But that went off very well. Interestingly enough, that treaty was signed on the anniversary of the signing of the Japanese surrender aboard the Missouri, September 2, this was in 1947 and that was in 1945.

Q: It was two years since.

Adm. D.: And, of course, there was a plaque in the deck of the Missouri making the spot where the table was where the document had been signed.

In any event after all the gaiety was over we were in Rio for a week or so and I'd been very busy attending a lot of social events, mostly, I had a senior patrol officer ashore, a commander and we must have had as many as 2,000 people ashore there at once, bluejackets and officers. I sent for him after we got to sea and said, "How many shore patrol reports did you have?" He said none. And I said, "What? I can't believe it. How is this possible. There had to be some kind of a dispute with a taxi driver or bar tender or something?"

"Well," he said, "number one, we had a good patrol ashore, but the reason for this is that the first thing I did was make friends with the chief of police, who told me that he had put every potential known disturber in the jail while we were in port. He just went out and grabbed all the bad guys and put them in the clink."

Q: That's possible elsewhere, isn't it?

Adm. D.: That's right, so there weren't any bad people around to make trouble for our sailors. These people were well behaved.

Q: Does it say something, too, about the education program you had on board the Missouri, wherein the men were properly taught and indoctrinated before they arrived?

Adm. D.: Maybe so, but what I actually did was write a letter, a notice saying several things. I was trying to summarize as briefly as I could what our foreign policy was. In those days even, even now, you hear people say we don't have any foreign policy, but we do fundamentally. We believe in a whole lot of things. For example, self-determination, which is no small principle. But I wrote that out and then I went into the matter of conduct ashore and why it was so important for these men to conduct themselves with decorum, and I explained to them, also briefly, about the temperament of the Brazilians and that they could expect nothing but friendly association with them, and I sent this to every ship attached to the task force with a directive that this was to be read at quarters so that every member of the crew aboard each one of these ships would have this from me, that this was what I expected, and they could supplement this in any way that they saw fit.

Maybe that had something to do with it.

Q: This sort of thing is entirely optional with the skipper or with the commander of units of the fleet, is it not? I mean it isn't a personnel policy of the U. S. Navy?

Adm. D.: No. Only my responsibility was, in this aspect

of my duty, to put on a performance that the United States could be proud of. I didn't want any incidents of any kind. I just wanted to make sure that we didn't create one through misbehavior or ignorance, and we were prepared, of course, quite naturally with some real discipline to move in on our own people if any of them were out of line. Well, that wasn't necessary.

Q: You certainly were amply rewarded!

Adm. D.: Really it took me completely aback, I just couldn't believe it, but that was the case and, of course, I got all kinds of congratulatory messages.

Q: Now, your mission was to bring the President back to the States?

Adm. D.: That was it, along with his family and his staff, a whole flock of newspaper people.

Q: All of them were quartered on the Missouri?

Adm. D.: Yes, and we had one incident. There was a lady reporter from Maine, Miss May Craig, and Miss Craig was a woman's lib leader in those days.

Q: How did she get on that tour?

Adm. D.: She was accredited to the White House and wished to return aboard the Missouri along with the other reporters. Charlie Ross, who was the press secretary, didn't want to tell her no and, of course, it would hardly have done for the President to move into that sort of a situation, so Charlie Ross consulted me and I said, "Well, I won't have her aboard." And he said, "Fine, will you tell her?" I said, "Certainly." My reason was that the only place that she could have been quartered was in the executive officer's cabin, which was just off the wardroom. The wardroom was filled with ship's officers and all these reporters and it just wouldn't have done. It would have made her uncomfortable, it would have made them uncomfortable.

Q: I don't know that would have made May uncomfortable!

Adm. D.: Well, maybe not, but it would have made everybody else uncomfortable. So I told her that I was so sorry but it wasn't feasible. I had Mrs. Truman and Margaret aboard, but that was a different matter because they were in the Admiral's cabin. The Missouri was fitted as a flagship.

I got to know Miss Craig later and this was a lot of propaganda. She really was essentially very, very gentle and very kind. I got to like her very much.

Q: She had to have a trademark, though!

Adm. D.: Yes, she had it. Her hats were pretty marked and rather eccentric, but she was all right. At any rate, I did have to tell her no, and she later forgave me for it because when I did go to the White House she was a member of the Correspondents' Association, or at least she was accredited to the White House.

We took off from Rio on a twelve-day trip back to Norfolk and in many years at sea I've never experienced such good weather, twelve days of almost absolute calm. There was no motion of the ship at all, clear skies, balmy. It was just wonderful.

Q: Very fortunate for at least one of your passengers, wasn't it?

Adm. D.: Probably fortunate for a good many of them, and on the way, of course, we crossed the equator, so we put on a real "crossing the line" ceremony, complete with Davey Jones and all the rest of it. And I remember one of the things we tried to find was who was the most senior shellback - I don't mean in rank, but who had crossed the equator earliest. Well, my first experience was during the war. I had crossed the equator several times. It finally occured to me that, maybe, Admiral Leahy had crossed the equator. Leahy, of course, was chief of staff to the commander-in-chief, and I had put him in my cabin and I used my sea cabin for this voyage. So I asked him when he crossed the equator for the first time. He seemed to be very patient with me and he said, "Wel, in 1898 aboard the USS Oregon we came round the Cape to get into the Battle of Santiago."

Q: Probably was shovelling coal at that point!

Adm. D.: Exactly, he was in the black gang and was shovelling coal. He was a passed midshipman in those days. So he was obviously the senior shellback. But we had a lot of fun. We did initiate the crew and urged the President then to make a speech. We didn't have any shellbacks anywhere around in the staff or the reporters, and, you know, the paddling and electric shocks and all that kind of stuff. I signed cards for every member of the crew and every passenger on board certifying that they had crossed the equator, and many of the reporters probably still have them because for years they'd probably break the cards out and then come up with some tall tale about what they'd been through in this ceremony.

Q: How did the presidential party occupy itself?

Adm. D.: Well, they got into the ship's life, the ship's routine. Calisthenics, for example, in the morning. The reporters, where they got these I don't know, but they broke out some tee shirts with "Truman Athletic Club" across the chest, and they'd get out on deck with the crew and go through morning calisthenics, and, of course, we did all kinds of things like, clay pigeon shooting and volley ball was a great thing. Margaret had a great time playing volley ball. You may think that time would pass rather slowly and a trip like that would be pretty dull, but far from it, and, of course, there was business to be done as far as the President was concerned.

Q: He had to be in communication, didn't he?

Adm. D.: Yes, he did. It gave him a wonderful chance to collect his thoughts without interruption with members of his staff. And we fired guns and shot down drones and did all kinds of stuff.

Q: Well, the fact that he had to be in such close touch with the State Department and others must have put some burden on you as skipper, didn't it?

Adm. D.: It didn't actually put any kind of a strain on me, but the arrangements were that the President had his own personal code and the only people on my end that held it were my communications decoding officer and myself, and these messages to him came over the Navy's communications circuits, obviously, and would be brought to me by my communications officer for me to handle. A good many of these messages were simply routine, but they were day-to-day business. I remember one incident that told me a lot about President Truman.

One evening I got a message addressed to him and took it in to the admiral's cabin, where he was seated at a table with most of the members of his staff. I remember they were playing cards, so I stood beside his chair and handed him this dispatch. He read it and handed it back to me and said, "Tell the SOB he's going to have to shoot his way in." I said, "Aye, aye, Sir," and left. That's all he said. His staff were dumbfounded. They didn't know what was in the message or what the reply meant.

Q: There was no context there!

Adm. D.: No. So afterwards he told them, of course, that what the message had to say was the State Department saying that Tito was making noises about invading Trieste. This seemingly off-the-cuff decision of the President - I found out later that it wasn't, that he'd been thinking about the situation in the Adriatic, knew a great deal about it. Apparently, he'd been expecting some feeling out on the part of Yugoslavia and he was just going to stop it. I don't know what I sent back to the State Department except exactly what he said. There's no way that you can improve on that language. It's not very diplomatic, but I never knew what happened or how Tito finally got the word that we were not about to put up with any foolishness.

Q: Actually, we had various units of the fleet in the Mediterranean stationed up near Trieste, didn't we?

Adm. D.: They weren't in the Adriatic. We had some forces in Trieste but the British did, too. Not very many. Later, when I was in the Mediterranean myself I visited Trieste and inspected their facilities.

Other than that rather dramatic incident there weren't any items of major importance to me at any rate, and there certainly wasn't a burden because I was up most of the time anyhow.

We came into Norfolk and the President disembarked at the naval base and came back to Washington along with his party. It was about time then for the Missouri to go in for minor overhaul in the Navy Yard in New York, so I took the ship in. It was a pretty routine, humdrum sort of a thing. I got a call from Admiral Fechteler sometime in December, mid December as I remember, saying when can you come down to Washington. So I said, "Well, I can catch a plane tonight or first thing in the morning."

Q: He was chief of Personnel?

Adm. D.: Yes. And he said, "Well, there isn't quite all that much rush." So I said, "If I'm coming I might as well come as soon as I can. What's the conference all about?" He said, "There isn't any conference. You're being detached." So I said, "For what?"

He said, "You're not supposed to tell anybody this, but you're being detached to report as naval aide to the President."

And I said, "I'm thoroughly enjoying what I'm doing, this is just wonderful, but I have no choice, obviously, if the President wants me, but I'm not crazy about it. What about my orders? Who's going to relieve me?"

He said, "Forget about orders. We'll take care of that. Your exec will take over until we can find somebody." So I said, "Bill, I can't just walk off this ship without reading my orders. I just can't disappear." So he said, "Well, you'll just have to figure that out." So what I did was to write myself a set of orders, which by tradition you're

Dennison #4 - 145

supposed to read to the crew. Apparently nobody pays any attention to what these orders say, anyhow. I said I was detached to proceed without delay to report for duty in Washington, D. C. So I did. I read my orders and turned the command over to J. B. Colwell, who was my exec. Colwell later became a vice admiral, too. And I came down to Washington.

Still nobody was supposed to know what I was doing. I stayed at the Army and Navy Club and I think the first night I was there the news tickers that they had in those days came up with this announcement that I had been appointed. So I reported to the President.

Q: This was all before you saw him on this occasion?

Adm. D.: Yes. I reported to the President for duty as his aide, and he said he was delighted to have me. I didn't know for a long time how it had happened, whether he'd asked for me or just how I got there. Well, it turned out he hadn't asked for me. What he'd done was to ask the Secretary of the Navy for the names of an officer or several officers that the Navy Department thought would be suitable and they came up with my name. And, of course, he'd cruised with me and knew me slightly, so he said that he'd be delighted to have me, and I told him that I was delighted to have an opportunity to serve him.

Q: Admiral, is there any truth to some of the stories I've

heard to the effect that when he first asked for a naval aide from the Department he said he did not want someone from the Naval Academy?

Adm. D.: Whether he ever said that or not, I don't know, because Commodore Vardaman, who was a real thorn in the side of the Navy Department, a Reserve officer, and General Vaughan was there as military aide, and I think that they were somewhat prejudiced against professionals, although I never detected that in the President. But he did have Vardaman and then Clark Clifford, who was another Reserve officer, briefly, and then James Foskett, a non Naval Academy graduate who served very briefly. And then finally the President asked the Navy Department. What he wanted was a professional, obviously. Whether he ever said he didn't want one, I rather doubt because of just knowing him and knowing the set-up there. But there was a strange thing in this connection.

My name did go up to him, he did approve, I did report, and after I'd been there briefly, General Vaughan, the President's military aide, got the reporters together out in the lobby of the East Wing and announced that he was going to be the military aide and that I was to be his assistant, and General Landry, who had reported for duty, was to be the Air Force aide and another assistant.

Q: Landry came in about the same time as you did?

Adm. D.: He came shortly after me. When the Air Force found out I was going to be there, why, they wanted to have an Air Force aide. This took me completely by surprise and upset me considerably so I talked to my dear friend Charlie Ross and one or two other people on the staff and told them that I didn't like this at all, that I was ordered as a Presidential aide and wasn't told I was to be assistant to anybody, and I didn't like it. I was upset about it. Well, these people liked me and under stood it completely, so Ross went in to see the President and he was very upset on the grounds that Vaughan had no right to be holding a press conference to make any such announcement.

Q: Ross was the press secretary!

Adm. D.: Yes, he was the President's press secretary. So a big uproar started and the President stepped in and said forget it, or words to that effect, "Dennison is my naval aide and you must forget this military aide idea." And that's the way it was.

Well, I found out not long afterwards that this indeed had been the plan, the only trouble was that they forgot to tell me.

Q: It had been the plan to make Vaughan the over-all military aide?

Adm. D.: Yes, to have one aide and several assistants, but nobody told me, so I'd reported to the President as his naval aide. I never could understand why I wasn't told in the first place. If I had been, I would have said I would like to decline, I don't think that's the kind of a job for me. I don't think it would have worked either.

Q: What was Harry Vaughan like? There were so many stories about him. What was his ability?

Adm. D.: I could tell you about him. He was, of course, a Reserve officer. He was completely dedicated to President Truman. The President told me one time that, years ago in Missouri when he was running for some judgeship or something, some minor post, Vaughan took on a campaign when all they had in the treasury was something like $1.20 worth of postage stamps - this was almost literally true - and Vaughan had gone to work for him and they used the $1.20 on penny postcards to 120 people to get his name into the picture. But that's the kind of a fellow that Vaughan was.

Q: Was he a lawyer in his past?

Adm. D.: No, he wasn't a lawyer at all. I don't know what his background was. He went to the University of Missouri, I believe, but he didn't have any means to amount to anything. Vaughan was completely misunderstood, I think. Somebody described him once as looking like an unmade bed. He didn't wear his uniform very well. He smoked cigars, though the image didn't come through. People thought he was a heavy drinker, but I've been with Vaughan day after day on I don't know how many occasions at Key West and other places. He would have about one drink a week. He just didn't drink. And he was one of the most generous men I ever came across. He'd give anybody the shirt off his back, literally. He taught Sunday School, he and his wife each taught a class, deeply religious people, and he really is a dear friend of mine although we are completely different in many ways. I don't have any kind of political background and he does. Vaughan served in World War I and briefly in Australia in World War II.

I think he did feel that professional officers looked down on Reserve officers. I've run across that a number of different times, which so far as I'm concerned is absolutely not the case. I've known some extremely capable and very fine Reserve officers. But he was completely misunderstood, misreported. The President understood him completely and being so loyal himself to people who worked with him and worked for him he backed Vaughan up to the hilt. At the same time, Vaughan never did anything in major affairs. He wasn't involved at all with the State Department or anybody else, the Defense Department. When General Eisenhower was Chief of Staff, for example, and he had anything he wanted out of the White House he would call me because I had known him slightly. I don't know whether this was because of professional ties or whatever, but that's the way it was.

Speaking of General Eisenhower, the President was responsible for General Eisenhower leaving Columbia and going to be the first SacEur, for good reasons. He was accepted by everybody as he was. NATO had to really get off the ground and get rolling, and he was the man to do it.

Q: He had all the contacts established.

Adm. D.: Yes, he was the only one. Even today I think only an American can be SacEur or SacLant, because the European nations never could agree on any one of them taking the job, and of course, the Europeans now who are qualified for high command are damned few because they've never commanded large forces. But for many reasons he was the man and the President had no trouble convincing him of it.

Q: Actually, while he was at Columbia I'm told that he spent maybe 50 percent of his time on defense work.

Adm. D.: I've no way of knowing but I wouldn't doubt it at all. But as time went on and it appeared that he had political ambitions and you remember nobody knew for sure whether he was a Democrat or a Republican, they didn't know what he was, and finally he turned out to be intending to run on the Republican ticket. He came back to the White House in uniform to report to the President - Of course, this was proper.

Q: He came back from NATO?

Adm. D.: Yes, and the President, knowing that I had known Eisenhower, sent me out to National to meet his plane alone to bring him back to the White House. Well, I got out there and there was some kind of a small rally going, with a speaker's platform and a band and all the rest of it, so I sat in the limousine and waited till the brief ceremonies were over, then got out and greeted General Eisenhower, told him I was there on behalf of the President to meet him and escort him to the White House.

This was around noon time. So he got in the car. Eisenhower was in the right rear seat and I was across from him, and the driver took us around the Lincoln Memorial and the Reflecting Pool. The streets were pretty well crowded with government people. It was a nice day. And many of them recognized General Eisenhower and he was waving at them, and he turned to me and said, "Bob, you know, you and I were brought up in our professions to believe that the way to keep yourself out of trouble was to keep your mouth shut. Now I find myself in trouble for doing just that." Of course, he hesitated for so long and dallied for so long about whether he was going to run or whether he wasn't going to run.

Q: And was beset by delegations going over and all that!

Adm. D.: I took him to the White House and the purpose of going there was for the President to decorate him with the Distinguished Service Medal and he invited Mrs. Eisenhower and members of Eisenhower's family - a very small group - and at an intimate ceremony the President decorated him himself. So they started out on that kind of a friendly basis.

The President told Eisenhower one time he'd be glad to advise him if he had any political ambitions and give him a little bit of guidance, which would have been a wonderful opportunity from a real master. Of course, later they had this unfortunate falling out because of General Eisenhower sitting on the same speaker's platform during the campaign with Jenner and McCarthy.

Q: That was in Wisconsin?

Adm. D.: Yes, and one of them on the floor of the Senate had called George Marshall a "living lie," and General Eisenhower was supposed to have taken out of his speech some flattering references to Marshall, who really made Eisenhower. But that's another story and it was finally patched up years later, and I was there when it was patched up.

Q: Well, when you went there as aide you were given to understand that you never would have to be involved in politics, were you not?

Adm. D.: The first thing the President told me when I reported for duty was, "There's one thing I want you to understand, that you'll have no business whatever with the Democratic National Committee," and, of course, I understood immediately what he was getting at and said, "Thank you very much. I do understand that." As a matter of fact, I never had anybody try to involve me in any political matter. The

President certainly didn't. He had a standard lecture he'd give me every few months, that I'm a professional sailor and I don't know anything about politics and I shouldn't dabble around in it, I should stick to my own business, remember that I was in the Navy, and so on. Every time I'd give him the same answer that I thanked him and got out of there quickly.

Q: He kept on reminding you of this fact!

Adm. D.: He didn't have to. I never voted while I was on active duty because I didn't think it was appropriate to vote for my own commander-in-chief.

Q: That's an interesting point of view and I've heard it expressed by other naval officers and yet I have never understood it.

Adm. D.: Well, look at it this way: you, as a naval officer, are bound to serve whoever the commander-in-chief is and you shouldn't care. If you get yourself emotionally involved in politics and you don't like Candidate X, who turns out to be elected, that should have no possible bearing on your performance or your attitude. Maybe it wouldn't. Maybe you'd say, well, it's every citizen's privilege and perhaps duty to vote, but I just never happened to feel that way for the reasons I just said. I mean in the Civil War when the troops would elect their commander, Reserves or whatever part of the Army it was - I remember my grandfather who got to be a captain in the cavalry - where the people would elect their own leaders, suppose that the guys that wanted to elect somebody else took the attitude that this particular one who was elected wasn't qualified. They're bound to be involved emotionally some way.

I've just believed all my life that professionals had no business in politics, even to the extent of voting in national elections. I don't say it's right. It's just the way I happen to believe.

Q: I'm very glad to have that explanation. As a naval aide, what were your specific duties at that point?

Adm. D.: I could pass that off easily by saying whatever the President told me to do.

Q: But you did have some assignments?

Adm. D.: Yes, because, in the first place, the ceremonial part of it, attending ceremonies with him or introducing people to him in a receiving line and all that, was a very minor part of the job for the two of us. And the President's way of operating - remember he had a very small staff - was to give assignments from time to time that, in his mind at least, had some bearing on our capabilities. For example, a committee of Congress investigated the granting of construction subsidies to the American President Lines, the U. S. Lines, American Export for the construction of ships. The SS United States was one of them. And the committee, on looking into it, determined that these subsidies were excessive because under the construction subsidy law the government is permitted to grant up to a certain percentage for what are called defense features. In other words, something is built into the ship that wouldn't ordinarily be required for, in this case, a passenger liner - the SS United States was the fastest ship on the seas apparently -

Q: And in time of war, she could be a troop ship?

Adm. D.: That's exactly the idea, and she had a tremendous troop capacity. I think her speed was something over 40 knots - 43 or 44 knots - and she was a big ship. But the U. S. Lines took the position that this subsidy that they got, which was quite sizeable, was exactly what was needed to build the kind of ship that we wanted, the government. Well, the government didn't take that point of view.

Q: Who had allocated, who had been responsible for allocating the subsidy?

Adm. D.: The Maritime Commission, I believe, was the one. At any rate, the law was tortured, if it wasn't broken in fact. So the President said something had to be done. How was the government going to get this money back? How were they going to settle this thing?

It was clearly the job of the Executive Branch. It wasn't really a congressional job. Warren was the attorney general - I mean comptroller general.

Q: Lindsay C. Warren?

Adm. D.: Yes, and he wanted to move into the act quite properly. We had no way to do anything about it, so the President sent for me, and, I suppose, to get back to your question why he would give a certain assignment, in his mind a maritime matter was something I ought to know something about or find out about, so I was appointed informally to, in effect, coordinate maritime affairs for the Executive Branch, namely, the President, because almost every department of government, State, Defense, Treasury, Attorney General, Commerce, Labor, almost every department has an interest in maritime matters in one way or another. Well, who the hell coordinates all this? There isn't any statutory position. The Maritime Administrator, or the Maritime Board, or the Maritime Commissioner didn't have that kind of authority.

So the first thing the President did was to reorganize the Maritime Commission out of existence. It was headed by an admiral who I must say wasn't very capable. So he put in a reorganization act to get rid of them. He put up the Maritime Department, a two-headed affair, retaining part of the Maritime Board's function and the Maritime Administrator within the Department of Commerce.

The first thing I did was get hold of Porter Hardy and said, "How can I get together with Lindsay Warren (in the meantime I had told Hardy what I thought ought to be done, namely, give the President a chance to get this thing

Dennison #4 - 157

straightened out) -

Q: You had to do a certain amount of homework and investigation?

Adm. D.: Oh, my God, yes, I did.

Q: I was hoping you'd talk about it.

Adm. D.: Then I said, "Why don't we have a lunch aboard the Williamsburg. You persuade Warren to come along with you and meet me and have lunch and talk." So Hardy said, sure. That's what happened. Warren came down and we talked. I did convince him that we meant business. The President was absolutely sincere about this, and he was going to see to it that the government got a just settlement out of it.

Well, Warren agreed and he said, "I will lay off. I won't move in General Accounting on this at all to give you a chance to see what you can do."

Q: Meanwhile, had the congressional committee laid off, too?

Adm. D.: They had finished their hearing on this report but nobody had taken any action on it, except the GAO which was about to. It wasn't clear that the law had been broken, but one of the witnesses, for example, in the Defense Department testified that this was like putting a fat boy into a tight suit. Maybe it was going to burst or maybe it wasn't, but it was clearly unfair.

It's a long story and I won't go into what happened, but in the end we had to resolve the disputes within the government. The Attorney General took one view and the Secretary of Commerce would take another about what the settlement should be or if there should be any, and how they went about collecting it, because the company could take the position, "OK, if you won't pay the subsidy or want us to pay you back, you can take the ship." Well, what would the federal government do with several passenger liners? This was kind of a tight-rope situation, but in the end -- and this went on for quite a few years -- we did recover not the full amount, but we got the Attorney General and the Secretary of Commerce and the Secretary of Defense and everybody to agree. That took a little bit of doing because the President told me one time, in another connection but something that applies here. He said, "You know, I don't command anything. Here I am commander-in-chief. The only military person who commands anything is the squad leader. I spend over half my time trying to persuade people to do the things that they know damned well all along that they ought to be doing anyhow."

This is what happened here. He could get out an edict, and he did write some pretty strong -- well, actually, I wrote letters for him to the Attorney General, for example, saying, "Surely the United States isn't helpless in this matter. There's something we can do."

But in the end everybody came around and we did get a settlement out of these lines, which greatly pleased Lindsay

Warren.

That is one example of how he assigned tasks.

Q: Would you complete that story by telling me about the naming of the first administrator there, Maritime Administrator?

Adm. D.: Yes. The President sent for me again and said, "Who are we going to get to be the Federal Maritime Administrator?" And we did get Jack Koehler, the Assistant Secretary of the Navy, an attorney now living in Washington, as an interim incumbent to do a little housecleaning, to get rid of a lot of unnecessary people and a lot of dead wood, and get ready for an administrator to be able to step in and take over. The President wanted to know who this fellow was going to be, and I said, "There's only one man in the country that I know of who could do it, and that's Admiral Ned Cochrane, whose name is well known. He's a naval constructor, Chief of the Bureau of Ships, respected in maritime circles, a very capable man who'd retired and was up at MIT." So he said, "All right, get him."

I called Cochrane and told him about this job and that he was the only man we thought could handle it, the only man with stature in the turmoil who could possibly take over. You see, there were a lot of ruffled feelings and a hell of a big upset here.

Q: You were invading lots of empires!

Adm. D.: That's right. He said, "Leave me alone, I've done

my job, I've earned my retirement, and I'm having a great time up here doing exactly what I've wanted to do for many years, and I don't want it." So I said, "OK," and went back to see the President and said, "I'm having trouble. Cochrane doesn't want the job."

He said, "Get hold of Admiral Cochrane and tell him I'd like to see him in my office the day after tomorrow, and you come in with him."

So I called Ned up and said, "The President wants to see you the day after tomorrow at ten o'clock," and he said, "OK." What else could he say?

So we went in to see the President and there were only three of us there, the President, Cochrane, and myself, and the President said:

"Admiral, I understand that you don't want to take the job as Federal Maritime Administrator. Why?"

Well, that's the last word that anybody said, except Cochrane. Cochrane gave him the whole pitch about how hard he worked and what he was doing and what he'd done and all the rest of it, nobody said anything. Finally, Cochrane said, "Besides, I'm too old to take this great responsibility." All the President said was, "Admiral, how old are you?" Remember, the President wasn't exactly a young man.

Q: No, he was not a chicken!

Adm. D.: The President was older than he was, I believe, and Cochrane stopped, his mouth sort of dropped open a little bit, and he finally said, "OK, Mr. President, I'll take it!" Beautiful!

Q: The fact that this administration was set up and that the Assistant Secretary of the Navy was a temporary head and he succeeded in getting a retired admiral as first administrator, did this result in any closer relationship between our Navy and the maritime set up?

Adm. D.: Oh, yes, it did. The Maritime Commission was an independent agency, and I'm sure there'd always been a great deal of interest both ways. Obviously, the Navy has had an interest in merchant shipping, a vital interest in the maritime service, the merchant marine, but it didn't hurt a bit to have a man like Cochrane in there. Not that he was going to lean over backwards to favor the military but he did have a thorough understanding of what the military problems were, the naval problems.

One more example, in passing, to give you a little more of a clue as to how the President made assignments.

In 1948 Secretary Johnson of Defense in one of his economy moods decided to close down some naval hospitals. One of them was a hospital in Long Beach and this hospital had to do principally with taking care of paraplegics, and it caused a tremendous uproar that the paraplegics in that area would have to go some place else and they couldn't do it. Movie stars tried to get some publicity by taking sides in this case, and it got blown up all out of proportion. So the President again assigned me to head up a committee of myself, Dr. Howard

Rusk, and a Dr. Abramson, who himself was a paraplegic. Howard Rusk was a noted specialist —

Q: His rehabilitation center?

Adm. D.: Yes. He has a rehabilitation center in New York now.

Q: He's quite a man!

Adm. D.: Yes, he is, so was Abramson. And here am I, non medical, but at least I knew enough about how to organize something and how to conduct this survey. So we had meetings with representatives of almost every imaginable group that had any interest, Disabled Veterans, American Legion, Veterans of Foreign Wars, and on and on and on. We heard everybody, we visited a number of hospitals - veterans hospitals - and finally ended up with a comprehensive report, not only on this particular problem but on the Veterans Administration hospital set-up in its entirety, and there were many, many things wrong with it and a great many things were not entirely the fault of the Veterans Administration either. Congress never came up really with clear policies in many areas. For example, how many beds should a hospital have?

Q: Yes, it was a piecemeal thing that grew that way.

Adm. D.: Yes, and very much of a political matter, too. We finally wound that up and ended up with persuading the VA to employ Booz, Allen, and Hamilton, a management consultant firm, to put in a report on the whole VA structure, including the medical department. This was pretty farreaching and in the end the solutions arrived at were mainly acceptable to everybody.

Q: This wasn't a minor project. How long did it take you?

Adm. D.: Oh, I've forgotten but it probably was six months at least, just like most of these projects. The maritime business started out looking like a one-shot single operation, but then they grow, and there were many other things that I did.

Q: One of your duties, you were in command of the Williamsburg, weren't you?

Adm. D.: No, we had a commander of the Williamsburg.

Q: Were there other yachts in existence at that time?

Adm. D.: I wouldn't call it a yacht but we had a boat called the Lenore, which was around for a good many years and carried reporters. The Williamsburg had a captain, but the naval aide was responsible for the Williamsburg and for the operation of Shangri-La, which is now called Camp David, which was manned by personnel who were nominally assigned to the Williamsburg, and for the stewards in the White House mess, which I established - the staff mess.

Q: Oh, you established that?

Dennison #4 - 164

Adm. D.: Yes, I started it.

Q: A very convenient thing it proved to be!

Adm. D.: Yes, it sure has. No, I didn't command the Williamsburg. I commanded her as naval aide.

Q: That's what I meant. You had over-all responsibility. Did the President use his yacht very frequently? Was this an outlet for him?

Adm. D.: Yes, indeed it was. He was not a very good sailor. I only made one trip with him at sea, and that was from Washington to Key West, but he did like to go aboard the Williamsburg, mainly to get away from his office for a little while - for weekends, for example. The routine was that we would go aboard, and he would have invited a number of friends to play poker with him, and I was there to stand between him and all communications. The Williamsburg was much more than just a so-called yacht. This was in our emergency plans as one of the command posts for the President. We had all kinds of contingency plans where he could be. I was responsible for drawing these plans for the Executive Branch.

Q: You mean in case of an atomic attack?

Adm. D.: In case of any disaster, but that's what we were talking about. The bomb shelter in the White House, for example.

Q: It was built at that time?

Adm. D.: It was one of my concerns, too. And the federal government's plans had to be coordinated with the President's plans, and there were headquarters set up all over the countryside for various agencies of the government and a microwave communications net was set up to link these various places. Shangri-La was another, and all this means a lot of communications equipment and people. But the Williamsburg wasn't the isolation that you might think. In other words, when the President was aboard her, just like when he was at Key West, he had the illusion of being away for a while, but, believe me, he sure wasn't. I know because I was between him and his communications.

Q: In his time, the so-called little black box came into existence, didn't it?

Adm. D.: You mean where he was supposed to be able to control the weapon?

Q: Yes.

Adm. D.: Well, they didn't call it that. He had, of course, the authority - it was his ultimate authority in any event.

One revealing thing about his contingency plans or emergency plans. I discussed with the President many times about this facility in the White House, the bomb shelter, and also the plans for using the private railway cars. We had several emergency locations across the river to station these cars. The Ferdinand Magellan was his own car. I forget just where we had her. The Williamsburg, airplanes, automobiles, the whole bit.

I had to consult him about these plans and one day he said, "There's one thing I want to tell you. I want you to make these plans. Obviously we've got to have something along these lines. But I don't intend to leave Washington. How would it look if the President of the United States in some kind of danger would run for the hills and leave the people here. I'm going to stay here, and all I want, if we can possibly arrange it, is for access to radio and television so I can get on the air and talk to people and let them know that I'm still doing business at the same stand."

And we did. We had television cables guarded and protected and we had radio cables, and God knows what all, or whether they would ever have been able to get into a station is another matter. I mean you never know what would happen. But that was his attitude, and that was another one of my responsibilities. I suppose you could associate it with being naval aide, but I don't know just how! At any rate, that was it. I did draw up an emergency plan.

Q: Yes, and it continued under that arrangement. I remember talking to Pete Aurand, who was naval aide to Eisenhower, and that was one of his duties. When the President expressed this attitude that he wouldn't leave Washington was, of course, before the Russians had the A-bomb wasn't it?

Adm. D.: I really don't remember the timing but what we were talking about was atomic attack against us, and it doesn't seem we would have been doing serious planning if we weren't faced with that possibility.

Q: One other place was the Little White House. Was that under your general supervision?

Adm. D.: You mean the one at Key West?

Q: Yes.

Adm. D.: Of course.

Q: Tell me about that. I mean how that came into being.

Adm. D.: It came into being not as what it got to be. One of the naval aides, Foskett, I guess it was, persuaded the President one time to go down there for a visit to get some sunshine. It wasn't a Little White House and it wouldn't fit the picture, I think, if you put in your mind what a Little White House would look like. It was simply a set of government quarters within the naval compound. The plot of ground it was on was a fairly good size. It was easy to guard because it had gates and what not. It was within the wall and within the outer gates of the base itself, but the administration building had very thoughtfully been placed between this house and the water. You couldn't see a damned thing, really, when you were on the front lawn or in the house itself.

It was an old frame house.

Dennison #4 - 168

Q: It sounds kind of bleak, as you describe it!

Adm. D.: It was. It really wasn't suited for his purposes, but for some reason or other - and I can understand why, I guess - he thought this was just great.

The first trip I made down there with him not long after I took over I was horrified and said, "My God, we can do better than this for the President of the United States." So I said, "Do you mind if I do a little rehabilitating and changing and what not, if I can do it without spending very much money? That place has got to be decorated and it's got to be changed one way or another."

So he said, "All right, go ahead." The guy at Key West who headed up the civil engineering outfit was a very talented man, very able, very capable. He got hold of several firms of interior decorators in Miami and got competitive bids and all that.

Mrs. Truman had been down there and would have no part of it. It really was dismal. It wasn't decorated, what there was was nondescript furniture.

Q: So he had to go by himself when he went down there?

Adm. D.: Yes, and he did most of the time anyway because she wasn't interested in being the only woman around there and Margaret didn't want to sit down there. But we did get the thing decorated and made some structural changes - nothing elaborate, and there wasn't very much money spent either. The decorator we had was really talented and he equipped that place after we'd changed the structure of some of the rooms and so on with furniture and with colors that were in key with the environment of Key West, and it was just absolutely lovely.

The President's room was in one corner of this two-story structure. The walls were painted a rather deep shade of blue and the ceiling was painted a deep shade of blue and, with the lights dimmed, this ceiling would sort of — you weren't sure you were looking at a ceiling or were looking at the open sky. It was a strange illusion. He had some attractive paintings and very comfortable furniture and the President just loved it. I finally talked Mrs. Truman into coming down there. We had a double room for Margaret and Mrs. Truman decorated in white with a porch around the second deck that was private to them and went around past the President's room but nobody else could get to it.

Q: Is that something that was added to the structure?

Adm. D.: No, but the doors and the entryways and things like that were changed. I think we put in one or two bathrooms and changed the front entrance a little bit. It had a porch around one end of it, an L-shaped porch, but the dining room in the inside of the L and folding doors would permit you to open up the dining room, so on two sides of it you had this expanse of porch. Mrs. Truman and Margaret thought so much of it, they thought it was just great, and they liked it so much that they came down several times, not necessarily just to be with the President, but they wanted a chance to relax, too.

Q: That testifies to your success!

Adm. D.: Well, it worked out great. But, yes, that was one of the things I had under my jurisdiction. Of course, that made sense. This was a naval establishment and we did have the communications. We brought down our own telephone operators and our own switchboard. But the President had the atmosphere he needed and he had this feeling of relaxation, and he liked to wear sports shirts not so much because he liked bright colors as he liked the informal sort of thing. It gave him a feeling of informality and fitting into that kind of an atmosphere. Of course, the rest of us had to work like hell. He didn't have any secretary. I did. I had my chief yeoman who did all the President's work for him. Chief Yeoman Winkler.

Q: Winkler?

Adm. D.: Yes, Bernace L. Winkler, and he was wonderful. He was with me for something like thirteen years. He was with me in the White House, he was with me in London, he was with me in Norfolk. And the photographer who went with the President to keep his record was a photographer's mate from the Navy, Paul Begley. He was the one who was always with the President, on the Williamsburg, at Key West and every place else. He had some records, of course, that nobody else ever had because he was the only one there.

For example, on the Williamsburg for a meeting with Churchill, who came over with Anthony Eden and Ismay and a few others in December, just after he got back into power in the government, to talk things over. This was the time when Churchill finally agreed to have an American officer as SacLant, in spite of the fact the Council had asked for one and at the same time had asked for General Eisenhower, an American general. But he blocked it.

Q: That was a very touchy issue, wasn't it? For a long time.

Adm. D.: I was told by Acheson that when he finally had to give in he had tears in his eyes, but he agreed that it should be an American officer and forever after.

So, getting back to Begley, we had pictures of that, and I can remember on that occasion - again I was there - I thought it would be a great idea to take a picture of the Prime Minister and the President up in the after lounge of the Williamsburg where we had a false fireplace before we all went down to the mess and had dinner. Everybody was informal, enjoying talking, and all that. So I asked them both if they'd mind posing for picures. Of course not, so they got up and stood before the fireplace and Begley was about to snap the shutter when I took a good look at the background. Well, the background was a painting of the Constitution beating the hell out of HMS Java, off Brazil. I don't know whether you remember that engagement. So I stopped Begley and went over to the Prime Minister and the President and said, "I apologize, but perhaps you won't feel that this is an appropriate background." And Churchill pulled his glasses down on his nose, looked around, and immediately recognized what this was. He said, "Young man, that was many years ago. Go ahead and take your picture."

Q: Was this an innovation, to have a photographer with the President always to keep a photographic record of things?

Adm. D.: All I know is what happened to President Truman. I have no idea what President Roosevelt did. But Begley did a thorough job. He fitted in and was unobtrusive, thoughtful. Everybody liked him.

Q: What did you do with the press down at the Little White House?

Adm. D.: We housed them at BOQ and when we'd go out on trips some place they could go along in their own boat or automobiles or what not. They would come down and have a conference if the President sent for them, but when the President went swimming there weren't any press, he didn't want them. But Begley, I remember, one time went out when the President, Mrs. Truman, and I went out aboard a torpedo-recovery boat that had been converted to be a fishing boat for officer personnel down at Key West, called the Big Wheel, and Begley took a perfectly lovely picture of Mrs. Truman catching a fish and the President unhooking it from her line. Begley had it printed and showed it to the press secretary, among others. So the secretary took it over to where the reporters were, had a lot of prints made, and put them on the table, whereupon all the press photographers tore up these prints because they hadn't taken it. Well, somebody rescued one and sent it to the editor of his paper, not a photographer but a reporter, whereupon the photographer got a phone call, "Where the hell were you when this picture was taken?"

Then the word got around and more calls came in, and the reporters were beaten to death because their editors couldn't understand why in the hell this warm family picture hadn't been sent to them. They could have had it, but they didn't take it so to hell with it, it couldn't be any good!

Q: It's a wonder, if they had a union, the photographers, that they didn't have a down on you!

Adm. D.: I remember one time the reporters persuaded the skipper of a Navy blimp we had down there to take them over the beach when the President was swimming so they could all take his picture. Well, they weren't supposed to do that.

Q: Low-altitude pictures.

Adm. D.: Yes, it was an invasion of privacy. He didn't want reporters around and they shouldn't have wanted to be there. We met the blimp when it came down at the Naval Air Station and confiscated the damned films. That was pretty high-handed, but you can do it if you want to -

Q: It was within the family, with the Navy!

Adm. D.: It was in the family, all right.

Q: The Little White House ceased to be used, then, by the Executive after Truman, did it not?

Adm. D.: I think almost immediately. The Navy made two quarters out of it. They made it a double house, sort of a thing. It was very awkward and very unhandy, but they couldn't foresee another president using it and I suppose they were right. But it meant a great deal to President Truman. It was exactly what he wanted. It had big lawns where he could go out and sit and have buffet lunches and all that.

Dennison #5 - 175

Interview No. 5 with Admiral Robert Lee Dennison, U.S. Navy
(Retired)

Place: His office in the Davis Building, Washington, D. C.

Date: Tuesday afternoon, 27 March 1973

Subject: Biography

By: John T. Mason, Jr.

Q: As usual, it's a delight to see you, and I'm glad that we're getting along so well with this oral biography. Would you begin today, perhaps, by talking about the retirement of Fleet Admiral Leahy as Chief of Staff to the President and tell me the story of General Bradley, who was Chairman of the Joint Chiefs, and his insistence upon briefing the President on various events as they materialized?

Adm. D.: In 1949, I believe, Admiral Leahy left the White House. Since he was a fleet admiral, he didn't retire, of course, he remained on active duty all his life.

Q: It was my error in using the word "retirement" for a fleet admiral. But his reason for leaving?

Adm. D.: Well, you must remember, of course, that the National Security Act was passed which had statutory provisions for the position of Chairman of the Joint Chiefs of Staff, and General Bradley was the first officer to hold such a position. Admiral Leahy, of course, was chief of staff to the commander-in-chief under President Roosevelt and President Truman, acted

Dennison #5 - 176

as chairman by virtue of seniority.

So, principally in view of the fact that there was now a legal Chairman of the Joint Chiefs of Staff and because Admiral Leahy had performed his duties so proficiently through the years, he felt it was time to step aside and President Truman agreed.

Q: He was getting along in years also.

Adm. D.: Yes, he was and his health hadn't been too good. So General Bradley was made a five-star general and took over as Chairman. Somewhere early in the game he discovered that the President had instructed me to take over all of Admiral Leahy's papers and he wanted me to continue to receive all the dispatches, documents, and so on that Admiral Leahy had been receiving - and these came from various sources, such as the Atomic Energy Commission, the Joint Chiefs of Staff, the individual services and the State Department. So there grew to be quite a volume of information. Well, the President couldn't conceivably digest all this information and pore over it, so it fell to my lot to brief him on the essential elements of the information I was getting and to try to put the information together in some form of continuity.

Q: This was at the beginning of the day, was it?

Adm. D.: Oh, yes. Admiral Leahy and I were on very close terms and he gave me all the documents he had and I believe most of them are now in the files of the Joint Chiefs. He was a meticulous record-keeper, so his files were in perfect order and of tremendous value. When General Bradley found this out he had never heard of me and he was a bit suspicious of some naval officer being in touch with - in possession of the documents of the Commander-in-Chief. So he asked permission of the President to come up and have a talk with us, which, of course, was granted, and the President sent for me. General Bradley said that, since he was chairman of the Joint Chiefs of Staff, he felt that he should be the one to brief the President on affairs that were pertinent to the Joint Chiefs of Staff. The President, of course, agreed and asked General Bradley and me if we would go into the Cabinet Room next door and draw up some kind of a memorandum of understanding, which we did. It said, in effect, that General Bradley would exercise the proper responsibility of briefing the President on military matters, but that he would continue to see that I got information in the field of politico-military affairs which were Joint Chiefs of Staff dispatches and papers.

Q: I suppose, by that time, he had discovered that you were knowledgeable in that area, too?

Adm. D.: I don't know. He may have, knowing General Bradley, but he probably did have an inkling of what I'd been doing, but as far as I can remember we'd never met and this was quite a natural thing for him to do. I may be doing him an injustice to say that he distrusted me, partly on account of my being

Dennison #5 - 178

in a different service. Of course, you remember the B-36 episode.

Q: Very well!

Adm. D.: Bradley called admirals a "bunch of fancy dans."

Q: You weren't an admiral then, but - !

Adm. D.: No, but I had on a blue suit! So we agreed and the President said, fine. Well, things went along pretty good for a week or so and one day the President read something in the newspaper, some occurrence in Korea. He sent for me and, in a very gentle voice, asked me why I hadn't informed him. So I said, "Because, Mr. President, I didn't know it myself until I read it in the paper this morning. You remember our agreement with General Bradley." "Oh, of course." He said, "But I'm sure it won't happen again." Well, sure enough, it did happen again on another matter. This time the President asked me to send for General Bradley and when he came in to, please, come in with him.

General Bradley came and we chatted with the President and the President, again very gently, mentioned these two instances. General Bradley understood completely and was embarrassed and chagrined that he hadn't briefed the President. Quite naturally he hadn't because he had found out that it was difficult for him in his own busy day to find time and find it at the same time the President would be available.

Q: And to do it every day!

Adm. D.: Yes, it had to be done practically every day and it was something he hadn't really realized. After a very brief conversation, the President said, "Brad, don't you think we'd better go back to the arrangement we had before we got into the present arrangement? That seemed to work pretty well." In the meantime, General Bradley had found out that it wasn't feasible, no matter how correct and desirable it might be, for him to do all this personally and perhaps he found out that a lot of us are not exactly parochial naval types, but for whatever reason we did go back to the arrangement we had before. Our personal relationship was very friendly and very good.

Q: You, then, in effect, became the liaison between the Joint Chiefs and the President in terms of information?

Adm. D.: Not only the Joint Chiefs, but remember these other sources, too.

Q: Yes. The AEC and others.

Adm. D.: Again, I'd just like to point out that I never looked on myself - and I'm sure the President didn't look on me - as being an advisor. That's sometimes a pretty fine line because Admiral Leahy's position was quite different. He was chief of staff, he was a very senior officer, very experienced, and he was in a position to advise the President. So I restricted myself to briefing the President and only advised him when he asked my views on something. He was perfectly able to evaluate my views because he knew my background and, perhaps, my prejudices. When he asked me something, I felt perfectly free to tell him what I thought and, if appropriate, why I thought so.

Q: Isn't it absolutely essential for a president to have a few men whom he can rely on for reactions on any topic he chooses to bring before them?

Adm. D.: Yes, of course, but if you can put yourself in the position of advising somebody with the power of the president, the commander in chief, it makes you pause a little bit before you throw advice around too freely.

Q: But rather as a person from whom he wants a reaction to something, rather than in the nature of advice?

Adm. D.: Well, of course, one thing that I did, and it was perfectly natural, was when I felt that I wasn't competent to give him the advice that he really needed, I could give him my opinion and suggest that he consult whoever would be appropriate.

Q: Did he seek advice from you in the area of political and military affairs and foreign affairs?

Adm. D.: Yes, but don't forget he was very, very close to Secretary Acheson and General Marshall, at one time, and these gentlemen, of course, were so knowledgeable and had so much background, and General Bradley, of course. So he had plenty of competent people and the President's way of doing business was to ask people whom he trusted. I might give you an example of his reasoning.

Did I ever tell you about how he made a decision?

Q: No, I don't think you have.

Adm. D.: I asked him one time what his mental processes were in reaching a decision and what he told me explained why, in so many cases, people would come in to give him some advice and go out of his office believing that he had taken it, and that's exactly what he was going to do. In any event, he told me that the process was very simple - at least, it was simple to state it. He said that the first thing is to gather all the facts that you can, and, remember, that you'll never have all the facts because, if you had them, there wouldn't be any need for a decision.

It would be automatic. Having done that, you call in the people most knowledgeable and most responsible, but remember, that quite naturally and quite properly, the Secretary of Defense might take an opposite view or a different view of the problem than the Secretary of State, each one of them thinking of his responsibility for his own department. But after you've gotten advice from all the people whose opinion you respect, then you go off by yourself and make up your mind, weighing all the advice and all the facts that you've got.

The next step is probably the most important. Having made the decision, you never look back. You go on to the next one. Which is exactly the way he operated.

But, again, I've known many occasions when some high official would go out of his office thinking the President was convinced of his point of view to the exclusion of everybody's elses, which wasn't the case.

Q: His point of view was only one contribution to the total picture!

Adm. D.: That's right. And the President, of course, realized his various roles, which he told me so many times were really separate and distinct. One was Commander in Chief, another were his actions as President of the United States, president of all the people, as he used to put it. And lastly leader of his political party. And he had what, to me, seemed to be an unusual facility or faculty, that is, he could completely separate these three different responsibilities. One never infringed on the other. For example, he never let party political considerations enter into his decisions as President, and just as a very minor matter, you may have noticed in some of the photographs and books I have that he has inscribed he refers to himself as "your Commander in Chief" or "your former Commander in Chief" in later years. This was completely unconscious, I'm sure, but that was the way he saw our relationship and that's the way it was.

Q: How long a period of time was involved in making these major decisions following this system?

Adm. D.: Well, of course, there wasn't any pattern. It all depended on the complexity of the problem. Some decisions - for example, the Truman Doctrine - this was 1947, before I joined him, but this had to do with aid to Greece and Turkey. Now, in that case, he couldn't have had more than maybe forty-eight hours or maybe a few more hours to do something, because the British had made a very surprise sudden announcement that they were withdrawing their support from Greece, which left a real vacuum.

Q: Again, that was without consultation, was it not?

Adm. D.: So far as I know, it was completely out of the blue. I wasn't there, but I was given to understand that the notice was very brief. So the reaction was swift.

There were many long-range matters, such as national security which involved the creation of a single intelligence agency, the creation of another branch of the armed services, and other things, and matters of this nature and he had longer to develop his own position, but he never took any longer than he had to. He wanted to take one problem, analyze it, make a decision, and move on.

Q: It's a happy faculty to be able to not look back and torture oneself, having made a decision.

Adm. D.: Well, when you come to think of it, not only is it a happy faculty but it's an essential one in a man such as the President of the United States.

I remember the case of Secretary Forrestal. Here was a case where the Secretary was unable to make a decision and go on to the next one.

Q: Have you reflected on the manner in which the President arrived at this system, the true executive in action? He'd never had much experience as an executive before he came to the White House.

Adm. D.: The sources of the President's knowledge were so varied and there were so many of them, it was a source of constant amazement to me how he could pick up certain principles and certain procedures and put them away in his memory and then pull them out when he needed them. This may seem far-fetched to you, but you must remember the system for developing, say, an estimate of a situation in military terms. The Navy had its set way of approaching it. The Army did it in much the same way. You analyze the forces available and the forces opposed and, the courses of action open, and so on, and it finally came down, I think, to five steps to a decision on what you were going to do, which is an orderly process applicable to many, many situations.

The President, in his early days, as an officer in the Army, a Reserve officer, learned of this approach to problems and I'm sure that this guided his manner of developing his own procedure in later years as President of the United States. He learned to think in these step-by-step terms which he could separate out as separate ways - or, rather, not separate ways but separate elements in arriving at a final solution. And many things that he'd come up with as facts really were amazing.

Perhaps it's a trivial example, but I remember one day we were talking about the capitals of columns and I couldn't remember, if I ever knew, the difference between a Corinthian and an Ionic and a Doric, and the President - I forget what building we were talking about - mentioned that these were, let's say, corinthian and I couldn't help but say, "How in the world do you know that, or how do you remember it?" And he said, "Well, as you know, I'm a Mason and I studied very hard and somewhere along the line in reading for my examination to go up the ladder in the Masonic Order, I just happen to remember coming across this piece of information.

Q: And filed it away!

Before we leave this area where you were charged with keeping him informed on developments, did you maintain a plot room of any sort in the White House in those days?

Adm. D.: No. President Roosevelt had. He had what he called a map room, and it was, in effect, a war room, but President Truman didn't feel the need for it. He had the resources of the various departments. He didn't need a map or a chart.

Q: He didn't need visual aids?

Adm. D.: No. He loved maps, but we didn't have one and really it was better I think as the years have gone by. The idea of all executives having a command post or an information center or whatever they want to call it is bad. Not that they shouldn't be informed but what happens is that the officers in charge of these various rooms want to get in touch with officers in the field to get information so that they can be the first one to tell their boss what's going on. Well, this is not the way to run any kind of an operation. But, for whatever reason, we didn't have one and President Truman, I'm sure, never felt the need for one.

Q: Now, Sir, would you look at the area that involved Secretary Johnson when he succeeded Secretary Forrestal. You told me some time back about Forrestal's illness and his resignation. When Johnson came in one of his first acts, I believe, was to cancel the contract for the aircraft carrier United States. Was this instigated by the President?

Adm. D.: No. I'm sure the President didn't know what was going on until Johnson made this announcement, which was pretty typical of Secretary Johnson to go off on his own. In this particular instance, it may conceivably be - I'd have to check President Truman's memoirs to find out - that he did say something, but I doubt it, because John Sullivan, who was very close to the President, was Secretary of the Navy and at this particular time when the contract was canceled he was, as I remember, making a speech down in Texas and that's where he heard about it as a fait accompli. This, of course, led to a very embarrassing situation involving the President - or could have - and this forced John Sullivan to resign as Secretary of the Navy.

John Sullivan and I, of course, worked together quite closely on the State, War, and Navy Coordinating Committee and many other matters so, as he'd done before, he called me up late one afternoon and wanted to know if I could come down to his office in the Navy Department. I went down immediately, and I went into his office, and there were quite a few people there - I forget now who they were - and he was just about to dictate his resignation to Kate Foley, who was his personal secretary. Well, I came in at this particular moment -

Q: She'd been secretary to Forrestal!

Adm. D.: Yes, she'd been in the Navy Department for many, many years. An extremely fine woman and very, very capable.

I came in as he started dictating and found out, of course, immediately what he was doing was resigning because of this action of Johnson's, and was addressing the President. This was quite proper because he was appointed by the President, not by Johnson, but I thought something's got to be done about this, so I left the room and called up Charlie

Ross at the White House and told him what was going on. He said, "Well, hold onto John and I'll be down there." So he came down and the letter was read to him. He implored Sullivan not to send it. He said, "You and the President are close personal friends, and, of course, you're a member of the Democratic Party and this is just going to raise hell because you've said some things in here which, justified or not, don't seem to me to be the things to put before the President." How he happened to come up with this one, I don't know. "Whether it's legal or not, why don't you resign to Secretary Johnson?" and that's what Sullivan did.

This could have been very embarrassing and it was just really almost by accident that a clash between the President and Sullivan, at least on paper, was avoided. So, I'm reasonably sure that had this action been cleared by the President, Sullivan would have been told in a different way or it wouldn't have happened at all.

Johnson was a strange man. He came into office believing that unification was the cure to all the evils in the armed forces. He was openly prejudiced against the Navy, quite bitter about the Navy. We had considerable opposition within the Navy to unification because it had not been really defined, it was just a general term, and anybody that was opposed to "unification" was really beyond the pale in Johnson's eyes. But it sounded so much to the Navy like a merger of the armed services, leading to the same uniform and all kinds of things of that sort, and they were quite naturally opposed to it.

Q: There was also a very real threat that they were going to lose their air arm!

Adm. D.: Yes, they'd lose their air arm and all sorts of horrible things were going to happen. What was needed was a definition of exactly what the term meant, or get some other term, or stop using any term.

Q: What was the President's attitude toward this whole thing of unification?

Adm. D.: I don't think he accepted the Johnsonian interpretation of what it meant. It was quite clear to him and quite clear to many of us who were trying to think this problem through that something simply had to be done to get the armed services under over-all strategic direction. Remember, during World War II in many areas, for example, I happen to be familiar with the Philippines because I was there. Here, we had a situation where the relationship between, in this case, Admiral Hart and General MacArthur was not just strained there was practically no interchange of information or plans. You are, of course, completely aware of the history of the war in the Pacific. We started out with the two services really fighting their own different wars. We didn't have a Joint Chiefs of Staff. We were forced into it really because of our cooperation and involvement with the British. They had Chiefs of Staff so we followed suit, and, together, they were the Combined Chiefs. We needed that kind of a structure, so that there would be single strategic direction of the armed services. That was one reason.

Another one was, of course, this CIA business. The President was completely appalled not only by the amount of information he was getting and intelligence, but by the diversity. Somebody should be in a position, so he thought, and so do I, to coordinate this information so that there would be an expression by an authoritative voice. Sure, there were alternatives or varying interpretations, but one picture, an independent picture. That was another reason for unification, as the President saw it.

His view about the structure was that it was to be headed by a Secretary of Defense, this committee would take care of the combined business of the three services. There are many areas where this has to be done, particularly with as large an establishment as we had. So that was another reason.

Q: That's essentially what it was when Forrestal was Secretary, wasn't it?

Adm. D.: It started out that way because he didn't have a deputy and he didn't have a large staff. They finally built up one, but not nearly as large as it finally became, because Forrestal, not being an executive in the sense that

President Truman was, couldn't operate that way with the various service secretaries and so on. He had to have somebody to advise him and to help him and so on, so it just finally grew.

Johnson was the first to have a deputy, which was Steve Early.

When Secretary Johnson took over, he felt a need, and quite a proper need, the way things were going, for a capable deputy. I happened to be in his office one day - I forget why, transmitting something to him from the President probably - and he told me that he was trying to find a deputy. He'd tried a number of people and he told me who they were, which I've forgotten, but he wasn't having any luck and didn't really have anybody in mind that he felt was suitable. And he was right, he didn't. And for some reason - but it couldn't have been a very good reason - I said, "Well, you've got a potential deputy right here in this building." They were having at that time a conference that they had every year and have had every year since, I think, called the Joint Orientation Conference, or something like that. They invited a number of leaders in industry and various other fields to come down to Washington once a year and have sort of a get-together. They went to various military installations and were briefed in the Pentagon and so forth. When I told him that, he said, "Who is it?" I said, "Steve Early."

Q: He being the Roosevelt - ?

Adm. D.: Yes, he was with President Roosevelt. He was a staunch Democrat and all that, and Johnson was very, very political minded. He said, "My God, I don't know why I didn't think of that. That's just fine."

Then I got to thinking what the hell have I done? So I went back to the White House and immediately went in to the President, and said, "Mr. President, I've done something unforgiveable. I was talking when I certainly should have been listening." I told him what I'd done and he said, "Bob, it isn't a bad idea. Don't feel bad about it. It's true I had other plans for Steve Early but I'm sure this would be a good place for him." Whether he really thought that, I don't know. He was so kind and gentle. I'd really done something I never should have done.

That's how Johnson got Early.

Q: Johnson was certainly noted, and justifiably so, for his economy measures in the services, cutting down to the raw bone. Was this something that the President shared? Was it his desire that this be done?

Adm. D.: What he desired was reduction of the budget of the armed forces. No, he didn't want to kill off all our military potential by any manner of means, but exactly what instructions Johnson got that had filtered down through the Bureau of the Budget, of course, he cut his cloth to fit the pattern, and when it came to a matter of judgment as to what areas to cut, perhaps the Bureau of the Budget had a great deal to do with that. I've never gone back to really check it out and see how specific instructions were or whether they could be appealed or had been appealed.

Johnson, in any event, got blamed for some of these fairly drastic actions that he undertook.

Q: You told me, sir, on another occasion about Johnson succeeding Forrestal. Since then I've heard a story, which I suppose is current, about Johnson's appointment and I bring it up to you so that you can say there isn't anything to it, if that is the case. The story was that Johnson was head of the American Legion, I believe, or Veterans of Foreign Wars, or something of the sort. Anyway, he was instrumental in supplying funds for the presidential campaign, making possible the whistle-stop train, which was so useful to President Truman in his re-election campaign, and as a result, according to this story, Johnson was promised a job in the adminstration, whatever he wanted.

Adm. D.: Well, I think that's a story that's plausible, but I don't think Johnson was head of the American Legion. I think he was very influential in it and, of course, again he was a dyed-in-the-wool, card-carrying Party member, the Democratic Party. I think it's too much to give him credit for arranging financing of the President's train, for one thing. It would be more likely somebody like Ed Pauley. While I can't say it isn't so, the chances are 99 to 1 that it isn't so the way you put it. That may have had some part in it.

Q: Well, when we came to the outbreak of the Korean conflict we saw the resignation of Johnson. Why was that?

Adm. D.: I've forgotten the timing and the exact circumstances. A lot of these things that Johnson had done in the aggregate commenced to look sort of bad.

Q: His independent actions?

Adm. D.: Yes, and he seemed to be some times taking over a bit too much power. A small example is the one that I think I've mentioned before when along with Secretary Matthews of the Navy they struck Admiral Burke's name - Captain Burke's name - from the Navy selection board's report.

Q: You have not told me that story.

Adm. D.: Well, this is a good example of how they operated and throws some light on Johnson and Matthews, as well as on the President, so I think I might put it in the record.

Q: Matthews was the successor to Sullivan?

Adm. D.: Yes, and this was a typical Johnson appointment. The President really wasn't concerned much about who was the Secretary of the Navy. I don't mean he singled out the Navy, but since we had a Secretary of Defense he relied a great deal on his recommendations. Of course, there were certain requirements. He should be a Democrat, if possible, although

Secretary Lovett became Secretary of Defense and he was a Republican. The President appointed him, but that was different.

In this case, Sullivan resigned. He was a Catholic and a very fine one. So Johnson decided the thing to do was to appoint somebody to succeed him who was also a Catholic, so he recommended the appointment of a super Catholic, Secretary Matthews, who was very prominent in the Catholic Church. He had a chapel in his own home and he was a devout man. I'm not criticizing him a bit, but I'm pointing out that he was identified very strongly with Catholicism. Well, this was Johnson's reasoning, you see. There might be a kick-back. Sullivan resigns and he was a Catholic, so the thing to do is put in another Catholic. That was the primary requirement, a political requirement, of course. Well, it turned out that we used to call Matthews, Rowboat Matthews because, as far as anybody knew, he'd never even seen salt water.

Q: He was from Nebraska, as I remember, wasn't he?

Adm. D.: I think so, yes. But in the particular case of Captain Burke, we were down in Key West - I was, with the President - and the report of the Navy Selection Board came down there. Obviously, the Secretary didn't realize that the mail, such as we had, would go to me. I was the naval aide and I always handled those things. When I read this board action and saw that Captain Burke had been selected for rear admiral and that his name had been stricken with a red pen - red ink - and the board had been re-convened and they had selected another officer to fill the slot that Burke would have been in. I knew that the President hadn't taken any such action. I would have been the first to know about it. He'd never seen the report until it came up in that form.

Q: Did he know Burke?

Adm. D.: Yes, he did. I'll tell you right now what happened after that. When I got a selection board report or a plucking board, too, as they had in those days, I'd take it to the President and he'd never ask me but one question, had any injustice been done. And each time I was able to say no. I knew the officers and I knew the board and I knew who hadn't been selected. I was perfectly sure there wasn't any injustice, anyway. It's one of the best systems for selection for promotion, I think, in the world. A naval officer takes his responsibility as a member of the board very, very seriously. They're restricted, of course, by the precepts given to them by the Secretary of the Navy to select an officer with certain qualifications.

I knew the President hadn't taken any such action in the case of Burke as to strike his name. Under the law, then, and I think now, the Selection Board's report is to the President, not the Secretary. It goes through the Secretary, but their statutory responsibility is to the

Commander in Chief. He acts on it. He can strike a name, send it back to the board for reconsideration to select somebody in lieu of this officer. He doesn't have to say why or anything. I've seen him do things of that nature with Army reports, but never the Navy's. So I was a little disturbed about this business of Burke, more than a little, and about Johnson's and Matthews' action. I got some documents together out of the library at Key West and got up early in the morning. The President always got up extremely early and went down to the living room to write letters, all alone. This particular morning I had this load of stuff under my arm and went in and stood at attention in front of his desk, one hand anyhow, and he looked up and said, "What's on your mind?"

I said, "I want to talk to you about a selection board report and I'd like to have you let me do some special pleading and separate myself for the moment from being your naval aide and simply speak to you as a naval officer."

He said, "Take the stuffing out of your shirt and sit down and tell me what the problem is!" So I did, and I showed him this report. Then I briefed him on Burke and I said, "This man is a classmate of mine, senior to me, and I have no personal axe to grind in this at all, but we are friends. But this is clearly an injustice, and besides that, it's illegal." I reminded him of the laws on it. He said, "Give me that report," he took it and stuck it in his desk, then he said, "You know, I think I remember Burke. I went down to Norfolk once and went aboard Admiral Mitscher's flagship, a carrier, and I was very much impressed with Mitscher and Burke was his chief of staff." I said, "Yes, that's right."

He said, "I remember meeting Burke. I think that anybody Mitscher would have as chief of staff must be good." And I said, "I agree." That was the end of the conversation.

We went back to Washington. The report usually went back immediately. My phone started to ring and finally Matthews got hold of me and wanted to know what had happened.

Q: The report hadn't come back?

Adm. D.: Yes. The President hadn't approved it and sent it back or taken any action. So I said, "I don't know, Mr. Secretary. I gave it to the President. He has it, as far as I know. I haven't got it." Well, nothing had happened. I thought that in the pressure of other things he had forgotten, although he never forgot anything.

A few days after we got back the President sent for me and said, "Secretary Johnson and Matthews want to come up and talk to me. I think I know what it is. It's this selection board report. I want you to be out of here when they come. I'll handle this." I said, "I'm sure you will, Mr. President." He said, "You go in the Cabinet Room and I'll call you when they leave." I did and after a little while he opened the door and said, "Come on in," and he was grinning from ear to ear. He said, "Well, you friend, Burke, it back on the selection list. The other officer who had no part in this is also going to be on the list. So that's the way it is. The best part of it is that Johnson and Matthews are taking the position now that this happy solution is their idea!"

Q: I thought they wanted him off, in the first place.

Adm. D.: At first, they did, but they'd gotten the news that the President had this thing. He was fully aware of what had happened and who did it, and he didn't like it. So, rather than having him tell them that, which he was fully prepared to do, they just came up with this thing voluntarily. So everything turned out fine. The President didn't have to raise hell with them.

But things like that, in the end, just got too much.

Q: What was their opposition to Admiral Burke in the first place?

Adm. D.: Because he was opposed to "unification" and he was at one time head of some outfit called Op-23, I think it was, or something like that, which in the Secretary's eyes was absolutely subversive! I mean they were opposed to unification! Whatever the hell Burke was doing in Op-23 or anything else, he was doing what he was told to do by his seniors. This was completely beside the point of what kind of a product are you putting out. It wasn't Burke. Sure, he had some bright ideas on it himself, but he was scarcely acting independently. But, for whatever reason, Johnson felt that this kind of thing on the part of the Navy was just terrible and Burke was the personification of this opposition.

Q: Let Burke be the scapegoat!

Adm. D.: Yes, just as Denfeld was.

Q: Tell me that story, Denfeld and his forced resignation.

Adm. D.: Again, this was an arbitrary action by Matthews, probably with the concurrence of Johnson and maybe more than concurrence. Anyway, the B-36 inquiry, of course, is a matter of record all over the place. You must have plenty of accounts about that. But it was a bitter battle and the Navy side of it, headed by Admiral Radford, was opposed to the rapidly increasing Air Force and they called the B-36 the "billion-dollar blunder" or some such thing as that. There was a real battle, but it was mostly aviation, and Denfeld was supposed to make a statement as the Chief of Naval Operations at a hearing before Congress - I think it was the House Armed Services Committee, but I'm not too sure which it was - and Matthews asked me if I would sit in on the preparation of his speech to ensure that he didn't put anything in it that would cross wires with the President's policy, which I did. Denfeld had a committee headed by Admiral Colclough, who was

Dennison #5 - 201

then Judge Advocate General -

Q: Don Griffin was in on that, too, wasn't he?

Adm. D.: I don't remember. I just remember Colclough. But there were quite a few. Maybe half a dozen. And they prepared a statement taking the position that the Chief of Naval Operations would take, and it was a good statement. Unfortunately, when he gave the statement, he put in something extemporaneously saying, in effect, that he supported completely the views expressed by Admiral Radford. Well, he became the lightning rod instead of Radford.

When this became public, Matthews and Johnson went into a rage and they fired Denfeld - here again, how much the President had to do with this, I'm not clear. He wouldn't have told them to do it, I do know that. But I remember how I heard about it. I was in my office in the late afternoon when a friend of mine in the press called up to ask me if I knew this or had heard it. I hadn't, so I went right over to talk to the President, and I said, "I'm really upset about this." Denfeld is an old and dear friend of mine and I know he's just gotten the news. Would you mind if I went up to his quarters at the Observatory to talk to him? I doubt if anybody's there with him, except Mrs. Denfeld."

Q: As a friend?

Adm. D.: Yes, sure. He said, "Of course not. I want you

to go. You're old friends and I'm sure he needs companionship, so go."

Well, I did. Next day I got a call from Matthews - he was furious, saying, "I understand that you prepared or helped prepare Admiral Denfeld's statement." I said, "Yes, I did exactly what you asked me to do, and there was nothing in that speech that would in any way cross wires with the President. I didn't write it, and certainly the way it was delivered was not the text that I saw."

Then he went on to say, "I understand that you went to Admiral Denfeld's quarters yesterday evening."

Q: He must have had a system of spies!

Adm. D.: I don't know how he found that out, but I said, "Yes, Sir, I did." He could hardly speak. He said, "That's the most disloyal act that I can possibly imagine. Here an officer's been fired and you go up to see him." I said, "I don't agree it's not a disloyal act at all, and I can tell you another person who doesn't agree with you."

He said, "Who's that?" I said, "The Commander in Chief." His face fell a mile. He stood in absolute awe of the President, quite naturally, and that really stopped him. There was nothing he could say after that. What I said was perfectly true. I told him what the President had told me. I asked him to go and he said yes, certainly, "he's an old friend of yours."

So here again was an instance of Matthews and Johnson,

and when I talked to the President about Denfeld I didn't have any inkling at all that he knew in advance that this was going to be done or why it was going to be done, or anything of the sort. Just another example of this high-handed action by the two secretaries.

Q: Actually, it's my understanding that Denfeld had seen his reappointment, as it was signed by Secretary Johnson, and this was put on file until the proper time. Then this reversal came.

Adm. D.: I think that's right. If I remember, I sent him a copy of it in the normal course of events. It seems to me I remember some columnist dug that out.

Q: In the summer of 1950, I think it was in August, there was an incident involving President Truman and the Marine Corps which is of considerable interest. Would you tell me about it?

Adm. D.: Certainly.

As I mentioned before, President Truman had an unfortunate habit of getting up early in the morning without a secretary and writing letters to people in his own handwriting. They were very informal and almost without exception were to his family and friends. This time, he got up in the morning and wrote a letter to a congressman whose name I've forgotten -

Q: Gordon McDonough.

Adm. D.: Well, somehow or other that name President Truman associated with some Army colleague of his in World War II. Why he didn't look this man up or check him out or why he didn't ask somebody whether this was the Gordon McDonough that he was thinking of, I don't know. But he didn't.

Q: And it wasn't in response to a letter?

Adm. D.: No, no, it was just old buddies chatting with each other, one former Army guy to another one. In this unfortunate letter, President Truman mentioned - I forget the exact language - something to the effect that the Marine Corps had a better propaganda machine than Joe Stalin. Now, that may or may not have been so, but it was unfortunately worded. The further astounding thing was that this congressman released the letter, so it was published and commented on.

Q: Did he ever give reasons why he did that?

Adm. D.: I don't know. Believe it or not, this drew more telephone calls, more letters, more telegrams into the White House than any other single incident in his administration.

Q: And instantaneously, I suppose!

Adm. D.: Yes. Matters that went on for years, like comments on the Taft-Hartley Act went on for a long period of time, but this immediate response really flooded the White House, and a good many of these letters and phone calls and telegrams came to me. The mailroom naturally would do that. You couldn't put all that stuff on the President's desk. But he got enough of it from the papers and what he knew and heard.

Q: Real flak!

Adm. D.: It was just unbelievable. It was emotional. Maybe not unbelievable because the Marines are that way. But these were letters from daughters, wives, former Marines, everybody.

Q: Probably underscored what he had said about them!

Adm. D.: Well, they picked up this likening them to Communists, you see. If he hadn't mentioned Stalin, it would have probably been passed over -

Q: The association.

Adm. D.: Yes. The terrific propaganda machine they had, that's one thing and, of course, probably a good many people who sent in all this stuff and had never read the text. They just got a general impression, third-hand or something. But for whatever reason, it really inundated the White House. So the President sent for me and Charlie Ross, his Press Secretary, and he said, "You've got to do something to get me out of this." So, what to do?

I was reminded of a story that I'd heard about Judge

Rosenman's advice to President Roosevelt. Roosevelt had made a speech in Pittsburgh, extemporaneous, and in this speech he made some remark about labor that really brought the roof down. He was damned and condemned all over the place, so he sent for Mr. Rosenman and said, "You've got to get me out of this. What do I do?" And Rosenman thought a moment and said, "It's very simple, Mr. President. All you've got to do is deny you made the speech."

Q: He just wasn't there!

Adm. D.: But in this case, President Truman put this one in writing.

Q: It was in writing?

Adm. D.: Yes, but he hadn't said really what the people thought that he'd said. He wasn't talking about the Marines being like Communists or anything at all. At any rate, this was a mess. So I said, "Well, I think what you must do is to write a letter and explain to the Commandant of the Marine Corps and ask him to publish the letter to the Marines." Ross took a very pale view of that. He said, "The President of the United States can't apologize." I said, "I don't see why not, if he's made a mistake and I assume that he has."

And the President said, "I don't see why he can't either."

Q: That's implying that he's infallible!

Adm. D.: Yes. Don't admit that you are fallible, that's

the policy, I guess. So he turned to me and he said, "Draft me a letter. Take Rose Connolly in and write it for me." So I did. I knew exactly what I thought he wanted to say and I hoped he would. So I brought this draft back in in a few minutes and gave a copy to Charlie on my way in. The President read it and took out his pencil and pen and changed a few sentences and some words, so it really ended up as Truman's letter. Then he called Rose Conolly in and said, "Please type this for General Cates," the letter explained what his feelings were and he didn't mean to create a wrong impression and would General Cates please circulate this widely to the Marine Corps.

Then he turned to me again and said, "Wasn't I invited to some Marine Corps reunion here?" I said, "Yes, Sir, you regretted with apologies because obviously you can't be going to all these things here in Washington." He said, "Well, I've decided I'll go. When is it?"

I said, "I think it's tomorrow morning." So, with that, Ross got up and brought in the Secret Service - Jim Rowley was head of the White House detail, he's now head of the Secret Service, and some of his people, and they protested. They said, "Mr. President, you don't know what's going to happen if you do go. Emotions are so high and somebody's likely to throw a pop bottle at you or assault you or do something, and we don't think you ought to expose yourself to it."

The President thought about that for a minute, and said,

"I'm willing to take a chance. Nothing's going to happen to me anyhow, so I'm going to go." He turned to me again and said, "Call General Cates, who I assume is going to this," and I said, "I'm sure he must be," "ask him to stop by the White House tomorrow morning and pick me up!" This was typically Truman. So I called up General Cates and translated this to mean "please stop by the White House and accompany me and please be here at such and such a time."

So Cates drove up to the South Entrance and the President's car was there. The President and Ross - I forget whether anybody else was there or not, I don't think Vaughan was - got in. Cates had his own car. We went up to the Statler, now the Statler-Hilton. Nobody knew we were coming. Of course, the manager, Herb Blunk, knew. They had a good many White House functions there or functions where the President attended. The Secret Service, of course, were all around inconspicuously. We went up to the Ball Room and waited outside the door and General Cates went out on the stage. All the Marines there - this was the Third Division, I think, applauded and yelled. They expected a "rally round the flag" speech.

Q: Might even attack the President!

Adm. D.: So, all Cates did when he got them quieted down was to say, "Gentlemen, the President of the United States" and Truman walked right on the stage. There was absolute dead silence. Everybody was completely surprised and taken aback. They just couldn't believe it. All of a sudden you'd think the roof had fallen in, all this applauding and yelling. They admired his great courage. Hell, no one even thought of throwing anything at him. They thought he was just great.

He spoke so well extemporaneously and he did this time and told them exactly what he thought of the Marine Corps, what a fine group of people they were and what they'd done for our country through the years, and about the friendly rivalry between the Marines and the Army, and so on. It was a very simple talk but so obviously was sincere, that he really respected the Marine Corps and admired them. Well, after this very brief talk, people were crying, the chairman of the group, probably the former commanding officer of the division, took a medal off his own uniform and pinned it on the President! It was very demonstrative, I'll say that.

Finally, the President was able to get away and we all went back to the White House. Cates did publish the letter and that killed it. What he had to say there was published. This was typically Truman. He was absolutely unafraid of anything. But he really liked to pull the Marine Corps' leg. His relations with the Marine Corps were not distant, but this may illustrate what I just said.

I used to remind the President when it was time for him to see the Joint Chiefs of Staff or make a visit to some Army or Navy installation, but he never did much for the

Marines. So I kept pestering him about it and said, "Why don't you let me set up something for you. You've been to Benning and Eglin Field and all those places, and all over the place, but not Quantico!" He finally gave in.

Q: This was after or before this incident?

Adm. D.: I think it was before. I'm pretty sure it was. He finally gave in. I should have realized that he was going to get back at me one way or another. So I set it up with the Commandant, Lem Shepherd, who was a very splendid officer and man and an old friend, as many of the senior Marines were. They were going to put on a show at Quantico. He brought in all his top brass and they were going to meet the President on the dock. So, at the appointed time, the President and I pulled up to the dock -

Q: This was in the Williamsburg?

Adm. D.: Yes, the Williamsburg - and disembarked. They had the whole show, gun salute, honor guards, and all that, and the President reviewed the troops. When this was all over, he called Shepherd and all the senior officers around him and said, "I appreciate very much these honors and I'm ready to go on to the demonstration, but before I do I'd like to ask a question. On the way down the river, my naval aide told me that in good times when things were going smoothly the Marine Corps wanted to be separate from the Navy, but when the going was rough it wanted to run back and get under the tent again. Is that true?"

Of course, I never said any such thing! And, thank God, neither Shepherd nor any of the rest of them ever believed I had, so they made some joking response to it, but the President sure got even with me for pestering him!

Q: Would you talk about General MacArthur and his ultimate dismissal by the President? This whole episode, I believe, began with the meeting of MacArthur with the President on Wake Island on October 15, 1950.

Adm. D.: Certainly. You mentioned MacArthur's dismissal and, it may be quibbling, but actually he was relieved.

Q: I'm sorry I used that word, I know it's not the correct one!

Adm. D.: Well, you read so much about MacArthur being fired, dismissed, discharged, or something, which was not the case. Yes, I'll be glad to comment on it.

I think probably the beginning, or the part that you're interested in surely, begins at Wake Island. I was ill at the time so I didn't go with the President to Wake, but he told me about it several times and I talked to other people who'd been there, and it's been recorded in various places. There were no official minutes kept or records, but the private secretary of one of the State Department people overheard from the next room some of the conversation and did make some notes, which are not verified, so as far as I know there is no authentic record, except from the participants.

Admiral Radford was there and his version of what happened is different from my recollection of what the President told me in several respects.

Q: In the first place, Sir, why was it necessary for him to go half way to Korea or more so?

Adm. D.: Well, remember, we had a pretty hot situation in Korea and this was typically President Truman. I asked him that question myself - this was after the event. I said, "I think that MacArthur probably misread this. Your coming to him and thereby putting him in a superior position, instead of asking him to report to you."

He said, "I can't believe that, but my reason for doing it was simply because he's the responsible commander out there, and I felt it would be wrong to take him as far away as Hawaii or the West Coast or Washington, surely, from his command. I think he ought to be there or as close to there as he can get." It never occurred to the President that there were any overtones or undertones in his going out there.

At any rate, the President wanted to be briefed by General MacArthur as to what was the trend of the war. And, again, according to President Truman, MacArthur told him two things, among others. But these two things were critically important. One was the assurance that the Chinese - or Chinese Communists - would not intervene, and the second was that the Eighth Army would be out of Korea by Christmas - and Wake Island, as I recall was sometime in October. Now, the government's policy had been to avoid the spread of hostilities into Manchuria. They didn't want to enlarge the war, they didn't want to take on the Communists. They didn't have any idea what Soviet Russia's attitude might be or how they would back up their position in case it was anti-U.N. or U.S., which it undoubtedly would have been. So, for many reasons - for example, we didn't want to bomb the power plants on the Yalu River, we didn't want to take any action inside of Manchuria. There were some of the fundamental principles we were operating under and there have been debates ever since as to the wisdom of them - whether we wouldn't have been better off to drop an atom bomb on Manchuria or do something drastic. I can't help, from what little I know about history, thinking that the President's decision was rational and wise and best for our country.

In any event, the Chinese Communists did intervene, and our troops were unable to come out. We don't have to go into what happened in Korea from October on, but it wasn't good.

Q: We finally were driven out of the Seoul area.

Adm. D.: Yes, we were pushed down to the tip and things looked pretty bad, and they were pretty bad. General MacArthur, unfortunately, made some statements on the record which were widely circulated, that were contradictory to the expressed U.S. policy. Obviously, this couldn't be tolerated. You can't have a commanding general of the U.N. forces taking a position opposed to the policy of his own country. So, something had to be done, and the President decided that General MacArthur had to be relieved.

Q: Had the President disbelieved the optimism that MacArthur had expressed?

Adm. D.: No. At the moment, he believed it. He didn't really have any facts to the contrary. This was supposedly a seasoned, reasoned view of the man who was responsible for the actions in Korea. The President may have felt, well, this is almost too good to be true but let's hope at least that the Chinese Communists aren't going to intervene and maybe we can get that army out of there. Whatever he believed I don't know, but he told me what General MacArthur had told him. So, when the President decided he would consider relieving MacArthur, as was his practice, he consulted senior people, General Marshall in particular, and General Bradley, and others, who knew MacArthur and had known him all their military lives, knew his record, exactly what sort of a man he was, what sort of an officer he was, and, as I remember, each one asked permission of the President to go back and look at the record and think it over. I believe it was General Marshall who came back to the President - all those he consulted said MacArthur had to go - and said, "I think the only mistake here is that you're at least six months too late."

So, with his senior responsible people agreeing with him on this dramatic action, he proceeded. Now, remember, this was politically very, very unpopular. MacArthur was a great hero. So, if the President had been acting under purely political considerations, he might have issued a statement denying or refuting what MacArthur had said and let it go at that. But that wouldn't have been right. So he took this generally unpopular step.

Q: May I interrupt, Sir, to ask you if - I think it was General Krulak who told me once that MacArthur had requested permission from the Joint Chiefs for the use of atomic weapons in Korea. Was this a factor in the decision?

Adm. D.: I think not. I'm not even sure that that's the way it was, but I know there were many suggestions for the use of atomic weapons, and it could well be that when the situation deteriorated so badly that MacArthur did. But this was contrary to our policy and, again, we didn't want to enlarge the war and we certainly didn't want to get into an atomic war. In this case, not with China because they didn't have the capability, but with Soviet Russia. But MacArthur had to go. So the President relieved him. MacArthur left and he had really a hero's trip back home across the country. He had a big celebration on his initial appearance when he landed back in the United States in San Francisco, which was really reported to be quite a show. Then he came on to Washington - I don't remember whether he stopped any place else - I believe he addressed the Congress and was given a tremendous reception and ceremony on the Washington Monument grounds.

Q: It was on that occasion, I think, when he addressed the Congress that he said, "Old soldiers just fade away."

Adm. D.: It could well have been, but he didn't say it quite soon enough, I guess.

The President asked me if I would represent him at this ceremony. He knew that I knew MacArthur. I'd been with him in the Philippines and knew his family. Naturally, I was glad to do it. I would like to see the General and his wife and son. So I went and sat down on the platform with the MacArthurs and came back and reported to the President how things had gone, and he was pleased, and he said, "You know, MacArthur's done this all wrong. If he had any political aspirations I'd have been glad to advise him," and I'm sure the President would have. He said, "What he should have done was to come directly to Washington and report to me. Not make speeches to the people or the Congress or anybody. Then, having done that, if he wanted to go out and make speeches or campaign or whatever he wanted to do, that's fine and it's quite another matter."

This was in contrast, of course, to what happened when General Eisenhower left SHAPE to campaign for the presidency.

Q: Did General MacArthur actually call on the President at any time?

Adm. D.: I know he didn't before this speech. Whether he did after or not, I really don't remember. It would seem to me incredible that he wouldn't, when you think that he was a gentleman -

Q: He was still on active duty -

Adm. D.: Still on active duty. He'd been relieved but "it's ours not to reason why" sort of thing. So, without knowing whether he did or not, I would have to say that I believe he must have. But that was President Truman and he was very cautious about relieving MacArthur and careful. He didn't do it until it turned out there was no reasonable alternative, no acceptable alternative. And, again, let me remind you this was a very unpopular decision, completely misunderstood, deliberately by a good many people who really knew what the facts were.

Q: I remember the tumultuous reception before the Congress.

Adm. D.: Well, he was a hero, and he did have a lot to his credit. I don't mean to say that he didn't, but he was a strange man.

Q: Since you mentioned the difference - the President's remarking that it was quite different from General Eisenhower - it's natural to lead into some comment on him and the manner in which he and the President had a disagreement.

Adm. D.: You mean first upon his return to Washington?

Q: You told me about his return to Washington, but you did not tell me about the falling out of the two ultimately.

Adm. D.: Did I tell you about their reconciliation?

Q: No.

Adm. D.: Remember that when General Eisenhower returned he reported to the President. It was generally known and widely known then that he intended to run for the presidency on the Republican ticket, which he did. The President admired Eisenhower. He'd put him over there in SHAPE in the first place. He respected the way he operated. He came back in uniform and reported to the Commander in Chief, was decorated by the Commander in Chief, and then went out to campaign. Unfortunately, however, he was ill advised politically because the incident that really turned President Truman against him occurred during the campaign when Eisenhower was to make a speech in Wisconsin and appeared on the platform with Jenner and McCarthy. These two senators were bitter against President Truman and the administration, the State Department was riddled with Communists and all that sort of thing. General Eisenhower, in his speech had some kind things to say about Marshall - General Marshall, who after all was a great general and big man. On the floor of the Senate one of these Senators had called Marshall "a living lie." Well, when General Eisenhower delivered his speech, he deleted references to General Marshall and, of course, had willingly appeared with these two senators who were so opposed to General Marshall and everything that he stood for. Remember that General Marshall really made General Eisenhower.

Well, that's the kind of thing the President simply could not forgive, and he didn't for many, many years. There was a complete falling out.

Q: Did he communicate with General Eisenhower on this subject?

Adm. D.: He must have one way or another, but not to my knowledge. I'm sure he didn't remonstrate because there'd be no use in that. He might have expressed disapproval somewhere along the line because Eisenhower certainly got the word. Anybody who had the faintest understanding of President Truman would realize how this sort of behavior would impress him, or fail to impress him.

So, here was the parting of the ways and the bitterness was really there. When President Eisenhower came to the White House to go down to the Capitol with President Truman for his inauguration, he didn't leave his automobile, he wouldn't come into the White House. The President told me that on the way down to the ceremony, Eisenhower said, "I wonder who it was who was trying to embarrass me by ordering my son back to the States to come to this ceremony."

Q: He must have known!

Adm. D.: I think it was a surprise. You mean he must have known who ordered it?

Q: Yes.

Adm. D.: Well, he should have known. But when he said that, the President said, "Well, I did," which was a perfectly natural thing for the President to do. He thought that this was a day when a man's family ought to be there. It was a great occasion. So that didn't help any. That was the reason for the falling out between those two, and it went on through the years until President Kennedy's funeral. President Truman came back, Mrs. Truman was ill, but his daughter Margaret came with him and they stayed at the Blair House. The President called me and a few of his staff to please stay with them down there, or be with them, because he needed some help. He needed some staff. He needed someone to stand between him and all the people who wanted to see him. Many of them he wanted to see, many of them he couldn't. All of us, of course, said yes.

Well, the morning of the funeral we were all sitting in the living room when a Secret Service man came in and said that President Eisenhower was on the telephone, so I went out of the room and took the call. I told the general who I was and, of course, he knew me. He said, "Thank goodness I got hold of you. What I've been trying to find out is whether President Truman would like to ride with my wife and me to President Kennedy's ceremony." I said, "Well, General, if you don't mind holding on I'll find out, or do you want me to call you back?" He said, "No, I'll hold on."

I went in and told the President what had happened and he said, certainly. So I went back and told President Eisenhower that the President would be delighted to go with him, and what time would General Eisenhower stop by? It was all arranged, so the Eisenhowers picked up the President and went to the cathedral. They didn't go to the cemetery and they didn't feel like marching or walking, which the procession did. So they went down to St. Matthews Cathedral, sat together, and came back to the Blair House. The President asked the Eisenhowers if they wouldn't like to come in, which, of course, they did. The President and General Eisenhower sat on a sofa, then each had a highball, and started talking, reminiscing, and really it was just like old home week. There was no sign of any animosity. They remembered only happy things and their association when General Eisenhower was at SHAPE - Supreme Headquarters, Allied Powers, Europe - and it was just wonderful.

This went on and on and we were sitting there just fascinated listening to it. Nobody needed any priming or any reminders. There might not have been anybody else in the room.

Finally, again, whoever was at the door came in and whispered in my ear that there was an Army colonel out there in the foyer who had a statement to make to President Truman and President Eisenhower. I went out to find out what the colonel had in mind. Well, he wanted to make a statement, so I said, "about what?" He said, "Mrs. Kennedy has sent me over with her apologies for overlooking inviting President Truman and President Eisenhower back to the White House after the funeral because she has with her General de Gaulle and other heads of state and, quite naturally, somebody overlooked these two distinguished former presidents, and she wants to ask them to come on over." Blair House is practically across the street from the White House, you remember. I said, "Forget the statement and just go in and tell them what you just told me. Don't stand at attention. We can relax and I'll be right there with you, so no problem."

He went in and I said, "Gentlemen, this officer has a message for you. Excuse me if I interrupt." Both of them looked up and said, "Sure, go ahead." So this colonel told them just what he had told me. General Eisenhower spoke up first and said, "I understand completely. It's perfectly natural. I'm not in any way offended, but please tell Mrs. Kennedy that my wife and I are very tired and we've got to drive back to Gettysburg this evening and we're going to leave very shortly."

Then President Truman spoke up and he said, "Colonel, please tell Mrs. Kennedy, that I'm not offended, I understand completely, it's completely natural, and I'm honored and pleased that she'd invited me but I, too, am tired and I must get some rest. Thanks again."

The colonel left to deliver that message. So both of them had another highball and sat there and talked some more.

Finally, it was obviously getting to be late and time to go, so General Eisenhower and Mrs. Eisenhower left. The President walked down the steps with them and out to the car. There were Secret Service all over the place, of course.

Q: Yes, that was the scene of a previous event that was not very happy!

Adm. D.: No. You mean the attempted assassination of President Truman. After they got in the car, the President leaned on the door and they talked again for a few minutes across the door sill - the window sill, and that was it. It was complete reconciliation. Even a stranger would have been privileged to hear that conversation. Not knowing the history, he would never have realized that there'd been a hiatus in their relationship for some considerable period of time.

Q: Had there not been some sort of contact during the changeover from one administration to the other, other than the ride to the Capitol? Had there not been some attempt to effect a changeover in staff and so forth and do it smoothly?

Adm. D.: Yes, there was indeed and that was an interesting story, too, because President Truman told me a number of times about his experiences when he had to take over the presidency from President Roosevelt when he died. As you remember, he was Vice President. He'd not been briefed by President Roosevelt at all. He didn't know what decisions the President had made, what his plans had been, and this was in April, remember. The war in Europe wasn't over and certainly not with Japan.

Q: Potsdam was coming up!

Adm. D.: Potsdam was coming and President Truman went completely unprepared, unbriefed. He told me what a tremendous job he had going through stacks and piles of documents and letters and papers, and consulting with people who presumably knew what was going on. Admiral Leahy, of course, was of invaluable assistance. There was the continuity as far as the war was concerned, and Leahy, of course, went to Potsdam with him.

Well, with that so imbedded in his mind as his own experience, he thought quite properly that there should be some orderly transfer. You see, up to then the practice of the president had been when he left the White House - of course, President Roosevelt died in office so it was somewhat different - everything went out, all the records left, no continuity. It was a complete breakoff, then start all over again. The President invited General Eisenhower to come down to the White House and spend as much time as he wished, like a week or two weeks or whatever, and General Eisenhower regretted. His reasoning is understandble.

Dennison #5 - 225

He didn't want to make it appear to anybody that he was identified in any way with the decisions the President might be making. He wanted everybody to realize that he didn't have any voice, he was simply there as an observer until he had some official standing. So nothing was done, except at the very end of the administration Eisenhower sent to the White House a group of people who were to be on his staff who were to go around and talk to various members of President Truman's staff and find out what it was that they were doing and what unfinished business there was. They came 'round to see me, among others, of course, and asked me what I was doing. When I told them, they said, "My God, this is quite a different operation from just being in the Navy." And I said, "Yes, it is, but that's the way it is. The President doesn't have a very large staff, and all of us are doing a lot of different things.

That was the only contact, and that was insufficient because, for example, some of the things that I was doing, particularly this coordination of federal maritime affairs, that was dropped. There wasn't any continuity there. Nobody continued it. But Truman had done his very best to see that there was some orderly checking, but it didn't happen that way.

Q: President Eisenhower apparently changed his attitude because when he, when it came time for him to turn over to Kennedy, he made elaborate efforts which weren't too successful.

Adm. D.: Well, you see, that's the natural way for a military man to think. When you're relieved you don't just walk off. You leave records and you brief your successor. He doesn't have to agree with you, of course, but he is entitled to know what is current, what the plans are. The President thought that way and naturally General Eisenhower did.

But the successor is another matter. I'm not aware what President Kenndy's views might have been, but in this case it's understandable. It seems a little far-fetched to think that just by being there he might become identified with some decisions of the current administration. But he could have sent down his staff far enough in advance to make a real study of what was going on and how things were being done. Not that they had to be done the same way, but at least they would have had the benefit of knowing what had worked and what hadn't, of course. General Eisenhower's concept of running that office was much more of a military concept than President Truman's. The idea of having a chief of staff, and the chief of staff really was the top executive apparently, and the contact between the remainder of the staff and the President was not direct nor was it frequent. In President Truman's case, the key members of his staff met with him every single day at the same time, so that each one could know what the other was doing and the President could find out what everybody was doing and express his wishes or advice or guidance or whatever he wanted to convey to them. In turn, we could get him to take action on important matters that we had before us and everybody there would know what was happening, which was invaluable.

Q: It seems that Truman's system would keep him more closely in contact with public opinion than would the staff system?

Adm. D.: Not only public opinion but what was going on, because in any staff there is likely to be a weakness in internal communications. One staff member doing something and either forgetting or not realizing that his colleagues should know all this or really not having an opportunity to talk to them because everybody's busy. Here was the President and, according to his usual practice, we all had the same chairs to sit in around his desk or in the corner or on the couch or wherever it might be every day. And the President went around in the same order. I remember the first man he always talked to was Admiral Leahy, and so on around the table or around the desk. We didn't bother him with a lot of trivia or gossip, but he did have an idea, more than an idea, of what matters were being taken care of, and this was his chance to say, "Well, I think you'd better think about this or think about that, or please forget the whole thing," whatever he wanted to say.

Keeping track of public opinion, this went more into the press conference area, and here again, before the President held a press conference he had a staff meeting. Our individual job was to ask him questions in our fields of competence that he might have to answer, national defense or foreign relations, heaven knows what, and give the President a chance to think through what he probably would respond to such a question.

Q: Did he actually give answers at that point?

Adm. D.: Oh, yes.

Q: This was a rehearsal, then?

Adm. D.: Yes. Or he would ask for any suggestions, and it started out with the press secretary who'd been talking to reporters for a week or some time preceding this scheduled press conference. He knew the kind of things the reporters would ask questions about. Some of the questions you couldn't possibly foresee, some of them were so spontaneous. But, in any event, after this ritual where we all had a chance to tell him about things that were going on and things he should know about and posing questions, we had the embarrassing job of trying to think up the toughest questions, the most needling questions that we could think of.

Q: That's the kind a reporter would ask!

Adm. D.: Yes, the kind of antagonistic questions that might come up where there's some reporter who really didn't know what was going on himself. It was kind of embarrassing to try to needle the President, even if that's what you were supposed to do! But that's how he found out what was going on. Of course, he read and talked to a great many people. He read all of his papers. He was an avaricious reader, read everything.

Q: Did he in any sense show concern for his press conferences? Was he afraid of lapsus lingua or something of the sort that might reverberate around the world?

Adm. D.: No, he really enjoyed them, and they started out in his office. The reporters would come in and they all had chairs, and they sat in the same order, not seat by seat, but, for example, on the President's left in the front row the first three chairs were occupied by the wire services, and so on - pretty much according to protocol, their own protocol. The conferences were always ended by Merriman Smith, in those days, saying "Thank you, Mr. President," and everybody had to get up and beat it to a telephone. The conferences got larger and finally moved across the street to the old State Department Building. There was an auditorium there, a good-sized one.

I never saw the President really thrown because he enjoyed this give and take.

Q: There was no opportunity to review the record, I mean, of what he had said before it went out?

Adm. D.: No, and that was one great problem because -

Q: Did he permit direct quotations?

Adm. D.: Oh yes. He didn't give the appearance of being cagey at all. There were a lot of questions he couldn't answer completely because there might be some critical questions on foreign policy that had to do with negotiations then under way, but I don't remember him ever being evasive.

He really enjoyed the reporters. Many of them were friends, if you can call that kind of relationship between a reporter and the President a form of friendship. They respected him, most of them did. People like Eddie Folliard, for example, of <u>The Washington Post</u>, one of the most capable journalists that we ever had around. He was a man of great experience. The President thought very highly of him, as he did Merriman Smith or Vacarp of the United Press. Smith was with the Associated Press. So it wasn't a bunch of antagonists taking on the President. It wasn't that way at all.

Q: He apparently had a better relationship with the press than most any of the recent presidents?

Adm. D.: Yes, I think because he was franker, more open, perhaps a little more receptive. He didn't try to steer the conferences. If he did, it was pretty damned subtle. Of course, he can control one thing that's pretty important, and that is who he calls on. He's got to have some control, and there he was as fair as he possibly could be. I mean he got a pretty good balance around the room. Of course, the most important people there as far as reaching more subscribers were the big wire services plus, of course, the great newspapers deserve a lot of attention, too. Most reporters, as you went down from the big metropolitan dailies to the small-town newspapers, and that's what most of them were, they were not representing the giants, they had to get something that had some relationship to local problems, matters that would be of importance locally, rather than nationally, the Taft-Hartley Act or something like that. And the President sometimes, I'm sure, was hard put to know how to respond to some of these questions about matters that really weren't of true national concern. He was so sympathetic and understanding that he knew what the problem was and if he possibly could contribute anything that would be newsworthy to some citizens in a small community, he would come up with it.

Q: Were the representatives of the foreign wire services included in his press conferences?

Adm. D.: Nobody was excluded. I don't recall whether Reuters, for example, in those days had one or not, but if they did he would have been there. There were foreigners there but I've forgotten what they were representing. It was quite a performance. The President was never the one who cut it off, it was always Merriman Smith who, when time was running out and they had to meet a deadline or something, that was it. They'd thank the President and then there would be a great clatter of running feet as they ran to the telephones. Television has changed that a great deal, of course. Late presidents have depended more on talking to a lot of people on television, rather than talking through the press.

Q: Yes, it's changed the complexion of the whole thing.

Admiral, when Secretary of Defense Johnson left office, the President chose General Marshall to fill in and he served only a year. What was the reason back of that?

Adm. D.: You mean why Marshall?

Q: Yes. He was an elder statesman by that time.

Adm. D.: It seems to me that under the law, he wasn't eligible. I think the law has something to say about that.

Q: You mean as a military man on active duty?

Adm. D.: Or whatever it is that he would be barred. I think it was in his case where Congress did sanction it, but he was a pretty obvious choice, when you think it had been sort of slipshod and really not well organized under Johnson. Marshall had a methodical mind and a fine mind, and he was the kind of man who could move into a mixed-up situation and straighten it out, make some sense out of it.

Q: And we were facing a conflict in Korea.

Adm. D.: He was the logical choice. I'm sorry I can't be more specific about the statutory business. The President depended on Marshall a great deal. Of course, he sent him on a doomed mission when he sent him to China to try to see whether he couldn't get some kind of a middle-of-the-road government or a coalition or something going over there between Chiang Kai-shek and the Chinese communists. That effort was bound to fail. There wasn't anybody of stature that could possibly do it. Then when he sent for him to come back and be Secretary of State, I believe it was, he thought Marshall was a great Secretary of State and I guess in many ways he was.

Dennison #6 - 234

Interview No. 6 with Admiral Robert L. Dennison, U.S. Navy (ret)
Place: His office in the Davis Building, Washington, D.C.
Date: Wednesday afternoon, 11 April 1973
Subject: Biography
By: John T. Mason, Jr.

Q: It's good to be with you again today, Admiral. Off tape, I brought up the subject of integration in the services and whether or not this was an issue during the time that Mr. Truman was President. You said that it, of course, was not a burning issue and you don't recall anything specific as to what the President might have said on the subject.

However, there was an incident that dates back to your command of the battleship Missouri and Admiral Nimitz. Do you want to recall that for me?

Adm. D.: Yes. Admiral Nimitz, of course, was at that time Chief of Naval Operations and after I'd had command of the Missouri for a brief time I received a letter from him saying that he wished to assign a Negro lieutenant for duty in the Missouri and what did I think about it.

Well, I thought about it and wrote back to him saying that any officer who was ordered to my ship, Negro or not, would be welcome on board and treated as any other officer, that he was a member of the ship's company and that was it. But, it appeared to me that if he wished to assign a Negro to the Missouri and did assign one, it had to appear completely artificial because, remember, in those days the <u>Missouri</u> was an extremely desirable assignment for any officer.

Q: She was the show ship of the Navy!

Adm. D.: She was the show ship and, as everybody remembered, they had a surrender plaque on the deck outside the captain's cabin and every time we put in to port there were thousands of people who visited that site and went through the ship. It was almost unbelievable, even in the poorest of weather. So a lot of people saw that ship and talked to the officers and talked to the men. But to have one Negro there when this was not a general thing throughout the Navy at that time, it would seem to me, to be phony. I transmitted those views to Nimitz and ended by saying furthermore, if you do this, make this assignment, you'll run out of maneuvering room - there's no place else to go. Why not start a Negro off in a smaller ship where normally an officer of his rank would start his sea duty and continue whatever sea duty he had.

Q: Not at the top!

Adm. D.: Not at the top, yes. Admiral Nimitz apparently was impressed. Whether he consulted other people, too, I have no idea and if he did what they told him, but the man was not ordered to the ship. At that time, of course, you must remember, too, that there wasn't any - as you just mentioned to me - real racial issue. It was just emerging

Dennison #6 - 236

and, while I can't remember any views that President Truman expressed in my hearing on the matter of integration, knowing him as I do or did I'm sure he would have been very much opposed to any discrimination but believing as he did that every citizen was equal under the law I don't believe he would have liked any artificial pump-priming sort of a thing or a quota system. He never expressed those views to me. I'm just deducing what I believe his views would have been.

It was a different Navy in those days in dealing with Negroes. We had many Negro petty officers and bluejackets who were fine, capable, respected shipmates and were just as much a part of the crew as anybody else. In other words, they were respected because they were capable men and honest men and really good shipmates. I've known many chief petty officers who were fine men. There were a number of Negroes in our ships in World War II of various ratings.

Q: As one reflects on it, it was something of a golden era, wasn't it, when passions were not so highly enflamed as they are now?

Adm. D.: That's right.

Q: There's another question - I don't know whether you have any comment to make or not. You told me previously about the special study you made of maritime affairs and of your suggestion of a coordinator - or administrator - for a maritime commission, but you stayed with this subject during the years that you were with President Truman. Were there any other events of note that you might recall?

Adm. D.: I think I've already recounted the case of the United States Lines, when the government was trying to recover what was considered to be an overpayment of construction subsidies to several shipping lines. There were no other similar or equally important matters that came before the President, but this one experience did bring out something of considerable moment. Here is an example - and there are many others in the maritime field - where almost every branch of the executive department, the Departments of State, Treasury, Commerce, Labor, and Defense, even the Attorney General, had their own interest in the broad maritime field and the specific one about overpayments, because the reason for the overpayment was the grants that were made for the defense features of these ships. In other words, high speed and greater troop capacity than they ordinarily would have had for purely commercial purposes.

In the case of a disagreement or a difference of opinion between the departments there was nobody to referee it, unless it was on a case-by-case basis, which is not the way to do business if you can avoid it. Furthermore there should be some mechanism so that these disputes really didn't become a sword's point matter, to get people together to talk, discuss, have conferences. That was the big lesson that came out of this particular thing. Unfortunately, when President

Truman left office and I went to other duties, President Eisenhower, either through lack of understanding or for some reason I don't know, did not continue to have somebody in the White House as sort of a watch dog over these maritime matters, which I think is an obvious need today.

Q: There is one development today, in that the Navy has an active duty officer in the Maritime Administration as an attempt to draw the two closer together for better understanding.

Adm. D.: I think that's a great move - Rear Admiral Miller. Yes, this is all to the good, but there's more involved than just the Maritime Administration and the Navy.

Q: Yes, there's still no over-all coordinator.

Well, Sir, the time came for the Truman administration to go out of office. This must have been in a sense a sad development for you?

Adm. D.: It would have been sad had it not been for President Truman. What I mean by that is that I knew full well why he didn't run again. I knew that he didn't want to run again, among other things, so to him it must have been a relief. He'd done his job superbly and I felt in my own small position that I'd served him well, he'd written me to that effect, and there was no place to go. I mean we'd done it up to that point. We didn't leave any great burning issues behind, just like walking off the battlefield and that sort of thing.

So, no, it wasn't really sad. To part company from such a great person had to be a wrench, but other than that, no.

Q: Before you went off to other duty, you had been selected, had you not, for flag rank?

Adm. D.: Yes, I was a rear admiral for at least a year, maybe longer.

Q: So this tangential kind of duty in the White House wasn't really harmful to your own personal career in the Navy?

Adm. D.: No. I remember one rather amusing incident. This is typical of President Truman's way of operating.

I went to him after a while and said, "I'm honored to serve you, there is no question about that, and as long as I'm here I'm going to do my job the very best that I know how, but I'm a professional naval officer, as you yourself reminded me, and maybe I'd better get back to my business of the sea."

He said, "Well, why don't I talk to the Chief of Naval Operations"- I believe it was Admiral Fechteler. "Why don't you get him up here and ask him to bring anybody with him he wants to bring along."

So, within the next few days, Fechteler did show up. I forget who was with him. The President chatted with him for a few minutes, then he said, "My naval aide, Rear Admiral Dennison, feels that perhaps he should get back to sea, get back in the Navy. I want him to stay here, but I'd like to ask you, if he does stay here, does that mean that there's any adverse effect on his naval career?"

What could the Chief of Naval Operations say?

Q: The only thing he could do was take some steps to ensure that it wouldn't!

Adm. D.: I hope he didn't have to take any steps, but obviously you can't tell the President, the commander in chief, that anybody serving him is going to suffer in his own profession! Again, this illustrates the way President Truman maneuvered sometimes. It was quite obvious that my White House duty had no adverse effect. For heaven's sake, I was appointed vice admiral, four-star admiral, by President Eisenhower. Then, of course, later to another four-star job by President Kennedy. There was no place else to go. That's it. Had it had any adverse effect I would have retired as a rear admiral. Fechteler was right!

Q: You came to the end of the Truman administration and you got a new assignment.

Adm. D.: Yes, and this was typical of Admiral Fechteler and the administration in those days. I had to go to sea, or felt I should, and there was a cruiser division in the Sixth Fleet, CruDiv 4, whose commander had been relieved in due course - or was to have been relieved in due course, I meant to say - but I didn't get away from the White House until after he normally would have been detached. So Admiral Fechteler saw to it that he was held on until I could take over that command.

Q: Until after Inauguration Day!

Adm. D.: Yes, which is exactly what happened. I joined the ship on its way - I think I said she was in the Sixth Fleet, she was being deployed to the Sixth Fleet - and that was fine. The only unfortunate thing from my point of view was that after I'd had it for a year and had done a pretty good job, I think, Admiral Carney - I said Fechteler, but actually it was Forrest Sherman, at that time -

Q: A little less than a year, I think. You went in February 1953 and you returned to the Department in January 1954.

Adm. D.: Oh. Admiral Carney, was then Chief of Naval Operations, so I was ordered back to the Navy Department, weeping all the way back!, to take over the job in Op-60, Director of the Strategic Plans Division, relieving my classmate Arleigh Burke. I didn't want any part of the Navy Department. I'd had enough Washington duty, I thought, for a while, but naturally I was assigned to it, and enjoyed every minute of it.

Q: Lapping back for a second to the Mediterranean, was there anything of significance in that period that you were there?

Adm. D.: Not really significant, but one thing happened that illustrates my feeling about the aviator-nonaviator distinction in the Navy. I think this is most unfortunate. It doesn't have to be that way. It goes back, of course, to the days when aviators had really no command outlet compared to their contemporaries who were practising their profession at sea, so when the carriers came along, the law specified that commanding officers of carriers had to be aviators and this grew so that practically the whole chain of command eventually was comprised of aviators.

Well, on this Sixth Fleet assignment Admiral "Cat" Brown was the carrier division commander and it had been the practice before, and was then, that that commander would command the whole task force - the whole fleet - including surface ships and submarines on exercises, and the cruiser division commander on those occasions was sort of a fifth wheel. He was just riding around in a cruiser as part of the force.

I thought I could see what might possibly happen. If anything did happen to Brown, maybe the commander of the Sixth Fleet, who was John Cassidy, just for the hell of it would give me command of the task force in one of these exercises. So I studied Brown's flight procedure, the signals he was using, and timing, and the captain of the <u>Baltimore</u>, I think it was, rigged a wind sock on a short mast and attached it to one of the turrets in front of the bridge. I had my staff get letter perfect on all procedures and the signals and what not. Now, this wind sock was not nearly delicate enough or accurate enough to give you precise direction but it was pretty close. If I needed to, I could have gotten further precise wind direction from one of the carriers.

Well, sure enough, this did happen. Something did happen to Brown. I think he had some ulcerated teeth or something. I don't know what it was. And Cassidy did put me in command. The skippers of the two carriers fully expected that the first thing I would do would be to hoist a signal to operate independently during these flight operations. I didn't do it. I just took charge and pretended I was in a carrier!

Q: Much to the consternation of the COs!

Adm. D.: Yes! They didn't understand that. But it worked. I did it, as I remember, on two different exercises. Obviously Cassidy was pleased. Everything went smoothly and if he hadn't known who was sending the signals or where they came from, he might well have thought it was Brown in his carrier who'd done it all the time anyhow. This, perhaps, didn't have any lasting effect because I don't believe that it was continued and it only happened in my case because of Brown's unfortunate temporary disability.

Q: But it was kind of a pleasant interlude in the established custom!

Adm. D.: Yes, and I mean I tried to make a point, and I think I did make a point. The point being, as I have said many times in many different places, our business is command and it doesn't make any difference to me whether it's a submarine or a carrier or a fleet of tug boats. It's all command. There are different techniques, of course, but this is part of your command manual that you better damned side have memorized in the back of your head. That's the only point I was making, that you didn't have to be an aviator to command carriers, and when I was commander in chief I made a particular point when I'd go to sea - I put my flag in a carrier. Of course, I was too senior to take over detailed operation of the task force, but I was there, not riding around in the screen.

Q: Was the Royal Navy very much in evidence in the Mediterranean when you were there?

Adm. D.: Yes - the reason I hesitated was because they changed rather rapidly as time went on but when I was there, at that particular juncture. Dickie Mountbatten - Admiral Mountbatten -

Q: He was in Malta, was he not?

Adm. D.: Yes, and he got to sea and took his ships into port every now and then - gathered up a group of ships. I remember one rather amusing experience with him. I got to know him very, very well as the years went on. Certain ships of the Sixth Fleet in the form of a task force - I believe we had one or two carriers and a cruiser and a few other things - was to pay a visit to Istanbul and anchor off the Golden Horn. Again, something happened to everybody but me and I was in command of that task force.

During our visit I learned that the Soviet government had protested our visit to the Turkish government on the grounds that it was in violation of certain provisions of the Montreux Convention - too many foreign war ships or something or other. We had some real "nervous Nellys" in the State Department organization over there, I thought. The ambassador was at Ankara, and I forget the senior official in Istanbul, I think it was a consul general, and he went to the extreme of telling me, for example, that I couldn't take my barge and go up the Bosporus into the Black Sea. I said, "The hell I can't! That's exactly what I'm going to do. I'm going to get the largest U.S. flag that I can carry in my barge. I'm going to get a picnic lunch and collect some friends, and that's exactly what we're going to do."

And I did.

When I heard about this note I talked with some of my Turkish friends, Navy friends, and said, "I just wanted you to get the word to your government that if we're embarrassing you in any way by being here I can get my ships out of here without embarrassing anybody. I can announce some exercise or reason for it." And they said, no, indeed "you won't do that, we don't want you to."

I said, "Why not?" and they said, "We've fought the damned Russians I don't know how many times, seven or eight up to then, and we're not afraid of them. We're just going to send a note back and say it's none of your damned business, in effect. Please don't go because this is what we want to do. We're not going to be pushed around by these people."

Q: They seem to have had more courage than our State Department!

Adm. D.: Yes. This fellow didn't go on to say they may have fought the Russians that many times but they got licked every time, too!

But, to get back to Mountbatten. My visit was to terminate the day that Mountbatten was supposed to come in with his ships, so I got my ships under way quite early in the morning and we were to meet the British task force in the Sea of Marmora, also quite early in the morning, before eight o'clock anyhow, maybe around 6:30. So when the British ships came in sight I sent a message to Mountbatten and asked his permission to fire a salute to him before eight o'clock. Of course, he replied very courteously that he'd be honored and delighted and would return it.

We weren't exactly in a head-to-head position. The British force was off our port bow. So I ordered the skipper of the flagship to leave the task force and to head over toward the British, who were coming along in parallel columns. My intent was to get over ahead of them and pass down between a couple of these columns and when the bow of my flagship overlapped the bow of Mountbatten's flagship we'd open up.

Well, so far so good! But after the <u>Baltimore</u> started to turn, or perhaps just about the same time, the whole damned British went into a turn to come over to head toward our task force.

Q: Anticipatory!

Adm. D.: Things were rapidly going to hell. I was tuned in on the British tactical circuit and I heard the typical British voice, probably Mountbatten's, calling something like "Indians, this is Chief. Queen Peter. One. Over." So I had my signal officer look up in the NATO signal book what "Queen Peter One" meant. It meant "situation deteriorating"!

Well, we finally got ourselves untangled. Mountbatten got back on course and we adjusted ours and started down the columns. We opened up with a salute and it was, of course, returned.

I remember speaking in London one time at the Ends of the Earth Club and telling about this incident. I pointed out that when I heard this signal I thought that maybe this was an echo of Lord Nelson's famous signal to engage the enemy more closely. But I was reassured after looking it up that it didn't mean that, but I did want to say that I got off seventeen guns before the enemy fired a shot.

Q: Incidently, Sir, as a footnote, what is the Ends of the Earth Club?

Adm. D.: This is quite an interesting organization. They have one - I wouldn't call it a chapter, but it's the same thing - in New York, quite an active group, and in London. They don't do a damned thing, as near as I can figure out, except meet once a year and have a big banquet. They're real good fellows and people fairly prominent in government, and more than that, in England anyway, with a heavy percentage of naval members.

At this particular banquet when I spoke the Minister of Defense, Lord Watkinson, presided, Mountbatten was there and spoke for the British. But that's about what it is. It's a large group and it's just good fellowship. I don't think they have any charter even.

Q: A very intriguing name!

Adm. D.: I'm sorry I can't tell you where it came from. I thought it came from Kipling - "when two strong men stand face to face, though they come from the ends of the earth" - I think that's Kipling.

Q: It sounds like him.

Adm. D.: But it turns out that it isn't where the name came from. I can't remember, but it's somebody you'd never suspect, like Keats or Shelley or some British poet.

Q: Going back to the Med for a moment. The state of Israel had been set up by that time. Did you call at Haifa, or was the Sixth Fleet permitted to do that?

Adm. D.: I don't know whether they were permitted or not. Probably not. At any rate, I never was in Haifa. We did have access to a great many ports on the coast of North Africa, for example, that are closed to us now. French ports, too, we were welcome there. And, of course, we've always been welcome in Turkey except the last few years because there have been a lot of student demonstrations and what not that have been really serious at times. We haven't paid any, or I'm not aware of any, visits there.

Q: In that time did the Sixth Fleet use the facilities at Malta to any extent?

Adm. D.: No. You see, we really were a seagoing force. We replenished at sea and we had our own tankers, supply ships, and periodically there was a replenishment exercise. The British were the ones who were using Malta in those days and they kept that shipyard pretty damned busy. They were the ones, through the years, that really kept that place going. Now, of course, NATO, along with the British, help finance Mintoff, the premier, who really, I think, has been blackmailing us because of the amount of money he wants to charge and is getting away with, really to keep him in power. I've known a number of Maltese and the ones I happen to know are very, very desirous of Malta joining NATO. Well, for political reason within NATO this doesn't seem to be in the cards. But they do have sort of an observer status at meetings. They attend the meetings of the Atlantic Treaty Association, of which I am a director.

Q: Was there any evidence of Russian naval force in the Mediterranean in the time that you were there?

Adm. D.: No. It was only later when they started streaming through the Bosporus and keeping 40 to 60 ships deployed. I happened to be in Istanbul last fall and I stayed in a hotel along the Bosporus and I could see, in this case, a destroyer every day - two or three of them - going down into the Med from the Black Sea.

Q: The picture in the Mediterranean is vastly different now from when you were serving with the Sixth Fleet.

Adm. D.: Indeed it is. It's ironic, I think, that the Soviets have taken a page right out of the book of the Royal Navy and the United States Navy on the political-military uses of sea power. That's exactly what this is. It's trying to make friends and influence people by having your presence there - in this case, aboard ship, which is a hell of a lot better than having an army camped some place.

Q: This is probably a subject that you'll talk about a little more when you talk about the Cuban missile crisis and the lessons that were learned from that?

Dennison #6 - 251

Adm. D.: Yes, I will.

Q: If there's nothing else that pertains to the Mediterranean, shall we go back to Washington?

Adm. D.: As you please.

Q: You got a very interesting assignment there. You were made director for strategic plans in the CNO's office in January of 1954. What was expected of you in that job?

Adm. D.: It was Director of the Strategic Plans Division and the number of it was Op-60. This was part of Op-06, the Deputy Chief of Naval Operations for Plans and Policy, a position which I later had. At the time I was Director of Strategic Plans, Admiral Matt Gardner was Op-06. The Strategic Plans Division, which I took over from Admiral Burke, was really the Navy Department's planning agency for matters that went to the Joint Chiefs of Staff. It was mainly that.

We would draw up papers for the Chief of Naval Operations, who was a member of the Joint Chiefs, to present to the Joint Chiefs of Staff, or, in turn, we would get papers that other services had put in and develop a position and recommand a position on these particular matters.

Q: Did you anticipate requests from the CNO on some of these papers?

Adm. D.: Yes, very often we were way ahead because, in doing this job, we had to be fairly close to our counterparts in the other services, the people who were actually doing the work, the planning, so we really had our ear to the ground and worked very closely with these people in the Army and the Air Force. So there was no problem about planning what to do. My God, the problem was finding out what you could do, what you had time to do, because some of these strategic planning matters are pretty complex, as you know. It's not something where you sit down with a small memorandum pad and write down something. Then we always had the task of trying to find out as best we could whether these ideas would be received sympathetically or antagonistically by the other services.

In other instances, of course, the Chief of Naval Operations would request some particular action.

Q: As director of this outfit, did you have the right to sit in on some of the sessions of the Joint Chiefs, in order to gauge their feelings and so forth?

Adm. D.: Some, yes. Later one, of course, as deputy, I was there for all their meetings. But our main contacts were with our counterparts who really were advising their chiefs what position to take or what to say. I mean a chief didn't go down there and speak off the top of his head very often. Sometimes, unfortunately, they did.

Q: Was there great divergence in the point of view on a given policy by the different representatives of the services?

Adm. D.: Sometimes, yes. Usually the greatest differences of opinion were in the area of the budget. How much money was the Army going to get, and how much the Air Force, and what for, what was the justification, how much would the Navy get, and, again, what were our plans? How many ships were we going to have, what types of ships, what did we want, what did we intend to ask for? You only get so much money, you know, and there has to be some kind of a compromise. Otherwise, we'd be abdicating and somebody else would have to tell us what to do, which has happened rather frequently in the last few years. The budget was the thing, and I remember in Admiral Leahy's time when Forrestal was Secretary of Defense, he told Forrestal that the Joint Chiefs of Staff would have nothing to do with budget matters because this would destroy the Joint Chiefs. Of course, he could get away with it then because he was chief of staff to the President, and he could make it stick. It didn't stick very long because we were in a tough situation, to be a service chief and, at the same time, realize that you've got to compromise -

Q: At the expense of your own service sometimes?

Adm. D.: Yes, sometimes it is. You hope to make a good deal and very often you can - more often than not, maybe. It all goes back to a justification for forces, and one of the great things that happened was that the forces were tailored to the war plans. In other words, you start out this process with a war plan and if this plan is approved it says in there what forces are needed.

All right, well, each unified command then is alotted forces. Again, you can't have a U.S. fleet in the Pacific and a duplication in the Atlantic - the same goes for the Air Force or anything else - so, Number One, there's got to be a firm justification for the need for these forces but not duplication unnecessarily. So each major war plan provides for the forces in that particular command being sent in part to some other commander who has need for them, and it's a matter of judgment that there will not be simultaneous action in two different oceans, or at least not to the same degree.

The war in Vietnam is a pretty good example of that. In order to get the forces to beef up the Pacific Fleet, the Atlantic Fleet had to contribute carriers and other types of ships, because there was a pressing and immediate need in the Pacific and not in the Atlantic.

Once the plans have been developed and approved, then, of course, the planning process goes all the way back to the commanders. They have to write their plans based on these master plans in great detail, develop contingency plans, some of which you find contain the need for forces that aren't in the master plan, so that's got to be revised. But once a force level has been decided - how many Marines do you need, how many amphibious ships, how many troops have you got to lift simultaneously - these are Navy problems and Marine Corps problems.

Then you get into the budget task. If your work has been done and done on time, you're in pretty good shape. Unfortunately it's very, very rare that it is completed. In other words, the planning cycle looks great on paper, but sometimes it doesn't seem to work out.

To get back to Op-60 and our counterparts in the other services, we had to develop principally the Navy part in various areas of the world and in the unified commands. Of course, that means that if you've got a certain size naval force afloat, then you've got to have certain back-up in the shore establishment, shipyards, supply depots, and on and on. So that any act that has anything to do with force levels reflects all through the defense establishment - new weapons and their support. Polaris, for example. It isn't just a missile on a ship, it's a system that goes back to the enormous installation we have down at Charleston, for example. Weapons assembly, testing.

This planning business is so important and it's a battle, believe me. I mean, so many different things come up that you can't really tell from one day to the next exactly what is going to happen. But basically you do know. I've given you a very simple outline, but that's the meat of the matter.

One thing, for example, that isn't in this chain but will give you an idea of some of the other things, it seemed to me that we ought to be able to avoid a great deal of inter-service hassling if the Joint Chiefs could determine the service identity of each unified commander. For example, we could assert that the commander in chief, Pacific, and the commander in chief, Atlantic, should be naval officers because of the direct concern over vast ocean areas and of what went on in these areas, as opposed, let's say, to an Army command mostly concerned with land warfare, CinCEur, in Europe is working primarily land forces, sure, he has naval forces as well, the naval component under Commander in Chief, U.S. Naval Forces, Europe, in London, and I was that at one time. A naval officer wouldn't seem ordinarily to fit into that kind of a job. As a matter of historical fact, CinCEur has always been either Army or Air Force.

Now for the Navy commands. The Pacific command has always been fought over, sometimes very bitterly and sometimes not, on the grounds that it should be an Army officer or an Air Force officer and so on.

So I said why not settle all this and decide before it becomes a matter of personalities or a matter of who the man is. Let's find out what service has the predominant interest and just establish the ground rule that he will be an officer of that particular service.

Well, we almost got it through the lower echelons of the planning systems of our counterparts in the Army and the Air Force, because it's a logical thing after all, and we were not talking about people, personalities. We were talking about service identity. This took up quite a bit of time and finally I forget what blew that out of the water, but it never was approved by the Joint Chiefs. I've forgotten now whether it ever got to them or not.

That's just an example of other related matters that Op-60 would be engaged in. Everything we handled was very highly classified. It was unusual to see anything in that job that wasn't "top secret."

Q: A propos that question which you dealt with, an obvious command like CinCPac at one point was in jeopardy for the Navy, was it not?

Adm. D.: It's been in jeopardy at more than one point. That's the reason, which I thought was not valid, why Admiral Stump was held onto beyond his normal tour of duty, because they felt that - the Navy felt that - if they tried to relieve him, it would immediately start up an assertion on the part of the Air Force or Army that they should have it. Then, too, there were some rumblings when Admiral McCain was due to be relieved just recently.

Q: It's a continuing thing, then?

Adm. D.: Oh, yes, it goes on all the time. CinCLant is not quite so vulnerable and I'm not sure why, because there's a lot more to it than just running ships around, as there is in the Pacific.

There again, to get back to the claim for command based on specialization, not in command but on being a member of a particular service and say, well, we've got

General So-and-So, there's an awful lot of, let's say, Air Force activity in the Pacific, or the Atlantic, or some place else, so we ought to have an aviator in there. Maybe we should, but not because he's an aviator. If we've got a hell of a good commander, it doesn't make any difference really whether he's a member of the Salvation Army - I mean so long as you've got the ability there. But to have a situation where the principal, if not the sole, qualification for command is the color of his uniform is stupid.

Q: Perhaps the fact that we were involved on the continent of Asia, Indochina, had something to do with the pressure for other than a Navy man?

Adm. D.: Yes, of course it did, and here again on quite a different point you have Washington, including the White House, dealing directly with the commander of forces in Vietnam - Abrams, for example.

Q: When you were in this job as director of strategic planning, was there a greater need for developing plans for this and that and every other thing because we had a most active Secretary of State who was credited with a policy of brinkmanship, so to speak?

Adm. D.: No, not really, because a great many of these catchwords - "massive retaliation" for example was a term that was thrown around so freely, and which was a pretty dangerous concept - then you had, speaking of Europe, the "trip wire strategy" where the purpose would be just to fire off an alarm, not really to oppose anything. "Graduated response" was another great phrase. That came in under McNamara's regime.

Q: Most of these, I expect, are PRs, aren't they?

Adm. D.: Are what?

Q: PR-inspired.

Adm. D.: I don't know. They're catchy. They're not subject to rigorous definition. If they are, the definition doesn't appear. It doesn't appear in "massive retaliation", which really means to bomb the hell out of everybody with atomic weapons. There's nothing in between in the area of -

Q: Conventional warfare is ruled out!

Adm. D.: Detente or something, yes. It means that you can save money because you don't need anything except strategic weapons. It's just ridiculous.

But, no, I don't recall that the Secretary of State had very much of anything to do with service planning. Of course, when it comes to the application of forces, they do have a natural concern - Lebanon, for example, or even Cuba - but it isn't really direct.

Sometimes you've got to go back to broad government policy. We had the Monroe Doctrine, which meant one thing to one person and another thing to another, although it was a pretty good idea to keep everybody out of America except Americans. This would control some of our strategic thinking, and Cuba, whether we should annex it or not, what we should do with it, became somewhat of an issue during the time of the Cuban missile crisis. Then, of course, we intervened in Nicaragua with the Marines. We've gotten ourselves in quite a few situations where the problem wasn't really so much how to get in but how to get out. We'd take over the territory, and particularly if you take over running the government or put in your own government, then you really are involved. Maybe you don't want to be that involved.

In Cuba, for example, one of the phony claims that was made on the part of the Soviets, one of the reasons for putting these weapons in, was to protect Cuba against invasion from the United States. Well, at that time, nobody in the United States that I know of felt that invading Cuba was the thing to do under any circumstances, even though our war plans did provide for it and we had a force all mounted and ready. We had also made plans, or I had made plans, my headquarters, what to do about setting up a military government, how we were going to run it, and, above all, how the hell we were going to get out. Who were we going to put in to run the Cuban government? It would have been years. We would have been there for God knows how long. These things have got to be weighed, but they start off with what is the national policy. Interestingly enough, I came across this copy of a letter written many years ago by Theodore Roosevelt to Taft, who was then Secretary of War -

Q: In the year 1907!

Adm. D.: Yes, in January, it was in reference to Cuba and says "there can be no talk of a protectorate by us. Our business is to establish peace and order on a satisfactory basis, start the new government, and then leave the Island; the Cuban Government taking the reins into its own hands; the course, it might be advisable for some little time that some of our troops should stay in the Islands to steady things. I will not even consider a plan for a protectorate, or any plan which would imply our breaking our explicit promise because of which we were able to prevent a war of devastation last fall. The good faith of the United States is a mighty valuable asset and must not be impaired." Now, here's a president speaking. This was an expression of national policy, which is a damned good one and it's stuck with us for one reason or another for a long, long time.

Q: Since you do express yourself on the subject of national policy, what about our consistency in terms of national policy? This must be confusing sometimes to strategic planners, such as you.

Adm. D.: I've heard, and I'm sure you have, through the years statements such as "we don't have any national policy in certain areas or even broadly," which is not so. I think the strategic planners, in this case, have to determine what national policy has any bearing on what it is that we are proposing. Now, war is another matter. Contingency operations, however, should be carefully tailored to fit into what our national policy is going to be or is. "Is" is a better word.

For example, Southeast Asia which we've just been through. Why were we in Southeast Asia, or should we be in Southeast Asia in the first instance? These are the things that have got to be considered. The decision finally was made by the President. Now, he doesn't act out of a vacuum, either. We have a number of national policies that are really firm convictions as well as just policies. For example, we believe in self-determination, and this is something that we've been involved in many, many times through the years. We believe that people should be able to elect and select their own government. We've said that. We've said it in Indochina.

Q: And that's consistency through the years!

Adm. D.: Sure. So this sort of thing means that in that kind of a war you've got to be planning not for occupation or, as Roosevelt speaks, in terms of taking over the government, but for eventually setting up a government that is freely chosen by free people. This is a very important point in our national policy.

Freedom of the seas. Many things that we do are directly related to our belief that the seas should be open to everybody. Commercial exploitation, for example, is becoming more and more important, for trade, which has been a British principle for so many years and, of course, ours, too. We're dependent upon imports. So our defense plan has got to take all these things into account. We don't start all over again and say that we don't believe in the freedom of the seas.

There are so many fundamental principles and policies that we were just talking about that planners have to know. They should be students of history, and not just military history. And always consider before you do anything in the way of planning what the hell are national interests. The answer may be there aren't any. But in these major plans there always is because we're bound by treaty obligations to a number of allies all over the world, mutual defense treaties with everybody and his brother. You can't ignore these when you're doing any planning. Are we going to have help from our allies in this particular field, or aren't we? How likely is this contingency to arise?

Q: Some of these mutual defense treaties, and when you combine them together as we did with SEATO and NATO and so forth, would seem to constitute some kind of a modification of the broad general policy that we had in past generations. How do you anticipate modification?

Adm. D.: Well, I think in that particular case, or those particular cases, where the United States really parted from traditional policy of avoiding entanglement with

with foreign states, which Washington is supposed to have said, through the years, and it wasn't a very gradual thing either, it happened very quickly when it finally got going, ended, I think - or began, whichever way you want to look at it - with the Truman Doctrine. This was a simple statement of U.S. policy against coercion of government by forces from outside that particular state. That was the essence of it. In other words, we're not going to stand around and watch some friendly nation be overwhelmed by some bully who's going to take over. This was the basis, for example, of NATO.

Q: Recognition of a new force that had come into the world!

Adm. D.: Yes, it really is. So, start out with that belief. We believe in the Truman Doctrine. We don't have to say we believe in it. It's a policy of the government. We know that. You don't have to reaffirm it unless the President wants to reaffirm it. As far as I'm concerned, if I'm doing any planning, this is one of the principles, one of the policies, that I have to consider in any kind of a war plan. How are we going to back up a policy like that? What forces do we need?

Planning, again, is not a simple matter. It's a complex matter, and this Op-60, for example, was the very heart of all our Navy strategic planning. That's where it all began, and still does. The other services have counterparts of Op-60.

Q: During your period there on this occasion the issues in the Far East, around Taiwan, were somewhat hot issues. Did this entail specific planning on your part?

Adm. D.: Yes. I'm just trying to think what particular thing was of concern to us.

Q: Quemoy and Matsu were very much to the fore.

Adm. D.: That was later. I can tell you an interesting anecdote about that situation.

I got to know the Chinese Minister of Defense rather well, a very well-educated man, a Harvard graduate, had a good many degrees, quite sophisticated. On this Quemoy and Matsu issue President Eisenhower spoke in terms of unleashing Chiang Kai-chek and all that, and our policy had been, our actions had been, to provide patrols in the strait and so on. We maintained forces out there. Now this was a matter of planning. Quemoy and Matsu, offshore islands, completely indefensible. Here they are within yards of the mainland. Nationalist China made a claim that these were part of Nationalist China and therefore they couldn't be taken over by the Communists.

Well, I talked to my friend the Defense Minister one time and said, "I know and you know, too, that this is a phony. You may have a legal claim, may have, I'm not too sure you do have, but why do you put these forces on the offshore islands, Quemoy and Matsu, right under the guns of the Communists? You can't support them, you can't defend

Dennison #6 - 266

them if they're really under enemy attack. I know what I think the answer is and I'd like to hear what you have to say."

He said, "Well, I know your country well, and I am inclined to agree with you, perhaps, about the legalistic position, but, knowing your country, I believe that if we'd start taking losses there, the United States public will be so sympathetic to our cause and deplore all this slaughter and so on that they will insist that the United States move in there and move into the Western Pacific in force."

That's a pretty cold-blooded way to look at it, but I'm sure that this was really the reason that they were doing it. It didn't work out that way. Even today, if the Communists put a shell or two in there for a day or so just to let people know that they were interested - I saw a picture in the paper just yesterday showing two Nationalist soldiers looking over the rampart with binoculars watching the Chinese Communists just a stone's throw away.

Q: At that time do you think the responsible people in the Chinese government on Taiwan really believed that they could some day or other go back to the mainland and assume authority?

Adm. D.: I think in the early days, when Chiang Kai-chek first went there and the people who went with him, yes, they felt they would. This was never possible, and we had failed miserably to really back up Chiang Kai-chek. I told you about Admiral Leahy being very bitter on this point.

Yes, I'm sure that Chiang Kai-chek and his party of people that went with him and the Army people believed that with a little bit of help from us, they would be able to go back and take over the government of China. But, remember, as time went on, these people became really deluded and died off or they were replaced by the Taiwanese, and it became less and less of a reality. It wasn't much of a reality to begin with.

I think the overseas Chinese, for example, perhaps millions of these people who were originally Nationalist - we have some in this country and some in ?Southeast Asia - wanted no part of the Chinese Communists, so they put money in the hands of the Nationalist government, invested money in Taiwan. This was because they had no place else to go. So they were a factor in some day getting back. They wanted to believe it. But, as far as the U.S. government was concerned, unleashing Chiang Kai-chek was really a phony. What the hell could he do? If you unleashed him he couldn't go any place. He couldn't do anything if he ever got any place.

This wasn't a commitment, but we did have a commitment, which we carried out, of protecting Taiwan, and the President - I've forgotten his exact words, except for this unleashing business - probably was implying that we weren't going to get in there and win with Chiang Kai-chek. We were going to unleash him and let him go and get blown off the face of the earth.

Q: Give him the tools!

Adm. D.: Yes.

Q: Reverting back for a moment to that doctrine of "massive retaliation," which you referred to some time ago, the fact that this was bandied about fairly generously and the American public apparently accepted it as a policy of our government, did this make it difficult for you people in strategic plans to work with the idea of conventional naval forces?

Adm. D.: Yes. You see, in the first place, if we had believed or had it been truly a matter of national policy, this would change our war plans completely. In other words, we'd have to put most of our ships into the development of strategic weapons, play down the so-called conventional forces. It would change the nature. This was John Foster Dulles. I don't recall that the President ever said that the national policy was massive retaliation. A lot of people, particularly Europeans, wanted to believe it because they took this to be an assurance that we would use atomic weapons in the first instance. And they still believe it. I don't think so. I didn't then and I don't now. It didn't automatically follow that if anybody fires a shot across the German border we're going to launch Polaris and the Strategic Bombing Command. I don't believe it.

But the best assurance that we'll never be faced with that decision is to have something in being in Europe to stop the idea of any incursions or invasions or the taking over of territory. That's where the difference in strategic thinking is.

Q: But back in the 1950s this thought was fairly widespread, was it not, in our government?

Adm. D.: Yes, it was. I don't think anybody came out in favor of massive retaliation. I won't say "anybody," but I think very few really thought it through.

Q: Thought of the implications.

Adm. D.: Yes. It was sort of a catchy thing. "Massive" is a good word and "retaliation" is "don't tread on me" sort of thing, but when you get into what the hell does it really mean in terms of the structure of our defense forces, what can we foresee in terms of what international effect it's going to have - it's looking back a long way but I never believed it. Nor do I believe it now. Of course, it's old hat now. I mean people finally realized how ridiculous it was.

Q: In that time did it make it more difficult for the Navy to secure funds for new ships and -

Adm. D.: I don't remember that it did and it doesn't seem to me that it had any effect at all. If it did, it was minor because, for example, we went ahead with Polaris. Nobody suggested let's stop that program. Or rather the other way around. Let's throw more in it. These were plans that had been established and were carried out. No, I don't remember. There was some debate on a related point, and that is what should the balance be between certain types of atomic delivery vehicles, but there was never any great beating of drums to discard or play down the so-called conventional forces and throw everything into the atomic weapons pile. As I say, these were programs that involved procurement. Polaris went on pretty much unchanged. I must say it was a needless annoyance. I mean, Dulles didn't think this thing through either. I think he may have felt that we had no alternative, we didn't have a conventional force and may not get one, so why the hell not say, well, our policy is this without any reference to whether we had or hadn't so-called conventional forces.

Q: The amazing thing to me is that this policy being expressed, or this idea being expressed, didn't meet with immediate reaction on the part of the public. Today, it would.

Adm. D.: Well, don't you think the public now is a little bit more aware of some of these problems. This is not really new. We did have a matter of national policy that was enunciated by the President, and I'm referring to the stated policy of President Roosevelt of unconditional surrender. That was a matter of national policy because he said it, and while I wasn't involved in the war planning then that I was later, if that was the way it was going to be it meant that we had to completely defeat the enemy, but more important to take over the government. This is what unconditional surrender means - destroy. It may have been a hell of a good policy for a few days, if our allies needed any reassurance that we weren't going to make an independent settlement, but this was a strategy in itself really, but as a serious national policy surely we haven't got a policy in any kind of a war where we're going to have unconditional surrender. It isn't in the cards any more. Wars are going to end now just as - Korea's an example and now Vietnam - in a limited war, which means fighting for limited objectives, you end up around the conference table to negotiate a peace.

Q: Not to just wipe things out. That probably is more in the realm of political pronouncements for its effect.

Adm. D.: I think everybody took it to be that, too, at the time, because really you don't have to say that as a matter of national policy, unless you want to tell your military leaders "make plans to take over the German government, or the Japanese government, put in military governments for the time being." Well, the Army is a great bunch of planners and I'm sure that they had such plans, because that's the way they operate and it's quite proper. You don't know, maybe we would have had to do it. But if we had to do it, it would be, to my mind, a matter that arose at the time. In other words, these guys wouldn't give up. We had no choice except to wipe them out, not because we started out to say we're going to go in there and kill you. What this said, if it did anything, was quite the opposite. It strengthened the resolve of our foes to fight to the bitter end because they were going to get wiped out if they didn't and they'd lose the country.

Japan, obviously, didn't read the newspapers or forgot about it or something, because they quit.

Q: Perhaps one more question we have time for. In this period when you served there in the Department, we saw the early development of plans for Polaris. Were you involved in that?

Adm. D.: No, I wasn't. Where I came into the Polaris picture was later, when I was commander in chief of the Atlantic Fleet, and there was quite a bitter dispute about which service would control these Polaris weapons. That's where I got in. But on the development of Polaris, how many we should have, or how many submarines we should have, no.

Q: Or the idea that perhaps the Navy should go in with the Army on the development of Jupiter, you weren't in on that?

Adm. D.: No. All that came along later, but when we get around to it I think you might be interested in this matter of who was going to control Polaris, because this was quite a bitter inter-service conflict.

Q: Indeed, I shall.

Dennison #7 - 273

Interview No. 7 with Admiral Robert Lee Dennison, U.S. Navy (ret)
Place: His office in the Davis Building, Washington, D.C.
Date: Wednesday afternoon, 9 May 1973
Subject: Biography
By: John T. Mason, Jr.

Q: Well, Sir, again it's good to see you for the beginning of Chapter 7. I think you want to begin today by talking about your assignment in June of 1956, as a Vice Admiral, to command the First Fleet.

Adm. D.: In June of 1956 I left the Navy Department to relieve Vice Admiral Hopwood as Commander, First Fleet. The headquarters of the First Fleet were in San Diego. We had a nominal flagship but the administrative head-- quarters were ashore, at the Naval Air Station.

Q: Your flagship being the Essex?

Adm. D.: I've forgotten what it was. It seems to me it was some tender.

Q: But the change of command was on the Essex?

Adm. D.: Yes. The Essex at that time was assigned to the First Fleet, but the First Fleet, which I'll describe in a minute, really changed from week to week or from day to day, while this particular ship which served nominally as my flagship was more or less permanent. We had the headquarters ashore, as I just said, at North Island.

Q: Tell me about the First Fleet, how it stacked up.

Adm. D.: I'll have to give you a bit of background to come up with an answer to your question.

During the war the Navy set up a number of what were called type commands.

Q: This was World War II?

Adm. D.: Yes. These were administrative commands, not operating. The numbered fleets after the war were cut down in number, both in the Atlantic and the Pacific, quite drastically. In the Pacific we ended up with the First Fleet and the Seventh Fleet. The Third and Fifth had been dropped out. And a similar thing happened in the Atlantic.

The type commands were established to take care of the overall problems of repair and support, mostly logistic matters, for the various types in the Navy. For example, the carriers, the cruisers, the destroyers. These commands stayed although the number of fleets was drastically reduced. So the Seventh Fleet was assigned to the Western Pacific and the First Fleet was based on the West Coast. Well, the type commanders, for example, aircraft carriers and in this case, ComAirPac, took these ships, got them into overhaul, and when they left to prepare for deployment they were under the operational control of, in this case, ComAirPac.

This seemed to me to be all wrong. First, we had planning responsibility for operations in Southeast Asia, and my war plans included grabbing all the ships I could and charging to the scene of the fire in Java, or wherever it might be. But I didn't have really control of the forces, and I had quite a number of disputes with Admiral Stump, who was then CinCPac -

Q: He was your boss, was he?

Adm. D.: Yes. He was CinCPac, unified commander, and commander in chief of the U.S. Pacific Fleet. He had taken the position, thinking of his own career, that in order to be an operational commander you should first by a type commander. Now, this had nothing to do with command, as I saw it. So I had one strike on me to start with because I never was a type commander.

But, on this question of operating forces, I talked with Stump a number of times and said, "This is all wrong, because our forces that are sent to the Seventh Fleet for deployment have not been trained in inter-type exercises. Sure, a carrier might be, a cruiser might be, or a destroyer, but for task force operations they aren't ready, and on the firing line is no place to learn how to operate a task force. Furthermore, we have no schools - using the term loosely - for task force commanders. We should have cadres, I think, of task force commanders and their staffs, so you have a group of people who are knowledgeable in handling task forces who are working together. Sure, you can't have a very big staff, but if you had a commander, chief of staff, plans and operations, and communications you have a nucleus that you can build up on very quickly."

Well, this was a new concept and I don't believe it's ever been put into effect, but it was badly needed then and I'm sure it is now. You just don't grab somebody and make him Commander, Task Force Umpty-dump.

Q: Especially when you're engaged in hostilities!

Adm. D.: Yes, it doesn't work. I pointed out to Stump my concern about being able to execute my war plan. In other words, I simply had a paper fleet. I didn't have a damned thing. We went round and round on this, and I said, "What I want is to have these ships, when they leave their overhaul, assigned to me, and I will be gathering together the various types as I get them, organize them into task forces or task groups, and take them out and work them out. I've been aboard some of these ships that are ready for deployment, trying to operate in simple task force formations. It's pathetic."

One day he said, "You know, Bob, you're just like Ernie King. You want to grab command of everything in sight."

I said, "Felix, that's the kindest thing you ever said to me!"

Finally, he gave in and I did get these ships. I did have scheduled exercises, I did put them through gunnery practices and all kinds of maneuvers. What I had told Stump before was really borne out because I've seen some of the most atrocious examples of mishandling by task force commanders until we really got them educated. They simply didn't know how to handle a group of ships, and it's simple. When I went on the bridge of a carrier one time, the task force commander ordered a rather erratic maneuver, involving a turn of ships in formation. The signal was done by voice over the tactical circuit. The normal thing is to ask one or two ships to acknowledge, so you get at least an idea that this message has been received, and a cautious commander will get an acknowledgement from the ships on the side of the turn. They're guys that are going to get run down if they don't get the message.

Well, in this particular case, we got an acknowledgement all right from the ships on the off side. When I pointed this out to the rear admiral he was astounded. It had never occurred to him. This is a simple thing, but I just mention it as being typical of matters that indicated the need for instruction.

Q: Had there been some unfortunate events because of this?

Adm. D.: No, there had never been any real tragedies, thank God.

Q: So, he acceded to your request eventually?

Adm. D.: Yes, and ever since then I believe the same policy

Dennison #7 - 278

has continued.

Q: Were you aided and abetted in this with Stump? Wasn't Hopwood on his staff?

Adm. D.: Yes, I think he was at one time. Of course, this was after Hopwood had left. I'd relieved Hopwood. My relations with Stump were just fine. He was a little hard to get along with occasionally, but he finally went along with me on what I thought ought to be done. Of course, I thought then and do now that I was right.

Q: How many ships would you have on the average passing through your command, in and out, in a given year?

Adm. D.: Well, the whole Pacific Fleet, whatever that was, because they all had at various times to come in for overhaul or something. And, of course, my job was to be an operational commander. I didn't have anything to do, nor did I want anything to do, with arranging and scheduling overhauls or personnel matters, except as they had to do with operations. At any rate, it worked.

Q: You obviously moved around. One of the photographs in this file shows your three-star flag flowing from the St. Francis Hotel in San Francisco.

Adm. D.: Yes. That's one of the things we did. We put on a fleet review. I believe it was on the anniversary of the Great White Fleet's being in San Francisco, and we got an amazing public response - flags and parades and God knows what all - and I put on a bang-up review of the First Fleet. Admiral Nimitz consented to be the reviewing officer and came aboard my flagship and sat there with other dignitaries, witnessing the review.

There was one interesting thing that happened. The ships were steaming in through the Golden Gate and there was, as usual, a fairly strong tide. They were in column because they had to pass through rather a narrow channel. The last ship, some amphibious type or service type, had been blindly following the wake of the ship ahead, which is stupid if you're in water where the whole body of water is moving with the current, instead of doing his own navigating, and the ship ran aground. This was a grand finale to the review!

Well, the flagship was loaded with reporters and fortunately we were able to squelch it and I'll tell you how. They all wanted to talk to Admiral Nimitz, so we had a press meeting. There were a lot of people. I guess we probably had it in the wardroom. The reporters started asking a lot of questions about what would happen to the captain of the ship, was his career ruined, and all that, and I said, "I don't know what's going to happen. I don't know what caused it. I just saw, as you did, that the ship stranded. Maybe the captain fell dead, I don't know. But we'll find out, you can be sure of that." That's exactly what happened, that's the purpose of our system.

I ordered an investigation or a court of inquiry. Then they started asking questions of Nimitz. Did he ever know of a case where the captain of a ship who stranded his ship and later was advanced in rank? And Nimitz said yes,"I did."

Q: Out in the Philippines!

Adm. D.: I happened to know about this incident, so I spoke up and said that Admiral was, of course, exactly right. He did strand his ship and I'd like to tell you gentlemen what happened. He took this small ship he had command of years and years ago into an uncharted harbor in Luzon some place, I believe it was, and as he was coming in he ran into soft mud. He backed the ship off with no apparent damage - there was no damage - and when he got back into port he reported himself to his senior as being guilty of stranding a ship of the U.S. Navy. He didn't tell me and of course I never bothered to look up and find out who his commander was, but whoever he was, he of course dismissed the whole thing completely.

So it was certainly a dramatic statement for him to come out with as a fleet admiral. He said that he'd stranded a ship. This sort of defuzed the whole thing.

Q: I can see that it would! Nimitz apparently was very fond of this incident. He told me.

Adm. D.: Oh yes, he was. The reporters didn't know this, of course. They just walked right into it and I thought, my God, I know it, I can speak up and tell them exactly what happened.

That's why my flag was over the St. Francis Hotel. I did quite a bit to build up an image of the First Fleet as an operating force for morale purposes. There were all kinds of reasons for it, some identity. The type commanders took a pretty pale view of me, of course, for doing what Stump accused me of, grabbing command of anything I could get ahold of. But our relations were friendly. I mean I didn't have real difficulty with any of them, and worked with them. But I did want to build up an identity for the Fleet. It took a lot of little things, such as developing a First Fleet insignia that you could put on a cigarette light or sweaters or shoulder patches or whatever.

Q: A little knowledge of public affairs.

Adm. D.: Yes, and incidentally my public affairs officer put on this show in San Francisco and many others. We put on a hell of a fleet review in San Pedro with the Secretary of the Navy, Charles Thomas, which was another big show.

But little things like this, insignia - I remember one humorous thing that is indicative of what I'm talking about. The Eleventh Naval District had a golf course and a golf team and they'd organized some kind of a league of all the naval activities on the West Coast for golf. I forget how many teams there were, something like 7, 8, 9, something like that, or maybe more. The idea was that these teams would play home and home matches. So I organized a golf team. I had a golf professional who was a chief petty officer on my staff. He was in the public relations department. Collett was his name. He later became a pro in Coronado and then went on to Houston. He was really the captain of the team. And I drafted people from the ships assigned to me as well as my own staff. We had fairly permanent people. One captain, one commander, a couple of lieutenant commanders, a couple of lieutenants, junior grade. Did I mention chief petty officers? We had some real fine ones. And two seamen, second class. It turned out that one of these seamen had been captain of the Stanford golf team the previous year and the other one captain of the University of Texas golf team.

Q: Some talent you had there!

Adm. D.: We had coaches who were former chief petty officers and were golf professionals. One was Billy Casper, who's a very noted golfer, as you know.

Q: Yes!

Adm. D.: The other one was Gene Littler. So not only did we have a whale of a golf team, but we had some pretty good instructors.

Q: Which carried your banner high!

Adm. D.: At any rate, when we applied for membership in this damned league, they wouldn't accept us. Nobody had ever heard of First Fleet golf. Of course, nobody ever had, we'd never had one.

So I got ahold of Chick Hartman, who was commandant of the district, and said, "Look here, this can't be. I've got a golf team and I'm going to play in this damned league." He said, "O.K., we'll have some kind of a qualifying tournament." When it came down to matches, I think we played eight men, and we had maybe fourteen on the squad. We'd pick different ones for different matches.

So they had this tournament and not to my surprise, but to everybody's else's surprise, we won every prize that they put up, individual low net, low gross. The team won everything, so we walked off with a couple of wheelbarrows of trophies. Well, everybody knew about us then.

When we went into this home and home match deal, I played. My score didn't count. I played the manager of the other team always, and our home course, as I recall, was Agua Caliente. At the end of the year, it turned out that we'd won every match we'd played and the average individual score - this sounds incredible - through this whole series of matches was something like 73.8. Every time we went out two or three guys would be sure to break 70. We just had terrific talent.

At any rate, it was great fun and did help -

Q: The First Fleet was something to be reckoned with, wasn't it?

Adm. D.: Yes, they found out there was such a thing!

These bluejackets were such nice young fellows. We'd go out to practice or play a match and I'd sit around with them. We'd have a drink of beer or Coca Cola or whatever they wanted. One of them went to Collett one day, he told me this story which I thought was pretty touching - these youngsters came to him and said, "Gee, we never knew admirals were like that." I told Collett to go back and tell them that admirals aren't such bad guys once you get to know them.

I just mention this as part of my attempt to build up an identity and make this really recognized as an operating force. It was a serious matter. I was amused not so long ago to get some stuff from the commander of the First Fleet, including a cigarette lighter with this insignia on it, shoulder patches, and I don't know what all. He didn't know that it was on my watch that we developed all this.

Q: They did, then, have a different status from then on?

Adm. D.: Oh, yes.

Q: And now it's been absorbed into the -

Adm. D.: It's been absorbed into what they call the Third Fleet based in Pearl Harbor. I don't just know how that's going to work out. Have to just wait and see, because there'll always be a need for inter-type training because that's the way ships operate now. You don't operate a squadron of destroyers, as a tactical squadron. That's really the heart of the matter. It's an administrative command. How this is going to be done under this new organization, I don't know. I understand it was dictated by economy, that they were saving billets or saving something.

Q: SEATO was in being when you were there and there were various exercises involving Australian ships and others. Was this in your cognizance?

Adm. D.: I don't remember any exercises with the Australian and New Zealand forces. I don't believe there were any, because I certainly would have remembered it. I've been in that part of the world a number of times while I was commander of the First Fleet for familiarization and discussions.

Well, that's about it as far as the First Fleet is concerned, I guess.

Q: Then you came back again. You couldn't resist the Department! You came back again, at a slightly higher echelon, however.

Adm. D.: No, I really didn't, because when I came back to be Op-60, after a brief time at sea, I remember I was really upset about it. I'd been in Washington all through five years with the President and I thought I'd done my duty.

Q: Just to be facetious, you said you had never been a type commander, but this was your type command, wasn't it?

Plans and policy.

Adm. D.: Well, thank God, in the end it didn't amount to too many years. But - yes, I was ordered back. I did have, I forget how long, two or three years I guess. I was ordered back to relieve Admiral Ruthven Libby and he, in turn, was ordered back to relieve me as commander of the First Fleet. I forget how long I was Deputy Chief for Plans and Policy, Op-06.

Q: You were there until the end of March 1959. You came back in the middle of 1958, I assume.

Adm. D.: That wasn't too bad.

Q: Perhaps one reason for your constant assignment back here was the fact that you knew your way around Washington, do you think?

Adm. D.: It may well have been because it doesn't hurt to know people in the other services or in the State Department. As a matter of fact, it's almost essential to have these contacts.

Q: The other week at the historical symposium over in Annapolis, when Admirals Burke and Anderson spoke, I think the gist of what they were saying is that to be successful in developing strategy and so forth, you have to have a certain amount of political savvy to get around in Washington and to be able to cope with the political elements.

Adm. D.: I think that's correct in a large sense. I would put it a little differently - that you have to know what is possible. You can't any more charge out as a single service and ram plans down somebody else's throat, particularly in these times of deep involvement of the State Department, and quite properly so. Really, the greatest asset, I think, for a naval officer in Washington is to know and understand his opposite numbers in the other services, and to be able to sit down and talk to these fellows. Don't confront them with a paper that says we're going to do so and so. The other services are full of extremely capable men. I think, for example, that the greatest single thing we have going in the area of developing understanding with other services is the Armed Forces Staff College in Norfolk, because this takes in younger officers, lieutenant commanders and commanders, who are thrown with their counterparts from Army and Air Force, get to know them, and this association, and, hopefully, friendship, lasts through their careers. Nothing can replace that. Not the National War College. That's too late. It's very valuable, of course, but -

Q: That's more senior.

Adm. D.: Too senior, really, for what I'm talking about. They're captains or colonels. This is valuable along the same lines but I don't think to as great a degree. They have a State Department, foreign service officer down there who's deputy commandant or something, a member of the faculty.

There are also Foreign Service officers as students. I've had a couple of them on my staff as political advisors who have gone through this experience, either as a student or executive, whatever his title is, and they get more out of it, I think, than professional officers - a knowledge of what the armed services are all about and that they're not just a bunch of stupid trades people. It's good from that standpoint, but again I think that staff college is by far the most important one. I never turned down an invitation to speak there. I always welcomed it.

Another place that I found stimulating was the Air War College, even back in the days when the two services weren't getting along too well, because these fellows want to know and I don't mind taking needling questions. I wasn't going to get insulted. I was sure of that. And it's all right. I mean I ought to be able to answer any kind of a question. A fellow's a little stupid if he doesn't have an answer.

Q: Admiral Wellborn underscored the point you've just made about the Armed Forces Staff College. He was superintendent or president for a period, and he said the mere fact that they had to live together and share all sorts of experiences was a tremendous asset.

Adm. D.: Charlie's absolutely right, and it's lasting. I've gone to so many parties - not that parties are important, but even back when I was commander of the Missouri -

Dennison #7 - 289

at many gatherings of people from the War College and the Staff College and they were a joy. They were great people. I made some lasting friends, too. I never went to the Naval War College, I never went to the National War College. When anybody asked me about why I hadn't, my stock reply was that I had to work for a living.

Q: During the time that you were there as deputy for Plans and Policy, we saw the enactment of the reorganization of the Defense Department and all its ramifications for the individual services, particularly for the Navy. Did it affect you in any way? Were you involved in the legislative process?

Adm. D.: Are you talking about the National Security Act?

Q: No, 1958, the reorganization.

Adm. D.: 1958 was the year that a very far-reaching amendment to the National Security Act -

Q: That's what I'm talking about. It was the reorganization of the Defense Department.

Adm. D.: Yes, we were much concerned about that. I think it was a great thing, absolutely essential. I may have discussed this with you before that there was much more to it than just a reorganization. Basically, from my standpoint in Op-06, what it did was to require that forces be justified on the basis of their employment in commanders' war plans - unified commanders'. This was a great thing. What it meant was that you couldn't run out and build an independent army or an independent navy or an independent air force. You had to show that these forces were in the right number and the right type for employment in executing war plans, and obviously you can't have navies of equal strength in each ocean. So the war plans had to overlap and the commanders, in their plans, showed that certain forces were going to come from some place else. What it meant in the end was that we couldn't fight two or three wars at the same time and anybody with any sense knows that - certainly not major ones.

Q: But it did take the control of the fleets out of the hands of - the operational control - the CNO?

Adm. D.: Yes. Didn't I tell you about my battle with Admiral Burke on this point?

Q: No.

Adm. D.: Well, remember first, that he's a classmate and dear friend. We've been together off and on through a good many years and in many battles. When he took over as CNO he was in name and in fact commander of the U.S. naval operating forces, and one thing the 1958 amendment did was to assign operating forces by the Joint Chiefs of Staff to the unified commander regardless of whether he was an Army officer, a naval officer, or an Air Force officer. He was

the operating commander, which meant that the Chief of
Naval Operations, in this case, was not. You must remember, too, that the titles of the military chiefs of the
various services are quite indicative of what they really
are.

The Chief of Naval Operations was true. It wasn't
true of the Chief of Staff of the U.S. Army, or, later, the
U.S. Air Force. They were chiefs of staff. To whom? To
the commander in chief, the President. In other words,
they commanded their own headquarters. The commander of
an Army was a pretty top guy - Third Army or First Army or
whatever. But when this act went through, it made it perfectly clear that the forces were assigned to unified commanders for operating purposes. The chiefs of the services
had responsibility for logistic support, pay, and all that
kind of stuff. And their separate budgets took care of these
matters as well as overhauls, in the case of the Navy, and
related things. And, of course, the shore establishment was
something else again. We're now talking about naval operating forces.

Well, I'd been needled on this point by Lemnitzer who
was Chairman of the Joint Chiefs of Staff at this particular
juncture. He told me that he knew damned well that Burke
was running the Atlantic Fleet, and I said, "Nonsense, he's
not. I am." I don't know whether I ever did convince him,
but it wasn't true. What was true, though, was that Burke's
staff and occasionally Burke himself would interfere in matters

that I thought were none of their damned business. I was just sort of waiting for a real shocker to come along, and it did.

We had a NATO exercise which I was commanding in my role as SacLant, and the Second Fleet under this NATO rule became Strike Fleet, Atlantic, in the NATO organization. The Commander, Second Fleet, became ComStrikeForLant. Well, an exercise came up and this involved a lot of planning. As I remember, the StrikeForLant was supposed to show up in the North Sea and launch a simulated strike from our carriers. It was essentially a fast carrier task force. We were to be joined by British carriers and, at the same time, one of my subcommanders, CinCEastLant, was conducting large-scale antisubmarine exercises off the coast of Ireland in the Atlantic. It was quite a large-scale operation.

One morning in my staff briefing they showed on the screen the deployment of the various forces, and it showed the Second Fleet, Strike ForLant, way to hell and gone out of position. They weren't on the course they should be at all. So I said, "Get a message off to Admiral Deutermann - who was an old friend of Burke - and ask him what the hell he's doing and to get back where he belongs."

In the meantime, Deutermann had bitched up the antisubmarine exercise. He'd gotten into the wrong area. It was just completely beyond my understanding. Well, it developed very quickly that what had happened was that Burke had sent Deutermann a message and didn't send me a copy, and in the message he suggested that it might be a great idea if Deutermann take this force to try to intercept something. He didn't know where it was either.

This infuriated me. It was just absolutely incredible. These forces not only were not under Burke's command, they weren't under even United States command. They were under NATO command, and my responsibility was to the NATO Council, not anybody else. This was what I was really waiting for.

Q: The best kind of gaffe!

Adm. D.: Exactly. So I went off to see Arleigh and I said, "I want you to keep your sticky fingers out of my fleet. What do you mean by sending a message to Deutermann to charge off and leave his responsibilities? When I first heard about it, I was going to fire Deutermann forthwith, but I thought there must be some reason for it. Now I find out that he was acting on your instructions."

He said, "I didn't order Deutermann to do anything. I simply suggested to him it might be a good idea." And I said, "You know Deutermann as well as I do. He took that as an order, and he didn't stop to inform me. Whether he thought that you had or not I don't know, but he just did this absolutely incredible thing, and I want it stopped, not only from you but from your staff. If anybody wants to know anything, why, call me."

He was getting madder and madder and finally he spoke up and said, "God damn you! I know you're right. While you were talking I was thinking what the hell I could do to you and I finally decided that the only thing I could do to you was cut off your fuel oil!" So I said, "O.K., let's leave it at that."

But that, you see, was because of my friend's, really, unwillingness to accept this change of the command structure. The operating force, as far as the Navy was concerned, was fragmented, if you want to use that term, between various commands, CinCLant, CinCPac, CinCEur. It was a great move, I thought.

Q: Simultaneously, it did something to the authority and power of the SecNav, didn't it? Was that detrimental in the over-all to the Navy?

Adm. D.: I don't recall that that particular act - I'm talking now about the 1958 amendment - had too much bearing on the Secretary. I think that what you're referring to really goes back to the passage of the 1947 basic act. If I've told you this before, take it out.

President Truman's concept was in this particular area, forgetting the CIA and a lot of other stuff, that there would be a Secretary of Defense, no deputy and no enormous staff, such as the Defense Department now has, terrific echelons between the Secretary and the services, for example, and the Secretary of Defense would have, in effect, an executive committee. He would be the chairman. The Secretaries of the three services would be members, and this executive committee would run the Department of Defense. This was simplicity for you.

At the same time, you see, the Secretaries of the three services lost their identity as members of the Cabinet. The only member of the Cabinet from the Defense Department was the Secretary of Defense. So they lost prestige. Then, too, they were affected by the changing role of the senior military officer in each service. They were operating more in the field of logistic support and general service policies and what not.

I may have misunderstood your question, but I think that this downgrading, if you wish to put it that way, really started back in 1947 and was aggravated by the fact that when the act was passed it never worked. Forrestal did not have a deputy. Louis Johnson simply couldn't function without one and this great staff that he built up further pushed the Secretaries out of the picture. They never functioned as a management committee when he was Secretary of Defense at all. But I don't relate this to the 1958 amendment.

Have I told you how Johnson got a deputy?

Q: Yes, Steve Early. I was thinking particularly of how the service Secretaries lost their cabinet status and that sort of thing -

Adm. D.: That was '47, not '58.

Q: In 1958 we saw a series of events in the Middle East

which must have affected your office considerably. It began with Iraq and then the same month the Lebanese affair and the British landing in Jordan, the whole picture, the whole Middle East being in a state of ferment.

Adm. D.: Are you talking about the time when we landed in Lebanon? Yes, we were, of course, involved in this. The whole affair was a little larger than just Lebanon. Admiral Holloway, you may remember, was commander in chief of U.S. Naval Forces, Europe, at that time, which is a naval component of the European Command. He had another title, which was sort of out of date even then and I had it too when I relieved him - CinCNelm., commander in chief Naval Forces, Eastern Atlantic and Mediterranean. This role really was more of a planning role, involving planning with the British for combined operations and one thing and another.

I don't remember any details of this, exactly what Op-60 was doing in all this, except you can believe that we were up to our necks in it.

Q: I'm sure you had some plans in being before the thing happened -

Adm. D.: Oh, yes, we never ran out of plans. You know, that's one thing that's not well understood. In the planning business, you don't sit around and wait for somebody to tell you to develop a plan. You and your staff figure out what contingency might arise after you've got the basic war plans out of the way and more important than determining what eventually is going to be done than anything else, because you've got a contingency plan for all kinds of possibilities, but they've got to have some relation to reality. But this is the area that keeps the planners so damned busy - to try to look ahead and see what situation is likely to develop and write a scenario of what could lead up to this situation, what actions are available to the United States, what should we do, what forces, what commanders.

I've forgotten in this Lebanon amphibious landing where those plans came from. Obviously, the supporting plans had to be developed by Holloway, but this was a touchy area of the Mediterranean - and this was not too bad an example of it - because of sort of overlapping responsibilities about who was in command, who's doing what, in other words talking about CinCEur. I've forgotten who Holloway's senior was in this operation, whether it was CinCEur or whether he was operating as CinCNelm. He was very fortunate in having Bob Murphy with him, and I think Murphy was very fortunate in being able to be there, too. He was one of the more experienced people in the State Department. Earlier, in World War II, he'd been all through this North African business.

Q: Of course, the Suez incident came along there, too?

Adm. D.: Yes, of course, this was, I thought, a pretty shady deal. I'm referring to the French and British, to go so far in their planning without really cutting the United States in on it.

Q: Why did they not do so?

Adm. D.: I've forgotten, if I ever knew, but I suppose because they felt that we would object, but if we had a fait accompli it would be another matter. It was the hell of an idea of begin with.

Q: And badly executed, wasn't it? I heard the story that Mountbatten was in Malta and was given only very short notice, he didn't have his ships in order or anything.

Adm. D.: No. The whole thing was absolutely amateurish. I can't imagine the British and the French getting into such a foolish thing. Well, I can, really, because look at Gallipoli as an example of stupidity.

Q: There is another incident that may bring back some recollection to you, and that was in 1959, as an outgrowth of this whole disturbance in the Middle East, we signed a defense pact with Iran, Pakistan, and one other. Did this call for some reshuffling of our plans and policy?

Adm. D.: I've forgotten. Perhaps you can refresh my memory. When was CENTO created?

Q: In that time period, there was again the Quemoy and Matsu affair and it really flared up and the and the Seventh

Fleet was called upon to escort Chinese vessels to supply the islands and so forth.

Adm. D.: Was this the time when President Eisenhower was going to unleash Chiang Kai-chek, do you remember? Or was it Eisenhower? In this case I don't recall the words that were given to the commander, Seventh Fleet. But you see we'd been patrolling the Taiwan Strait for some time with the idea of protecting the island from invasion by mainland China, which never was a real possibility. This Quemoy and Matsu support could be done because the only thing that we had to be concerned with at all were attacks from Chinese submarines or small surface ships. There wasn't any air opposition. But nobody ever thought, as far as I know, of landing forces on those islands because really the Chinese had flooded Quemoy and Matsu with troops and with weapons. This move, I suppose, bears out in a way what I mentioned to you before about the Chinese policy of getting deeper involved in the hope that we also would be dragged into the thing.

Q: That public opinion would be aroused.

Adm. D.: Yes, that United States citizens would have bleeding hearts over this thing and demand that we go in there. Again, I don't recall what order was given exactly, but I'm sure that there were no orders to participate beyond the protection of shipping. We didn't mount forces or alert the Third Marine Division.

Q: At this stage of your career one tour of duty seemed to meld into another. On the 1st of April 1959 you became CinCNelm, which was the other side of the coin, so to speak, from what you'd been. Do you want to talk about that period? There were lots of things going on. In the Mediterranean, for instance, the French were having a terrible time with the Algerians and I guess we were barred from North African ports, weren't we?

Adm. D.: I suppose we were. I mean we certainly had no idea of sticking our nose into Mers el Kebir or any place. You see, again, in this kind of a situation of unrest and even more than that in North Africa, my dealings as CinCNelm might be only with the British on the basis of my being CinCNelm. One thing is good to illustrate what went on.

I found out shortly after I got there that the British chiefs of staff were going to get in touch with our President, through Mountbatten, I suppose, who was a personal friend of his, and ask him for some action to be taken to plan for combined operations. And Admiral Holloway for some reason which I never knew had seen fit to not do anything about it.

I was on friendly terms with the British chiefs and I went to their meeting about this time and heard them discuss this matter, and I said, "I just really can't believe that there's any need for such action on your part. I have the authority to engage in planning and I will go back to my headquarters and I will write a letter to my own staff and send you a copy, as to what planning activities I wish them to immediately engage in." We discussed what it was that was their concern, and they were amazed. So I did just that. The chairman at that time was a marshal of the Royal Air Force, Dixon I believe his name was, a fine man, and he followed through on his part.

About this time I became involved one way and another with Duncan Sandys, who was Minister of Defense, and he thought I was just great.

Q: He was a son-in-law of Churchill.

Adm. D.: Yes. This became sort of embarrassing, but anyway I put out this fire of anybody getting in touch with our President to talk about something that was quite clearly within my competence. These plans would provide for certain amphibious operations and the one point of dispute always in these kind of plans, and the principal one, was who was going to command the operation. We always step up and say, "we are, the paramount interest is UK and we will do it, thank you very much." We've always been very touchy about putting our forces under any foreign command. The Navy has been very, very touchy about putting U.S. naval forces under the command of anybody in the Army. This was just a fact of life.

At any rate, about this time we were going to have a

combined exercises in the Mediterranean, a simulated landing against the coast of North Africa somewhere, Libya, I suppose. Sandys heard about it and he called me up at Romany House on a Saturday and said, "I understand that we're having these exercises and I'd like very much to go down and witness them." And I said, "Well, Mr. Secretary, that's just fine. I will provide you an airplane. I can't go myself because I have something very urgent, but I'll be glad to have my chief of staff there. We'll have people aboard to brief you completely on this operation and explain it to you, and I'm just delighted."

He said, "By the way, there's one thing I want to tell you. I would have no hesitation whatever in placing any British forces involved in this kind of an operation under your command. I've told the British chiefs of staff that this was a great thing, and this is exactly what had to be cleared up." Well, after he hung up the phone and I had a chance to think for a minute, I was reasonably sure that he hadn't told anybody in the Admiralty about this business of calling me up and going down with me or my people, instead of the Royal Navy or the Royal Air Force. Well, thank God it was Saturday because you can't get anybody in official London on Saturday. So I got on the phone and tried to call my friend the chief of staff of the Royal Navy. I couldn't raise, him, I couldn't raise anybody that amounted to anything. I tried but I wasn't too sure what the hell I could tell them except that Sandys had asked me and I had said that I'd be glad to have him. I didn't want them to hear about it second-hand or find out about it after it had been done, because it would have been embarrassing to them, really, not to me, to think that I knew that their own Secretary of Defense had by-passed them completely.

So I got out all the necessary orders. I think the plane was going to take off Monday or Tuesday or at some very close date, and Sunday I got another call from Sandys, thanking me again and saying that the Prime Minister had just called an emergency meeting of the Cabinet at the same time when he was prepared to go down and look at this operation. So everybody was taken off the hook, whether in fact there was such a Cabinet meeting, he bowed out. I'd accomplished my purpose in the way of being hospitable and getting him to tell me - I didn't ask for the command. It was very difficult for the British armed forces to get along with him.

Q: Did you get involved as CinCNelm in any of the Greek-Turkish disputes?

Adm. D.: No.

Q: Cyprus came up at that time.

Adm. D.: Yes. My God, that's been with us for years. One problem in this whole general area was to find mutual interests and it's pretty hard to do. In other words, what are the mutual interests in a particular situation of France, the United States, the United Kingdom, let alone Italy and

Portugal and Spain or anybody else? The Suez situation might be an example and Cyprus, of course, had been hot and cold and off and on for so many years. The British were there. It was just a problem from our point of view you just hoped would go away. Of course, you know damned well it can't any more than the Israel problem can go away.

Q: The mutual interests, and then the different levels of capability, too!

Adm. D.: Yes. It's one thing if you've got a mutual interest and something ought to be done about it, but it's another thing to find out who is going to do something about it. And it's pretty touchy to consider putting United States forces in an active role in a situation such as Cyprus, for example. Here we are involving ourselves in a dispute that concerns two of our allies and friends, the Turks and the Greeks. That's a quagmire no matter how you look at it. You couldn't win. There are so many situations where you just simply can't send the U.S. flag in there with forces and solve a damned thing.

Q: And then overlording the whole thing is the United Nations I suppose, which complicates the picture. It isn't a matter of three powers, it's a matter of many.

Adm. D.: Strangely enough, the United Nations hasn't in my time, and I suppose this is true now, really figured very largely in military matters. One example where they did get in the picture in a very big way was, of course, in Korea. But as far as military advice or sanctions go, no. Here you're talking, let's say, to the Security Council. The permanent members, of course, as you know, include Soviet Russia, France, the United Kingdom, the United States, and one time China, Nationalist China, and then the ad hoc members, or whatever they call them, serve. It's impossible, really, to get consensus on any matters of not exactly detail, but even major policy decisions, except such things as Korea. The Organization of American States is much the same, too. They are nice people to have with you for morale or prestige or something, I don't know what, but to get them to do anything -

Q: They're a little more homogenous than the United Nations, aren't they?

Adm. D.: Well, one thing, of course, in the United Nations - I mentioned the Security Council because that's the place where you'd expect things to happen, but the General Assembly and its operations, and particularly in that part of the world, are dictated, which I don't think is too strong a word, by the feelings and views of a black African vote. It's a bloc. And here the major powers of the world - I'm talking about the forum of the United Nations - have their hands tied. This has happened in many, many things that have gone into UNESCO or the General Assembly. There has been, of course, in our country, as you well know, a lessening of regard for the United Nations as an organization -

Q: Even a disillusionment!

Adm. D.: Yes, because we started out with such high hopes, but I still think we've got to have an international debating society and this is it.

But when you talk about a court of justice, some of the agencies of the Security Council or of the United Nations, no country is going to take orders from the United Nations, if they don't agree. We wouldn't, neither will anybody else.

Q: I guess you have to take the hyphen out of political-military and just say "political."

Adm. D.: Political, yes, and sometimes it's spelled with a very small "p"!

Q: Quite a different event occurred in December of 1959, and that was President Eisenhower's tour to the Far East and then returning stopping in Greece and Tunis and Spain and Morocco. Did you get involved in that trip?

Adm. D.: No, not directly. I would be involved, of course, in protection and surveillance, communications, and so on.

Q: But you didn't meet with him at stated places?

Adm. D.: No. Sometimes, from a President's point of view, perhaps more times than not, it isn't a good idea for him to be accompanied by top-flight military people, unless in war at the Yalta meeting or that sort of thing.

Q: It's an avowed trip that involves the military.

Adm. D.: Yes. So the military are always in the background.

Q: That leads me to a question about Spain. Did you have any dealings with the Spanish government?

Adm. D.: No, because that wasn't part of my terms of reference. I did have friendly relations with a good many Spanish people and I've made official visits to Spain, but, of course, as everybody knows, they're not members of NATO. We have a number of bilateral arrangements with them.

Q: In particular, as far as the Navy's concerned, Rota.

Adm. D.: I was going to say that this is the one that would provide a reason for me to go there and to talk to some of the Spanish senior people. They're very nice people, but they're awfully touchy, as a good many countries are. They don't want to be used, they don't want to be dominated. They've got tremendous national pride.

Q: They drive a hard bargain, too, don't they?

Adm. D.: Yes, they do. My personal views are that Spain should be a member of NATO. Of course, these views are shared by a number of people, but it's impossible to accomplish because of the feelings against Franco on the part of the Northern Europeans.

Q: And yet Portugal with a similar kind of government succeeded in becoming part of NATO!

Adm. D.: Yes, but Salazar was not a Franco really. He was a dictator, yes, but we had many reasons for accepting Portugal into NATO. Its strategic position was one. Of course, the same reasoning could apply to Spain, or it should be able to apply to it. The Azores were a tremendous asset.

Q: That was the trump card!

Adm. D.: It really was - is. I told you about being asked by the Joint Chiefs of Staff one time to come - this was while I was CinCLant, I think - up with a plan for what we would do if we weren't permitted to use the Azores. The reason it's important is because, well, one, is because it's a necessary stepping stone on a transatlantic flight of tactical aircraft. There are other reasons, of course. From the surveilliance standpoint in the Atlantic. This was shown in the Cuban missile crisis. A base for patrol aircraft and so on. So I was given this little chore. Hell, anybody with statistics on the range of aircraft, if he had a chart and a pair of dividers, could figure out why you had to have a strategic position some place in the Atlantic.

Q: And 800 miles off the Iberian coast is not bad, is it,

for an airfield?

Adm. D.: No. I'm sure I couldn't have sent a dispatch to the Joint Chiefs of Staff. I probably called up the chairman and said I've been thinking over this whole problem you sent me and I've got a very simple solution. And that is, all you've got to do is build another island.

Q: You mean in the same cluster?

Adm. D.: Yes, just next door. Strangely enough, just in passing, the use of Lajes airfield is restricted to NATO purposes. I mean, that's the agreement. The reason that Portugal is in this Azores deal with us is because she's a member of NATO, not because of her relations with the U.S. - of course, that has a lot to do with it, but, for example, there have been times when Portugal has not permitted United Nations aircraft to re-fuel or to stop off.

Q: We actually built the base on Santa Maria, didn't we?

Adm. D.: Yes.

Q: And then we turned it over to them.

Adm. D.: Well, again, no country wants anybody else to own real estate in its own country. We wouldn't But our relations with Portugal, even bad as some of our policies have been in Africa over the overseas territory, have been just great. I think I told you how the Portuguese treated me. It couldn't have been better.

Q: What was your relationship as CinCNelm with IberLant?

Adm. D.: None. You see, IberLant was a sub-area of NATO and Portugal was part of - well, the country itself, the only one, was assigned to the responsibility of SacLant. There was a subordinate command established - well, the command itself wasn't, but provision was made to have a CinCIberLant and he would have an international staff, he would be supported by the Portuguese government, by their armed services. His responsibility would be the IberLant area, which is a fairly small sub-area in the Atlantic, off the coast of Portugal.

Q: Taking in the Bay of Biscay?

Adm. D.: Yes. The idea was that this was a natural place to protect the entrance to or exit from the Straits of Gibraltar. Well, for a long, long time we didn't have a commander there. The French wanted it, the Portuguese wanted it, and the British, of course, didn't like the idea of having the French in there and so on. So for many reasons it never really got off the ground until much later when we finally put a U.S. commander in there, and he's still there.

Q: This was Fluckey.

Adm. D.: Is he the one who is there currently?

Q: He retired about a year ago, but he was there for a number of years.

Adm. D.: Yes, and Ed Miller was there. We did have a Military Assistance Advisory Group there, you know, and I think the commander of that also acted under NATO or under SacLant. The French were so hard to get along with. I told a good many of my French friends that if France would give me some more ships, I not only would agree to a French commander, but I would actually promote it myself, recommend it to the Council. But de Gaulle had earmarked certain ships for SacLant and then he put a restriction on them that we couldn't operate them anywhere except in the IberLant area. Well, this is no place to operate aircraft carriers. It's too small an area. True, you might want to, but you don't want to have just that and nothing else.

I may have told you what I mentioned to my French friends. What would you think if the United States gave me the U.S. naval forces and I couldn't operate them east of Bermuda. Of course, it's unthinkable.

But, for many reasons, it never came about. We had one exercise when I asked the French government to let me have a French admiral who was a good friend of mine to act as commander, and they agreed, and he did a hell of a job. They put a French ship in there to act as communications post. The Portuguese Navy turned over their whole naval headquarters there, and the exercise was extremely successful.

He did a whale of a job. I was going to use that as proof that the French could do it. I didn't give a damn what the British thought about it at that point.

But because of De Gaulle's attitude about the assignment of naval forces and about that time he withdrew his Mediterranean naval forces from participation in NATO. He didn't at that time withdraw their Atlantic forces.

Q: Was there a difference in point of view between the navy echelon and de Gaulle himself? Was the Navy more readily willing to -

Adm. D.: Yes, they could understand how ridiculous it was to pin down the assignment of forces to a small area. Sure, it might be that that's exactly where I would want to operate them, but maybe not. Sure, any naval person could understand that. I've talked myself hoarse many times protesting the geographical boundaries of sea in NATO.

I may have told you my reasoning on this. It goes for IberLant as well as having the Tropic of Cancer the southern boundary of the North Atlantic area for naval purposes. It became a matter of grave - not grave - but concern in the Cuban missile crisis. It's all wrong. The whole concept of the IberLant area was all wrong.

Q: It makes it too rigid?

Adm. D.: Yes. A simple operation like the transfer of operational control when you cross some arbitrary line, when you go from CinCWestLant or CinCEastLant or CinCIberLant into the Mediterranean and came back again, always in cases like this there's a gray area about who the hell is running the show when you cross one of those damned boundaries. Naval forces don't operate like that. Sure, when you cross from France into Germany, that's a different matter, but when you cross some arbitrary line like the Tropic of Cancer, you can't see it, you don't know it, there are no guards over it.

Q: This goes back to World War II and the mid-ocean point where a convoy changed.

Adm. D.: Well, it was far enough away so that this could be done without - it's not like the entrance to the Strait of Gibraltar.

Q: Yes.

Adm. D.: There was nothing rigid about it. Sure you had the latitude and longitude and all that sort of thing, but that was a bit different operationally. Again, IberLant, as you can see, had no connection with CinCNelm. It was entirely a NATO matter. So as CinCNelm I had no concern about IberLant at all.

Q: This is an observation on the Truman administration, is it?

Adm. D.: Well, you just asked me about the Bay of Pigs.

We're going to talk about this in detail later. It did remind me of something that I thought might be of interest to you.

The National Security Act provided for the creation of the Central Intelligence Agency and I think in some of our previous talks I've mentioned to you that it was an outgrowth of the National Security Agency, which had no statutory authority. But President Truman felt the need for some kind of coordination in the intelligence reports he was getting. He'd get reports from the Army and the Navy and the Air Force and the State Department, and the coverage was uneven. He wasn't sure who was doing what. Who was responsible for what. In other words, it was just too much stuff. My unpleasant job was to try to sort through this.

Q: It came evaluated by the different agencies, did it?

Adm. D.: Yes, but finally when the act created CIA, his idea was that this would be the central source of intelligence and an authoritative source. They were to operate abroad. They weren't supposed to operate in the United States. In other words, this was an FBI-CIA conflict as to whose responsibility certain things were.

Instead of that, the damned thing developed, among other things, into an operating agency, and the Bay of Pigs was one example of how inept they were in this field. They were responsible completely for the planning and the execution of this debacle. I thought then that this would result in some congressional action to get them out of the operating field.

Well, now, just two days ago in connection with this unfortunate Watergate affair, it develops that while General Cushman was deputy director, the CIA allegedly had some part in providing equipment and even man in performing illegal breaking and entering into the psychiatrist's office - the psychiatrist who was treating Ellsberg who was alleged to have stolen the Pentagon Papers. Cushman is an honorable man. He was deputy director because the law requires either the top man or the second man to be a military officer and the other a civilian. So, here again, you have an example, yet to be really proven, of CIA participating in operating matters and, even beyond that, this infringes on restrictions about operating within the continental limits. I hope that my friend Cushman is completely cleared of this because I'm sure that he either did the right thing or thought he was. I just thought you might be interested in the comparison between -

Q: What was intended and what has happened!

Adm. D.: Yes. We know for sure in one instance and maybe in a second.

Note: There is no page 316 - an error in re-typing.

Dennison #8 - 317

Interview No. 8 with Admiral Robert Lee Dennison, U. S. Navy
(Retired)

Place: His office in the Davis Building, Washington, D. C.

Date: Tuesday afternoon, 12 June 1973

Subject: Biography

By: John T. Mason, Jr.

Q: Today we come to the crowning glory of your great naval career, Sir, when you became CinCLant and SACLant in February 1960, having come fresh from the Eastern Atlantic and the Med.

Tell me about the scope of your duties as CinCLant and SACLant.

Adm. D.: I held three jobs at the time you're talking about. One was commander-in-chief of the Atlantic Fleet; the second commander-in-chief of the Atlantic Command; and the third was Supreme Allied Commander, Atlantic, in the NATO organization.

When I came to this job I came from Commander, U. S. Naval Forces, Europe, and Commander-in-Chief, Eastern Atlantic and Mediterranean. The first of these roles, Naval Forces, Europe, was a naval component of the European Command, and, of course, as you know, there was an Army component and an Air Force component. It was a typical unified command. In my role I had the Sixth Fleet under my command and CinCNElm, as I think I've mentioned before in our interviews, was really a planning organization for combined operations with British naval forces. Although we did a few minor exercises, that was the principal purpose of it.

Now, to get back to CinCLantFlt, CinCLant, and SACLant. At one time in the Pacific CinCPac was also CinCPacFlt. In the Atlantic my predecessors and I and my successors have also been commander-in-chief of the fleet as well as commander-in-chief of the unified command.

Q: Does this entail two separate staffs?

Adm. D.: Yes, there are separate staffs. There is some overlap but not much. The unified command staff in the Atlantic had been cut down drastically in size, with the idea, as it turned out in the Cuban missile crisis, that when the occasion demanded activation of the command - the command was not ordinarily activated - that the commander, in this case myself, would be given a number of officers from the Navy, Army, and Air Force to fill out the command staff, as well as forces. This worked well. It seems like piling one job on top of another, and it is, of course. It all stems from the Navy's original reluctance to go along with unification and the unified command structure. So what they did was pile whatever unified job came along on top of the existing organization. So CinCLantFlt became CinCLant as well. In other words as CinCLant he commanded himself as his naval component under the unified structure. That is an introduction to what it's all about. I don't think that fully answers your question, so if you'll just repeat what it is you want me to go on to say about it -

Q: Well, I just wanted some sort of a foundation for these great events that were to -

Adm. D.: I think that does it, and remember that the command and control of Polaris was a very essential element in all three of these commands. In other words, nominally CinCLantFlt was completely under national command, or CinCLant, whichever command channel the President wanted to use or the Joint Chiefs of Staff. And, if the NATO forces were activated, I, the same man, as SACLant and a U. S. national, obviously, would be in command. All we'd be talking about would be a change in call signs or something.

This is the way it has to be and it's the only reason this kind of a command makes sense, because if we had to transfer from one commander to another commander with a completely different staff at some hectic point along the chain of events we could very easily be in deep trouble. So, clumsy as this may seem and even though it came about through a negative reaction on the part of the Navy, it turned out to be a pretty good idea.

Q: And certainly you gave it the ultimate test, didn't you?

During your command?

Adm. D.: I did, indeed.

Q: And, incidentally, the Polaris aspect of it came to the fore at the very beginning when you assumed command.

Adm. D.: Yes, it did.

You might be interested in hearing how it came about that a naval commander was given the assignment of Polaris submarines as part of his force.

Q: I would indeed, and especially because Mr. Gates, a former Secretary of Defense, failed to relate this to me when I talked with him about the Polaris.

Adm. D.: Well, it happened in, I think, mid-1960 when Tom Gates was Secretary of Defense. It had been the practice - we had what we started out calling a General Motors picnic down at Quantico. The idea was to get all the top commanders down there once a year on a buddy-buddy basis. I think that was the year that my room-mate was General Curt LeMay, and we had speeches and conferences and consultations and briefings, and then in the evening we'd have a picnic and sit around and have a few drinks.

Dennison #8 - 321

I had known Gates, of course, and was on friendly terms with him and he knew me well enough. He was faced with a difficult decision - difficult for him because he had been Secretary of the Navy, he knew a lot about the Navy - but the decision was who should be given command and control of Polaris. Should it be the Strategic Air Command or should it be a Navy command? A case could be made and more than made that this was a strategic weapon. The Strategic Air Command claimed to have exclusive rights over these kinds of weapons -

Q: And it was made rather emphatically, I would think.

Adm. D.: Yes, they had fought us over carrier strategic bombing, carrier-delivered strategic bombing. So they put on a real strong pitch. Gates had been to Omaha, the headquarters of the command, several times. Tommy Power, I believe, was the commander at that juncture, a very able man. Gates was impressed and rightly so with their command and control system, whereby the commander, Power, had immediate control, direct control, over the bomber force. He didn't have to go through a whole layer of commanderss to get the word for them to take off and bomb. I've seen drills put on many times and it was good - a very thorough job.

So late one night, or very early one morning, a number of us were sitting around having a few drinks and finally everybody gave up except Gates and me. We got into a discussion about who would have command and control of Polaris. He told me about his views of SAC's performance, and he thought logically, since Polaris was launched by submarines, that they probably should be part of the Navy or a naval command, but he wasn't so sure that he could do this with a clear conscience.

I spoke up and said, "Well, of course, as you know, I'm a unified commander, I'm SACLant and I also have the fleet under my command, I'm commander-in-chief of the fleet. If you assign these Polaris submarines in the Atlantic to me as a unified commander, I will guarantee you that I'll put in a better command and control system than SAC has over his bombers. I will command them personally, not through a whole echelon of division commanders and squadron commanders and so on.."

He said, "That isn't what I've been hearing from the Navy." I said, "What have you been hearing?"

"I'm told that the Navy has such a great command organization that they'll control Polaris through the normal chain of command."

So I said, "Well, I don't know who's been telling you that, but that isn't what you're going to hear. I just told you what I will do and I'll guarantee it. I'd like to do it."

Apparently I impressed him that I did mean what I said and that I could do what I said, because he did make the decision to assign the submarines to CinCLant.

Q: Did he indicate his conviction that night, or was it a delayed decision?

Adm. D.: I've forgotten. The decision wasn't long in forthcoming because time was pressing and he couldn't leave this issue hanging. All the facts were in, and what Ihad to say to him was the last piece of evidence, I guess, that he needed to make up his mind. He did. He followed through and, as you know, well, everybody knows, that's exactly what happened to the Polaris submarines. He did assign them to the Atlantic command, so I did set up the command and control system. I don't think I have to go into exactly how it operates. The order to fire came directly from me and my headquarters, or wherever I happened to be, to the commanding officer of the submarine or submarines. There wasn't any commander between me and the officer who was going to press the button.

Q: And there was no one in between you and the White House?

Adm. D.: Orders, if time and circumstances permitted, would be transmitted through the Joint Chiefs of Staff. Of course, we drilled like mad and had everything down pat and the system was very good. One principal person who was a great help to me in doing all this is on active duty now. He is Vice Admiral Hal Shear, a very, very capable officer, and a submarine officer. Of course, I had ComSubLant right there near my headquarters. I turned over the Polaris submarine to the Submarine Force commander for training prior to deployment. The minute they were deployed that intervening level fell out of the picture completely, and they had only one boss and that was me.

Q: That meant that your command as CinCLant reached out beyond and included Rota and -?

Adm. D.: Rota is quite another matter. As you know, Rota is in Spain and the base is under Spanish command. We used the base principally for primary support of submarines deployed in the Mediterranean. The overseas base for Polaris is at Holy Loch in Scotland. In addition to Polaris submarines assigned to CINCLANT there is a smaller number assigned to the Mediterranean under the command of CINCEUR. We also have Polaris deployed in the Pacific under the command of CINCPAC.

Q: And, since this was part of the picture as it developed, what about the Polaris submarines in the hands of the Royal Navy? Do they come under SACLant?

Adm. D.: I believe not. Let me just clear up something.
Neither the Polaris submarines under CINCLANT's command nor under CINCEUR's command are earmarked to NATO and therefore do not come under the command of either SACLANT or SACEUR. Submarines belonging to the United Kingdom likewise remained under national command. However, the targeting of these submarine ballistic missiles is coordinated at the Strategic Air

Command headquarters in Omaha.

I've given you the history of how the Navy got command and control of the Polaris submarine.

I might put in a little anecdote here which will perhaps underline a few things I said.

During President Kennedy's administration he decided that he would come to Norfolk and go to sea. He did come. He brought down Vice President Johnson and a number of congressional leaders, both from the Senate and the House, and the Secretary of Defense and a few other people. Before going to sea, he wanted to visit my headquarters and be given a briefing on Polaris. My command center was built like an auditorium and on the ground level you're on the level of a tremendous screen on which we used to put track charts or information, tabluations, or anything. It's really a very sophisticated and very fine installation, and there's a tier of balcony seats where ordinarily one would sit to watch a briefing. Under this tier of seats, on the next floor down, which was on ground level, with the screen and all, is the command center with all the necessary communications outlets, telephones and print-outs from computers on computer display screens, rather.

So when these gentlemen came down, the first thing we did was to go into this center, on the ground level, and I got up on the platform to explain what was going to happen. I gave President Kennedy my chair at my desk where he could see everything. The reason I told them what was going to happen was because things happen so fast that unless you knew what you were watching you wouldn't realize what had happened. Just a lot of bang, bang, bang, and it's all over. So I went through this step by step, and finally, after I found out that nobody wanted to comment on anything, I gave the command to start the exercise.

Well, of course, all hell broke loose. Bells and buzzers and everything else started going. We had made tapes of telephone conversations developed for this purpose, and we played them over the loudspeaker phones, presumably from the President, the Chairman of the Joint Chiefs of Staff, and so on, getting the necessary instructions about the exclusion of any targets, the principal ones from the master list, and giving the order to shoot. I, in turn, had my telephone keys and telephones all manned. People would come in with keys and boxes under their arms and all the rest of it -

Q: Sounds like an impressive operation!

Adm. D.: It really was, and I was delighted to be permitted to put it on.

Then after the Polaris messages went out, we started sending the fleet war messages. Well, at that point, I stopped the exercise because we weren't interested in the whole show, just the Polaris part of it.

When I stopped the exercise, first I asked the President "Do you have any questions, Mr. President?" He didn't say anything and there was quite an appreciable pause, which seemed like a long time but was probably maybe six or seven or eight seconds. Finally, he said, "Can these missiles be stopped?" I said, "No, Sir. The submarines are reeling in their underwater antennae, the count-down has started, and there's no way."

Q: You can't change your mind?

Adm. D.: That was the answer. I don't know whether he liked it or not, but I've wondered often what he was thinking about, what could happen in a matter of a few seconds - not half an hour or fifteen minutes - for him to think about countermanding an order to shoot. Obviously, you couldn't tell a submarine commander "Now, I may send you a firing signal, but hold on till the last second because I might countermand it." You can't do that. When you tell a man to shoot, that's it. Nobody else had anything to say. It was so dramatic. It was just real. You could hear these voices coming in and hear the signals going out, and getting all these reports about what had been sent and what hadn't been sent.

It really impressed the President, and the rest of them, too. Then we did go to sea, but that's another story.

Q: You say this was very early on in his presidency?

Adm. D.: Yes.

Q: This leads me to another question. Obviously in that job you must have had many delegations of VIPs, did you not? Did you have a special program outlined for them?

Adm. D.: Yes, but it depended a great deal/on what nationality - we had a great many Europeans come, you see, so we had a security problem. We couldn't put this Polaris show on for them.

We usually put on a Marine landing exhibition, amphibious force landings. Tha Marines always put on a good show. And the usual intelligence briefings, which were geared to the clearance of the people who were listening to them.

Obviously, when the President comes down there or the Vice President and all these top-level people, you're not going to pull out a book and say, is anybody here not cleared for top secret?

To get back to your question: we did have a great many visitors and delegations come, and I encouraged them. I wanted everybody who had any proper interest, particularly people from overseas, to come and find out what we were doing and how we were doing it. Of course, they never failed to be terribly impressed by the power that was so evident in our fleet. The latter because many of them had very small navies and they didn't have anything like our amphibious forces or carriers.

Q: Did you have any particular thing you wanted to emphasize to a delegation of American VIPs - nuclear power and that sort of thing?

Adm. D.: Yes. Of course, if anybody had anything to do with appropriations, we could put them in tears with how much more we really had to have! I don't mean to say that all we did was deal with Europeans and Americans and North Americans. We put on several shows for the Latin-American CNOs. We put on one bangup review just off Puerto Rico one year, I remember. There wasn't a day, it seemed to me, when some VIP - and I mean real one - would be in Norfolk, and it took a lot of doing sometimes to handle all this. It was a sort of juggling act.

A: That was almost a fourth hat, wasn't it, that you had to wear and really had to?

Adm. D.: Right.

Q: Well, you hadn't been in your job very long when there began to be some indications of developments with regard to Cuba. I think the first indication you said you had was in April of 1960 that something was stirring, and that was in connection with Swan Island?

Adm. D.: Yes. I think you're leading up to what was called the Bay of Pigs -

Dennison #8 - 330

Q: Oh, the Bumpy Road, yes.

Adm. D.: That was the code name for the operation.

Q: Yes, and incidentally would you say it also had an earlier code name, "Crosspatch," which was deleted. Why?

Adm. D.: I don't really know, but I think it was probably deleted because perhaps Crosspatch was associated with the Swan Island communications business and not with this invasion attempt. But I became involved in it at the time it was Bumpy Road.

Q: You were going to tell me just a little bit about the Swan Island episode?

Adm. D.: Yes. This is leading in to this Operation Bumpy Road, which was an abortive invasion by insurgents.

The first I knew about Swan Island was in April 1960 when the Atlantic Fleet lifted people and some material to Swan Island, in the Caribbean, and constructed an airfield, a camp, and some other facilities, and put in a patrol of one destroyer - later that became a minesweeper - again in April. I never really knew what all went on on Swan Island, but I know that they were putting out broadcasts on schedule and some of them not on schedule, and obviously there were some additional communications that I wasn't familiar with.

Q: And you didn't ask for further information on it?

Adm. D.: I didn't get any. I never got an over-all plan for that operation, but that swiftly became a very, very minor issue, not that it ever was anything else, as far as that was concerned.

Q: But it apparently alerted you to the fact that -

Adm. D.: Something was going on, yes. And the involvement of CIA. But Bumpy Road itself came to my attention in September and the whole operation was a strange one, and I think before I get further into it I'd better tell you in a general way how it was run.

CIA were the ones who developed the idea and carried it out. The military obviously had to have some kind of an organization to handle their part in it, whatever it might turn out to be. So the Joint Chiefs set up a small staff under an Air Force major general, I think he was. I think it was General Dean, a capable man. He and a small staff were in the Joint Chiefs of Staff organization, but nobody except the Chiefs and a few other people knew anything about it. It was a separate cell. I had to have the same kind of a special staff, apart from my own staff, to handle Bumpy Road business. And any other commander who had any remote connection with it did the same thing.

So all this was going on completely apart and aside from the ordinary business of command. It really was an appalling situation because I'd been at my own briefings later on and seen fleet dispositions that were phony. My own operations staff was misled because I, through this special staff, would order some particular disposition, and that was dangerous.

Q: And a real strain on you as commander!

Adm. D.: Yes. It just is not the way to do business. In any event, briefly, that's the way this thing started. But the way I found out about the operation was really fantastic.

Vice Admiral Towner was Commander, Amphibious Forces, Atlantic Fleet. He came to see me one day with a story which is hard to believe. He told me that the commander of one of his LSDs was visited by two men down off Puerto Rico, or in Roosevelt Roads, or wherever they were, who identified themselves as being with the CIA and said they wanted, in effect, to requisition his ship to carry some landing craft and crews from, I think, Vieques, to a point off southern Cuba. This was to be in connection with some operation they couldn't tell him about.

Well, of course, he told them in short order that he just didn't own that ship and couldn't respond to any such request. He'd have to get orders through the Navy chain of command.

So, Towner came to me and told me this story. I immediately called up Lemnitzer and said, "What is all this?" Lemnitzer was chairman of the JCS. He said, "Don't you know?" I said, "I don't know any more than I've told you. What's it all about? I'm not going to turn my ship over to a couple of characters who say that they're from CIA or any place else." He said, "My God, I'll get ahold of Dulles or his deputy Lieutenant General Cabell, USAF.

Anyway, it turned out that Dulles couldn't come down, the general couldn't come down. They were out briefing General Eisenhower or something. So on 2nd November 1960 Bissell came down to brief me.

Q: Was there any excuse for having overlooked you up to this point?

Adm. D.: No. This was the first time I'd ever heard of such a plan. I told them how stupid it was. I think any military man who had anything to do with it could have told them the same thing. We weren't asked to approve anything, We were just being told that this was by direction of the President and this was what was to be done.

So here we were in November. And I was really appalled. I said, "Didn't it occur to any of you that I'm responsible, among other things, for the defense of Guantanamo? What do you think might happen? Are we likely to get a reaction?"

You see, this plan had been drawn up a long time before this and it was based on the idea that in the very early days of Castro, if invasion took place by some Cuban insurgents, everybody would run down from the mountains and from the countryside, join this movement and throw out Castro. Well, by the time they got around to executing it - Eisenhower postponed it until it passed on to Kennedy in the very early days of his administration - the picture had completely changed. Castro had armor. He had equipment from the Soviets.

Q: And he had supporters.

Adm. D.: It was a hell of a different picture, entirely different. The whole concept was stale and outmoded, and it turned out, as the operation unfolded, that CIA was becoming really apprehensive about what these people they had trained would do. In other words, they might turn against some other Latin-American country or they might do almost anything, instead of going in to Cuba.

I had to know more about what CIA's information was, about what was really going on in Cuba.

Q: How detailed was the Bissell report to you?

Adm. D.: It didn't satisfy me a damned bit.

Q: Was it that he was withholding information or that he didn't have it?

Adm. D.: He was withholding it, as I found out later. Even when we got really going in this operation, a lot of things had happened that were completely new to me. We nearly blew one of

Dennison #8 - 335

their ships out of the water - from this insurgent outfit - because they forgot to tell me about another operation that was going on not far from the Bay of Pigs landing.

Q: At one stage, I think the operation was scheduled to get under way on the 10th of November. Had this been canceled by the time he came to see you on the 2nd of November?

Adm. D.: Not that I remember. I don't remember what dates I had. It couldn't have been that close because a lot had to be done.

Q: Why had the President postponed it from time to time?

Adm. D.: Well, it got to be a pretty hot potato. You're talking about President Eisenhower?

Q: Yes.

Adm. D.: I think he realized that it was very risky and probably would be an unsuccessful operation. Whatever reason, I don't know, but it was passed over to Kennedy and, of course, he believed that it had been well thought through and everybody had approved it. Then, when it went into a real disaster -

Q: But, to continue your narrative, Sir, Bissell came on the 2nd of November to brief you and you were not satisfied with his information, so you took steps to get some additional information from the Joint Chiefs?

Adm. D.: I'd gotten some just a few days before that from a man named Holcomb from CIA, who came down to give me a little preliminary information.

My task on the surface was pretty simple. All I had to do was bring some landing craft into the transport area off the beach and turn them over to these insurgents, and that was all. They were going to make the landing some time in November, but later that was postponed indefinitely because they weren't ready. So it wasn't until the 10th of February that I got a request from the Joint Chiefs that one LSD would leave Roosevelt Roads on the 1st of March to carry landing craft whose identity had been removed. In other words, there was nothing on them that said U.S., but I don't know who would have thought they belonged to anybody else.

Q: Is that the meaning of the term "sanitized"?

Adm. D.: Yes.

Q: The identification marks removed?

Adm. D.: Yes. Crazy!

This was to begin on the 1st of March, this first movement. I had gotten assurances from time to time that U.S. forces would not be directly involved in this operation - would not be. The last assurance I got on that was on the 9th of February.

Q: General Lemnitzer assured you?

Adm. D.: Yes - from the President

Q: Did you see the President?

Adm. D.: My recollection is that he was the one who told me along with Lemnitzer, but I'm not too clear on that. My notes aren't clear, but I remember being in the White House and asking, in a different way. I said, "Am I likely to be involved in a bail-out operation?" In other words, I could foresee a disaster. And he said, "No" that U.S. forces would not be overtly involved. Well, of course, that didn't turn out to be the case, as you'll learn as I go on.

I relayed my concern and the reasons for my concern, about the lack of intelligence that was available to me concerning Cuba. I felt I had certain responsibilities; of course, I had over-all responsibility. The defense of Guantanamo naval base, of course, was important, and the defense of my own fleet forces, and, of course, proper concern for the safety of U.S. nationals that were in Cuba. So I had to know more than I knew, which wasn't very much.

As Castro took over and became more and more powerful, we lost certain sources of information, attaches and embassy officials, businessmen and so on, because of the harassments and restrictions that were imposed on them, and the Soviet ships that came in there and other merchant vessels were unloaded at night under strict security control. We were pretty much in the dark as to what was being put in there. We heard a lot of rumors. We did have some occasional aerial sighting. But it was pretty clear that these rumors relating to MIGs, tanks, artillery, communications equipment, and so on were substantiated eventually, but too late.

By mid-1960 intelligence-collection in Cuba was largely just conjecture, and at least one Washington source was estimating the armament of the Cuban forces by relating the total tonnage delivered to Cuba to what had happened with Soviet-bloc arms exported to Egypt and Iraq. That was really a crystal-ball operation.

Q: Did not the CIA have sources of information?

Adm. D.: They had very, very few, and I'll go on to tell you what I tried to guess. I had to come up with a Cuban plan and, as all plans of this sort do, it contained an annex on intelligence. I sent that on up to the Joint Chiefs and it was questioned because I didn't list certain Bloc weapons which they thought might be in there but they'd never been positively identified, to my knowledge. When I visited with Mr. Bissell, whom I mentioned a while ago, on the 2nd of November I did bear down very heavily on my need for intelligence - almost anything. Bissell and I agreed that I'd submit my intelligence requirements to CIA through the JCS with an advance copy direct to them.

I did that on the 20th of December and listed over 90 specific intelligence requirements on Cuban military and paramilitary forces, together with 29 equally specific requirements on Cuban counterrevolutionary forces.

Q: On the island?

Adm. D.: Yes. This was on the 20th of December.

Q: It must have entailed a tremendous amount of work in preparation for a small staff.

Adm. D.: Of course, it did. Now I got a reply on the 21st of February from the Joint Chiefs stating that my requirements had been referred to the services for fulfillment on a continuing basis. Out of the 90 requirements on Cuban armed forces, I got less than 12 of these requirements satisfied. This was unsatisfactory. It was too late, too sparse. No information that required clandestine intelligence effort was ever fulfilled.

Dennison #8 - 340

Q: You must have been pretty apprehensive in the interim period, as it became apparent to you the operation was going forward and you hadn't got your reply?

Adm. D.: Well, if I had been able to count on my role being restricted to what was told to me, it wouldn't have made a hell of a lot of difference, but I was looking a little bit farther ahead as to what might happen and what I might have to do.

Q: Isn't that the job of a good commander?

Adm. D.: I would think so, but this getting your intelligence requirements filled on a post-mortem basis is hardly the way to operate.

Q: It supports the record at least!

Adm. D.: One thing that I wanted to know and that was of direct interest to me was what did we know about what workers' unions might do at Guantanamo in the way of sabotage, espionage. I never found out anything about that, nor did I ever get any real information on the capabilities of the Cuban armed forces.

Q: Had the fleet been sending planes over for reconnaissance?

Adm. D.: No. We were forbidden to do that. All we had going

Dennison #8 - 341

on was a very casual and very limited strategic air cover. We did have an effort controlled in Washington for high-altitude reconnaissance to be followed up by tactical reconnaissance where this seemed to be indicated. But I didn't find that adequate. It wasn't sufficient in detail or in timeliness.

Q: And you didn't have a free hand to augment it?

Adm. D.: No.

Q: Why was Washington so apprehensive about it?

Adm. D.: Well, because it might be discovered and people would think that something was going to happen and God knows what all. I tried to get authority to fly tactical reconnaissance myself, but I didn't get it. We did have at one time, until October, information from strategic reconnaissance, again incomplete, of course.

Q: That's when the wraps were put on?

Adm. D.: Yes. On the 3rd of October we couldn't lift a finger. We had to knock off any effort at all.

Q: During this whole period, did you have recourse to the CNO, he being a member of the Joint Chiefs?

Dennison #8 - 342

Adm. D.: Sure, but there was not much he could do. He was in the same fix I was. The Joint Chiefs of Staff were really sort of sidelined on all this. All he could do really was sympathize. I kept pressing about this insufficient intelligence but never did get what I needed. One of the final words I got was on the 19th of January when I got word from the Joint Chiefs that the need for intelligence was recognized but the policy of the administration was not to authorize overflights by military aircraft.

Q: This was at the time when the administration changed. The 19th of January was the last day of the Eisenhower administration?

Adm. D.: That's right, yes.

In any event, I had requested authority to resume military photo reconnaissance five different times and was turned down. As you can tell from what I've said so far, I really didn't get the information that I felt that I needed and felt completely blocked. It made me go back to the question of U.S. involvement, which was at the base of all this.

You remember I mentioned a while ago about being sure that I wouldn't be drawn into any bail-out operations?

Q: Yes, the President himself assured you.

Adm. D.: On the 9th of February I was given a briefing by Vice

Dennison #8 - 343

Admiral Beakley and Rear Admiral Lowrance, who were then in Op-Nav, on the general concept of operations up to arrival in the objective area. In other words, they were talking mostly about my coming in there with an LSD and so on. The written directive I got from the JCS on that, which I got before the briefing but the briefing didn't add anything to it, said it was necessary to take precautions to assure that U.S. support of the Cuban volunteer force is not apparent and the support for this operation be conducted so that the U.S. might plausibly deny participation. And as late as D + 1 Day, which was the 18th of April, at three o'clock in the afternoon, I was informed "no intention of intervening with U.S. forces." That nailed it down pretty firm as to what our attitude was, and the result, of course, was that I was cut out from further information and, as I go on with this account, you'll find out how vital this was.

Q: This limited you and the fleet to a kind of an escort operation, and that alone?

Adm. D.: Yes, but you see the situation had so much potential in it for danger. Here we were giving covert assistance, so we thought. Anybody could recognize a U.S. ship or a U.S. military airplane. I mean nobody else has anything like that, certainly not in those waters, and I was worried about reprisal. Had I not found out anything about this I wouldn't have been able to reinforce Guantanamo or take essential precautions.

Dennison #8 - 343A

As we go along here I'll come to a part where it was thought that I could conduct air reconnaissance over the ocean areas, the Caribbean area, with aircraft out of Guantanamo. Well, of all the stupid things, that would give the Cubans perfect ground to say, "Well, we're going to move in there and throw you out." It had to be seaborne so it was out of range of our land bases, and it was. Later on, in my account here, I'll tell you how I did it. But this is incredible to me now, as I'm sure it is to you, how in the world we could get into such a mess as all this.

The first directive I had for support of operations came from the Joint Chiefs of Staff. It really was a personal memorandum from the Chairman to me. The Joint Chiefs of Staff as a body were not really involved in this. They acted only as independent service chiefs. This was outlined for a 10 April D Day. Here are the instructions I got:

One destroyer with CEF convoy - that's the Cuban Exeditionary Force - from a point in the southern Caribbean to a point southwest of Cienfuegos -

Q: You were picking them up at sea?

Adm. D.: Yes. From D - 2 until dark on D - 1. Then this one destroyer was supposed to be well clear of the coast by dawn. I was supposed also to provide combat air patrol over these ships from sunrise to sunset on only D - 1, and this patrol was to be controlled by the destroyer.

Dennison #8 - 344

Q: On the spot.

Adm. D.: Yes. The LSD was to transport three LCs, four LCVPs, from Vieques to an area southwest of Cienfuegos and transfer these craft at six o'clock in the morning on the 10th to the Cuban Expeditionary Force and then get out. The wind-up of all this was that this was all the Atlantic Fleet participation desired, units were to withdraw after mission completed and to be clear before dawn. No rules of engagement were provided. That left me still hanging. This all seemed a little bit too pat for me.

Q: When D Day was April 10, what was the objective? Was that still the Bay of Pigs, or was it Trinidad that had been previously - ?

Adm. D.: No, this was the Bay of Pigs.

I had someproblems even in carrying out this simple directive. I couldn't use planes from Key West without overflying Cuba. Roosevelt Roads was too far away. I didn't have any CVA, and I couldn't fly out of Guantanamo without disclosing that we were participating. Of course, there was no problem about getting a destroyer and we were kind of low on LSDs. But my main concern was the security of my own command and my readiness for contingency operations; for example, an attack on Guantanamo

Dennison #8 - 345

or even Key West wouldn't have been out of the realm of reason.

What I decided to do was to use the ASW force that I had. I took the ordinary S-2F squadron off that carrier and put on a fighter attack squadron which I had armed with rockets. That's where I got my aircraft, and I used two destroyers instead of one. I mean one destroyer is silly.

Q: This was all at your own discretion?

Adm. D.: Yes, a lot of what went on was at my discretion. I again warned the Joint Chiefs of Staff that we might get a reaction by air or otherwise against a U.S. target, again Key West or Guantanamo. I had taken certain precautionary measures on my own. I had an amphibious squadron with a marine battalion landing team embarked just off Guantanamo and I held some destroyers in Guantanamo that had completed their refresher training, and sent a 6-inch-gun cruiser, the Galveston, in to Guantanamo from Roosevelt Roads, and advanced the date of deployment of a VMF squadron in Guantanamo, and held an attack squadron that was down there and due to come back.

I did take these steps as precautions.

Q: What about Key West?

Adm. D.: I did nothing, really, about Key West except get the word to the commander at Key West, and of course the air defense command of the continental United States has defense responsibility.

Q: Then you had to bring him in on the plan, did you? The commander at Key West?

Adm. D.: So I had done everything I could think of, I kept Rear Admiral Clark in the Essex, which was his carrier, his ASW carrier. He was ready. All this would be under the cover of ASW Operations in the Caribbean area, except they didn't have ASW aircraft by that time. These aircraft I put on there, as I told you, were A-4Ds because they were compatible with this carrier and could combine fire and attack capability for the support of Guantanamo, if needed, and Essex had all kinds of general-purpose bombs aboard and rockets. That gives you some idea what steps were taken.

I told Lemnitzer what I had done and was ready to do.

Q: And then the date was changed again?

Adm. D.: You mean from the 10th?

Q: Yes.

Adm. D.: Yes. On the 5th of April I received word from the JCS that D Day was delayed at least 48 hours and probably a min-

Dennison #8 - 347

imum of 96 hours, and they asked me to send a representative up there to Washington to get the latest information and further instructions, which of course I did.

I got this message too late to cancel certain operations. For example, an ASW sweep of the Central American coast. They found no submarines there anyhow. Then I got a memorandum from the Chairman on the 7th of April changing the concept of U. S. Navy support and rules of engagement and giving me a new D Day, and it said it was necessary to take precautions to ensure that U. S. support of the Cuban volunteer force was not apparent and that support for this operation be undertaken so that the U. S. could plausibly deny participation. This was the key that ran through the whole operation, to start with, anyway.

Q: We would publicly deny that we were part of it. Was this a part of changed thinking in the White House at this point?

Adm. D.: No, I think all along we were going to keep our hands out of it. But I mean it was pretty obvious as I go along, or even up to now, who was back of this operation. There wasn't anybody else except us.

Then I got information that went on to say that there wouldn't be any expeditionary force convoy, but that I would provide area coverage with destroyers, and still I was required to be well off the coast on D Day, nowhere near the landing. I would be permitted to put up a combat air patrol during daylight on D-2 and D-1 only, and I was to avoid overt association with this expeditionary force. In other words, keep the destroyers at maximum range during daylight, don't get closer than 20 miles from the Cuban coast, and my air cover should not appear to be covering the expeditionary force!

Q: Then, what was the purpose of being there?

Adm. D.: None. And then again, for I don't know how many times, "USN support will not be used to support the landing operations." My rules of engagement were modified several times such as to withhold engagement to the last possible moment and to take action only when total destruction of the expeditionary force ships were imminent and not to attack unfriendly aircraft until they actually started runs with open bomb bay doors or actually strafing.

Q" It reminds me of Bunker Hill - "don't fire until you see the whites of their eyes"!

Adm. D.: Yes, but we knew on that occasion that we were going to shoot!

Another modification to the rules of engagement was to minimize the need to abort the operation because of U. S. engagement with Castro's ships or aircraft.

Q: What did that mean?

Adm. D.: It meant that if we were detected - in other words, if we engaged Castro's ships or aircraft - then it would become apparent that we were back of this thing and the operations, the landing, would have been aborted. They wouldn't have gone through with it. That was the thought, anyway.

Q: How many Cubans were involved in this operation?

Adm. D.: I've forgotten how many. I think they had six ships, if I remember correctly, transports. There weren't enough and they didn't land in the right place at the right time in the right year. There wasn't any right year, probably. In other words, we still wanted to be able plausibly to deny that we were supporting it.

Then I got some more instructions about the reschedule of the Vieques training exercise, 15-18 April, although actually none had been scheduled in the first place. I don't remember now just what that was all about.

Q: Was that a ruse, do you suppose?

Adm. D.: They just thought that would be an activity they could do without, I guess. Then I got instructions to prepare a compound on Vieques, which was later used as a refuge for these poor devils that we rescued from Cuba when the Castro forces beat the hell out of them. I had my FMFLant people, Marines, deliver the camp equipment for 1,500 men to Vieques.

Then again I got word that the CIA wanted to keep military aircraft 70 miles off the coast of Cuba from 14 April until the operation was completed. So I did all that, which was ridiculous, 70 miles. Then I had done what I was supposed to do and we got out of the general area at 5:44 a.m. on the 17th. About four hours later, about nine o'clock, I got a warning message from the JCS to provide combat air patrol for shipping outside of territorial waters during daylight on D Day and to provide a DD for air warning to this expeditionary force, which was beyond my original instructions.

This was the first indication that I might be called on to provide further support, although I fully expected it. Then I was asked by the Joint Chiefs of Staff to put some air early warning ships on some widely separated points about 30 miles off-shore. You see, we didn't know what the Cuban air capability was, and it turned out that they didn't have very much.

Q: These would be the equivalent of picket ships, would they?

Adm. D.: That's the idea. Again I was told that I couldn't put up a combat air patrol, and finally I was advised that two of the transports had been sunk and one damaged.

Q: Two of the six?

Adm. D.: Yes. I think it was a total of six. This was the first indication, of course, that we were in a real disaster. Then I got a message from Clark telling me that these expeditionary force ships were under heavy air attack and the steps that he was taking. He put up a combat air patrol for his own protection. Then we got a confirmation that these two transports had been sunk and that the Department of Defense had been requested to provide jet aircraft support, but there hadn't been any presidential approval of this request at that time. This was again on the 17th.

Q: And that was D Day?

Adm. D.: Yes.

Q: How were all these messages being transmitted, if they didn't come through you?

Adm. D.: These that I'm talking about did. They had a special cipher and special address and limited distribution and all that.

And here's a strange one. I'll tell you a little story about this one. I was directed in great detail by a dispatch from the Chairman of the Joint Chiefs of Staff to set up what amounted to a safe haven for these transports if they managed to get out and not be sunk, or any friendly ships, about 15 miles offshore, and establish a combat air patrol to cover them and all that. It went into considerable detail. It was really a tactical order addressed to me as Commander-inChief. I wouldn't have sent the thing to a captain. It was not just what they wanted done but exactly how to do it, how many destroyers to use. So I called up Lemnitzer on the scramble phone and said, "I've gotten a good many orders in my life, but this is a strange one." He said, "What do you mean?" I said, "Well, the last paragraph in it says that the Joint Chiefs of Staff interpret this to mean, set up a safe haven. This is the first order I ever got from somebody who found it necessary to interpret his own orders."

He said, "Where did you get this directive?" And I said, I got it from you." He said, "Who do you think wrote it?" I said, "You did." He said, "No, I didn't. That order was written at 1600 Pennsylvania Avenue."

I said, "Well, you can just tell 1600 Pennsylvania Avenue that I'm not going to do it that way. I'll do what they want done, but I'll use all the forces that I think are necessary. They don't know what's going on as much as I do."

So this thing really went from bad to worse. I did put up a combat air patrol and I did provide a safe haven. And of the four ships some were sunk and some of the landing force got on the beaches and on the little rocky pieces of island, really, and we did pick up some men. I'll get into a little more detail on that. But it was all extemporaneous pretty much from then on, and fortunately I did have the forces to do it. I had seen

Dennison #8 - 353

to it that I did. I never could believe from the very beginning that we weren't going to be involved in this thing.

Q: The Joint Chiefs must have been mighty sympathetic with the commander in the field?

Adm. D.: Oh, of course, they were. We were all in a difficult position. They knew what I was up against, and they well knew that I was going to do what I felt ought to be done in any event. I had to. I had responsibilities other than to CIA to support this silly operation.

Then, of course, here we were still trying to play that we didn't have any hand in it. I was to prepare unmarked aircraft for possible combat use, which I did. ComKeyWest began to get six F-3Hs ready. Then they latched onto the fact that I did have a PhibRon embarked and I was told to move them up within four hours' steaming of the landing area, which I had already done. I could see that one coming! And then I got this one about preparing unmarked boats for possible evacuation operation, which I had already done except the unmarked part of it. And the end of this one was like everything else I got "there is no intention of intervening with U. S. forces."!!

Q: The unmarked boats came from the destroyers, did they?

Adm. D.: I forget where I got them, but they were landing craft I think. As I pointed out, suppose these unmarked aircraft had been shot down with the pilot in a suit of dungarees, and no insignia what is he? A spy? And what about the crews of these landing craft that are invading with no marking on the boats? What are they?

I said, if we're going in there let's go in with our flags flying.

Q: If captured, the enemy is entitled to shoot them!

Adm. D.: They certainly aren't covered by the Geneva Convention anyway, for whatever that's worth nowadays. So it was just ridiculous.

Then I ordered the Independence and a couple of cruisers to speed up and get down to the general area, thinking that maybe I'd need attack aircraft from the Independence.

Q: It must have been absolutely impossible to maintain the kind of strict secrecy that they had outlined?

Adm. D.: By that time, yes. This was getting completely out of hand. I mean you can't move all these ships around and leave the whole staff completely in the dark, which up to this time they probably were. That was one of the problems about getting messages through. To get them to somebody who could do something about it. Just to send them to General Dean wasn't good enough.

Dennison #8 - 355

I did finally send in a sort of a situation summary on the 18th, and part of the things I had to say to the Joint Chiefs of Staff was that I too had been operating in the dark, which had been generated by not being completely advised of Cuban Expeditionary Force operations. The sudden laying out of requirements that could have been forecasted, and no intelligence assessment of the situation within Cuba. My own assessment was based on a very high degree of ignorance that the CEF operation was not going well and it was either inconclusive or total collapse and I expected strong retaliatory effort, probably against Guantanamo. Then I went on to say that it was inevitable that our participation would gradually become known to a degree at least by many people, including those in Castro's government. Time was not on our side and it was certainly important to do all possible to tip the scales in favor of the expeditionary force. I had no suggestions at this time beyond containing the measures I had previously outlined.

Again I got this unmarked aircraft business, to put six of them in the air between 6:30 in the morning to 7:30 local time on the 19th and defend the force against air attack by Castro forces. "Do not seek air combat, but defend forces from air attack. Do not attack ground targets." Now this was in extremis. Here were these poor expeditionary guys. I couldn't blast the Cuban forces that were attacking them. All I could do was to give them air cover to protect them against air attack only.

Q: What arms did they have, the Cubans themselves, in the expeditionary force?

Adm. D.: They didn't have anything like what they ought to have. They didn't have any armor or any heavy stuff at all, and presumably they'd been trained in guerrilla warfare. I learned later, I never figured this out, that they hadn't been trained in guerrilla warfare. They'd been trained in conventional army operations. This was different. This was beating it up into the hills and acting like guerrillas. They were just poorly trained and poorly equipped for what they were supposed to be doing.

Q: Did it seem to be, this force as it developed, predicated on some kind of support from our forces?

Adm. D.: I don't see how it could have been because if a third of what I was told about no U. S. participation got through to them, they certainly weren't depending on us to do anything.

Another one that was finally washed out, and there's more to this one than my own records show. I was ordered to rendezvous with some expeditionary force aircraft that were flying from Nicaragua, I believe, and my record shows that the idea was that I'd protect them against attack and let them go ahead and do the bombing of Cuban forces and so on.

Q: Furnish fighter support to them?

Dennison #8 - 357

Adm. D.: They got to the rendezvous point an hour ahead of the schedule and retired before my forces got there, in spite of the fact that I was there forty minutes before the time specified by the Joint Chiefs. Now I was told, though my own records don't substantiate this, that that expeditionary forces's air strikes were canceled by Kennedy.

Q: You mean coming in an hour early -

Adm. D.: and then leaving, yes.

Q: The White House was not in command of the expeditionary force anyway, was it?

Adm. d.: No, but they could have gotten word to them somehow. The CIA was doing it - to call them off. Don't forget that all through this I wasn't allowed any close air support. Never got it. I had to stay fifteen miles away and cover my own forces.

So, still expecting some reaction, I ordered that force of the *Independence* and a couple of cruisers to go to Guantanamo. Then we were in sort of a box as to how to get these expeditionary force people off the beach -

Q: Once it became apparent it was a fiasco?

Adm. D.: Yes. They finally got out a directive - I finally got one - to have a destroyer take people off the beach and to give them air cover. If the DD was fired on they were authorized to fire back. As I recall one of them was fired on and did fire back and knocked the battery out completely, whatever the battery was that was shooting at them.

We picked up quite a few people. Finally on the 20th I got a message that the JCS didn't see any need for any further combat air patrol in the beaches area and to put my PhibRon back to normal operations. But I decided to keep that PhibRon right where it was. I called that normal.

Then again on the 20th I got a message sending me some information on Guantanamo reconnaissance, but deferred action on my request to overfly and take pictures of the Guantanamo area. Finally I got an order to take charge of the expeditionary force ships that were left and personnel and get them to Vieques and to keep my destroyer patrol going off the beach for more survivors, and I got one strange one, that the commanding officer was authorized to ground his ship if it would facilitate mission.

Q: The landing craft?

Adm. D.: No, the destroyers.

And this is about the time things were getting real hectic. These ships came through where this safe haven was set up with a lot of soldiers on board and one of my destroyers damned near opened fire on it, thinking it was the enemy. It turned out to be the expeditionary force's abortive landing farther up the coast that I never knew anything about. They'd just gotten scared and took off, and came charging down through my area.

Q: Was this in addition to the six? That you'd been escorting?

Adm. D.: Yes - it turned out we picked up about 26 survivors from the beach.

I kept up patrols at various bays along the coast and continued sort of a mopping-up operation.

Q: Actually, how violent was the Castro opposition?

Adm. D.: Oh, they really put some power in there and just mopped them up. I've forgotten now what they had. I think they had some light tanks. You see, this was a sort of a cul-de-sac that they were in. There was only one way out of it and blocking it was a fairly simple job, and I'm sure the Cubans had advance information on all this and they knew where the landing was going to be and they were all set.

So that's about the story. I think I can tell you a bit more of the history of it. Again, it does seem incredible and if it seems that way it's because it was that way. President Kennedy, I think, was perhaps not deliberately misled. I think that when he took office with this operation shortly to come off he knew it had been planned for so long and he simply assumed

Dennison #8 - 360

that the capable people that were in the government and certainly in the military had approved it or had some knowledge of it and thought it was all right. So it was a fairly natural thing to do, to let it go. Of course, then he took the blame for it. The only blame really that attached to him was that he was the commander-in-chief and maybe he should have looked into it a little more carefully. I'm sure if he'd asked me what I thought of it I would have told him exactly that I thought of it. But in all those things there's so much momentum going that it's pretty hard to turn around or cancel. And I mentioned a while ago one reason was what would happen to these expeditionary forces, what would they do? Would they go and attack some friendly country, or what would they do?

Q: Once they were organized and were armed!

Adm. D.: They were organized and armed. Well, I think I've talked enough about the operation itself, but I think the principal interest in all this is the derivation of lessons learned and how we apply this experience to future operations. I think the lessons to be learned are valid for any kind of an operation from here on in.

So I did make a general summary of my observations - or summary of my general observations, and I divided these observations into five categories: lack of information, problems imposed by security restrictions, covert operations by military forces, changes in rules of engagement, and control and direction of operations.

Starting with the first one on lack of information, it's obvious from what I've said that I was operating very much in the dark and it turned out that nobody had the information, really. Certainly CIA didn't, they wouldn't need it and didn't take adequate steps to do anything about it. The obvious recommendation from all this is that military commanders have to be sufficiently informed so that they can do their job or take action necessitated by events. And in this case it was just inexcusable. Part of it was understandable because we were trying to keep our hand concealed.

On the planning information, I've already recounted the briefing I got from Mr. Bissell. I got a general concept as it existed on the 2nd of November, and this concept was radically changed before the final execution, but I never had an opportunity to study the detailed plan nor the effect of successive changes. The needed knowledge would have been helpful to Clark and myself when we were told to assist in the rescue operation. This lack of information made intelligent planning for evacuation or for direct support, if either one of these had been ordered, almost impossible. So, obviously, the recommendation in this case was that the commanders involved have to be informed at least in general terms of the nature of any plans, in this case by CIA, for operations in his area. It is obvious that commanders have to be prepared to support operations or to assume directing responsibility if the nature of the operation changes from the original concept.

There was a general lack of up-to-date intelligence on Cuba and by the middle of 1960 the intelligence on Cuba had been reduced to conjecture and extrapolation, except for political intelligence. I had no knowledge of the disposition of the equipment and the state of training of Castro's forces. I told you about the essential elements of information that I requested and never got a satisfactory reply to. Of course, we got a great deal of essential elements of information as a result of a post mortem, but this was too late to do any good. So, in this case, I recommended that the Joint Chiefs of Staff and CIA get together to review my requirements and satisfy them because I could see, among others, that we were going to be back in Cuba one of these days, as we were later on in the missile crisis.

Q: Do you know that they ever did get together?

Adm. D.: I doubt it very much. I never saw any results of it, if they did.

I pointed out in the course of my report that CinCLant needed to know and would continue to need to know the definition of his own responsibility and a great deal of information that was not then available to him.

Other problems were imposed by security restrictions. Granted that CIA operations needed protection and the utmost security during the planning stages, in any event. The result

Dennison #8 - 363

of it all was the number of people on my own staff and in the forces that were assigned to support the operation was minimal. It's dangerous to have a cell operating within your own staff, as I think I pointed out before. So the whole thing was a very dangerous set-up- as far as the command was concerned.

Q: Well, Sir, in the light of the various changes in date and direction and objective and all the rest, it must have made it extremely difficult for you, with this security business, not to confer with some of your staff members who weren't in on the thing?

Adm. D.: It did. It gave me a good many uneasy moments, I can assure you. Now, of course, the security restriction was carried much too far because from the moment I was directed to turn my forces back to the objective area the covert nature of our operation was completely negated. You can't conceal the presence of our own destroyers and aircraft from anybody.

Q: If they're sanitized!

Adm. D.: Well, any school kid would know the silhouette of a U. S. Navy fighter plane. At that time we ought to have gone back on our normal system of security, which would have obviated subsequent delays and so forth and transmission of orders and information. You can carry secrecy too far.

Now, on the matter of covert operation of military forces. We started out with an effort to conceal any U. S. military participation. I've already discussed the fact that this covert business should have gone out of the window when we got ordered back into the objective area. The use of unmarked airplanes and boats, I think, is something we never should do again.

For example, boat crews should be dressed in dungarees so that they will not be easily identified on the beach. This is stupid. I mean, you can't conceal the identity of aircraft and boats and I think that if you have pilots and boat crews who are not wearing the proper uniform or any identifiable uniform, that they're subject to undue peril because they've lost their military status and probably would be treated, at best, as spies.

Q: Actually, their rights are being violated, aren't they?

Adm. D.: Yes, of course, they are. And my orders expressed my views - orders to my forces - to ignore further attempts at concealment and said if we must fight to protect our forces in accomplishing a mission we will do so with our banner flying. Here we are operating inside of the enemy from our own destroyers and here we are at the same time saying, "Castro's forces aren't going to identify them as U. S. forces or the aircraft pilots or landing craft crews - they won't be in proper uniform nor will there be any identification of these aircraft and boats." The time had gone for any concealment, for heaven's sake. This was a stupid directive.

Q: A contradiction!

Adm. D.: Now take the rules of engagement. This is a pretty touchy thing, too. I've already recounted what I considered to be undue restrictions placed on me. The one, for example, about not attacking Cuban aircraft that were attacking the expeditionary force, and one of my orders was that my planes couldn't fire on the Cuban aircraft unless they had their bomb bay doors open and were actually making a firing run!

Q: Might be a little late!

Adm. D.: I would think it would be considerably late. My idea would be to intercept them well out and get them out of the area. If they wouldn't go, shoot them down. I mean there is such a thing as a doctrine of self-defense, too. When do you feel justified in shooting somebody who's threatening you? You don't wait till you see his fingers squeeze the trigger, I don't think.

Q: To somebody just listening, some of these directives sound like civilian orders, rather than military, I mean with the civilian's lack of understanding of the military situation?

Adm. D.: I think what I said about this order coming from 1600 Pennsylvania Avenue bears out what you just said. I'm sure that a lot of these came from the White House or from CIA, with very little understanding of what the situation required.

Q: Why then come with the signature or over the signature of the Chairman of the Joint Chiefs?

Adm. D.: That was one of the humorous things. To get an order interpreted by the guy who wrote it! They sent it anyway and said all they were trying to do was help me out, and I said, Thanks very much, but I wasn't going to carry it out the way I was told to, anyhow.

Of course, on this control and direction of the operation, I've commented enough on that, I think, but I'd just like to add that the plan was conceived, prepared, and executed by the CIA, and the Joint Chiefs of Staff were directed to support the execution. They, in turn, delegated the support to me as CinCLant Up to the point where my original support mission had been carried out exactly according to the plan, everything went all right, went smoothly. But from then on, the direction and control of the operation left a hell of a lot to be desired, and this resulted because of my lack of intelligence and detailed information on the over-all plan, by violation of basic military principles.

In effect, the CIA was trying to control in detail unplanned paramilitary operations being conducted 1500 miles away through the Joint Chiefs and me, the unified commander. This isn't the way you do it. The commander on the scene ought to be given a mission from a plan containing policy guidance and, if necessary, his supporting operation order may require approval by the authority directing the operation. That's normal. But beyond this, orders to the on-the-scene military commander should be limited to major directives regarding policy and objectives. This is all ABC stuff, really.

Q: To a military man?

Adm. D.: Yes, to a military man. The planning organization was wrong and I'm not so sure that what I have to say about that would be of any lasting interest. I've already commented on this creation of cells and the danger in that. It could have been organized in a much more efficient way without compromising any security.

Then again, I mentioned that because I didn't have the knowledge I should have I made certain decisions on my own, such as putting that amphibious squadron and battalion landing team down there and ordering certain forces into the area, getting fighter aircraft in an ASW carrier. This I believed to be within the competence of any responsible commander. You just don't do ABC because you're told to do ABC. You do D, E, and F, if you think it's necessary, and if they don't like it

Dennison #8 -368

they can fire you.

Well, the result of all this was that the President was much upset about how this operation was going, or had gone. He called Maxwell Taylor, who was in Mexico - I forget in what capacity.

Q: He was President of Mex Power and Light.

Adm. D.: I think he wished he'd stayed there! I'd known Taylor for a long, long time and respected him. Taylor was to be the president or chairman of a committee to investigate the Bumpy Road thing, and I was called, among others. The members of the committee were rather strange. Robert Kennedy, the Attorney General; Dulles, the Director of CIA; and Arleigh Burke. I appeared with a complete record of dispatches and in writing much of what I have just put on this tape.

I didn't pull any punches with them. I knew all these men, except Kennedy, and had worked with them. I thought this was such a horrible disaster and fiasco, really, that we ought to get everything out of it we could so it would never happen again. I was asked to speak and I spoke at some length, provided all the documentation that was needed, and when I got through I asked if anybody had any questions. Nobody said a damned word. They'd had it. So I asked Taylor if I could be excused and he said, sure, thanks a lot, and everybody got up and shook hands and thanked me. Then he asked if he could have this documentation and I said, sure, but it's my personal record and I'd like to have it back. He said, I'll return it to you. He is a man of his word, and he did.

I was told that the board or committee, or whatever it was called, didn't submit a written report to the President. They were asked not to get any of this stuff in writing. All of them did have some documentation, and one day they were asked to come to the White House and bring all the written material they had with them. When they got to the White House, they were met by the Attorney General, Robert Kennedy, and asked to come in the Cabinet Room and put all their papers on the table and then he excused them. They all left, leaving the documents they had brought with them on the table.

Why he overlooked inviting me to that tea party I don't know. Either he thought that Taylor had my papers or he overlooked it. But so far as I know, nobody has anything - I hope somebody, like Lemnitzer, has some diaries or something, because there's too much of value in this whole story to just have it disappear. But, so far as I know, the record that I have is the only one extant.

I think that concludes the tragic story of Bumpy Road. As I mentioned earlier, it should have been called Quagmire.

Q: Quagmire, yes. Thank you, Sir.

Interview No. 9 with Admiral Robert L. Dennison, U. S. Navy (Retire

Place: His office in the Davis Building, Washington, .DC.

Date: Tuesday afternoon, 10 July 1973

Subject: Biography

By: John T. Mason, Jr.

Q? Admiral, it's good to see you today as usual. Now we resume your story in the year 1961. In January of that year a very interesting naval event occurred. Some rebels seized a Portugese passenger vessel in the Caribbean, and the Portuguese government requested that the United States and other nations be interested in this and try to apprehend the vessel. Would you tell me that story, Sir?

Adm. D.: Yes, I'd be glad to. The Santa Maria that you mentioned is a Portugese cruise ship and displaces about 20,000 tons. It was the property of the Portuguese government. The Santa Maria incident is of considerable interest from three different standpoints. One, a capsule study of search operations, a naval matter. Second, a study in international relations, notably between the United States and Portugal. And lastly, it brought into focus the definition of "piracy" under international law.

This is a bit of background. The ship departed Curacao

about the 22nd of January headed for Port Everglades in Florida, and was last sighted at 9 a.m. on the 23rd between St. Lucia and Martinique. The crew was comprised mostly of Portuguese, 361. There were 13 Spanish crew members and one stow-away. The ship also carried 612 passengers, of whom 36 were American nationals.

On the 23rd the "Senior Naval Officer," West Indies, a Britisher, sent me a dispatch saying that the Santa Maria had been taken over by a group of about 20 armed men and that the destination was unknown, and also the reason for the takeover was not clear at that time, or exactly who had done it. In any event, I was asked through the Chief of Naval Operations to see if we could find the Santa Maria and discover exactly what the situation was with regard to the safety of the people on board and so on.

Well, it had been so long since the ship had sailed. The original destination was presumably Port Everglades. My resources were not unlimited, and it would seem reasonable to assume that she might be headed for Cuba, which is roughly through the same sea lanes as Port Everglades. So the first thing we did was to search those lanes by air to rule out that particular course. That would have been the nearest possible destination and the logical thing to do was to eliminate that first.

On the 24th I directed Commander, Caribbean Sea Frontier, who was Rear Admiral AlanSmith, Jr., to use maximum effort in a search for the Santa Maria. Commander, South Atlantic Force, who I believe at that time was in Trinidad, was alerted for possible participation. Smith in turn requested the admiral of the Netherlands Antilles to assist in the search.

The British government considered the Santa Maria incident to be an act of piracy.

Q: This was different from our attitude, was it?

Adm. D.: No, we took the same position initially. It was thought that the ship had been illegally seized for reasons unknown, and our main concern, whether or not it was an act of piracy, was that 36 American nationals were in jeopardy. It seemed under the law of humanity, if not international law, that the thing to do would be to try to protect these passengers.

Air searches were instituted from Puerto Rico and Commander, Caribbean Sea Frontier, also put three small ships to sea to assist in the search.

We got some background information from the American Embassy in Lisbon, advising that the Portuguese government had requested "friendly assistance" in capturing the bandit identified as Enrique Galvao, who was a Portuguese involved in a revolutionary movement and who led the operation to seize the Santa Maria.

Q: He's often referred to as Admiral Galvao. Was he actually an admiral in the Portuguese Navy?

Adm. D.: I think not, but my memory could be faulty. I think the man that you may be referring to is his senior who was a noted revolutionary figure. I think Galvao was the man on the spot. I forget the name of this other fellow.

Q: General Delgado?

Adm. D.: Yes, that's the man.

Q: He was a military man.

Adm. D.: Yes, that's right.

In any event, we didn't sight the Santa Maria on the 24th, but then after that time we commenced to be flooded with requests for the news media to accompany the ships and aircraft involved in the search operation. This pressure built up as time went on.

The Santa Maria was observing radio silence and since we didn't know where she was headed, and there was an immense amount of ocean area and, since time had elapsed, it made the search extremely difficult with nothing more than we already had to go on, which was very little. So I started calling on the Santa Maria's frequency with messages for Captain Galvao. These were disregarded at first, but finally he opened up to reply, and the gist of what I had to say to him was that we were interested in the safety of our American nationals and suggested that he was in a hopeless position, that we would find him, so to avoid all this unpleasantness how about going in to some northern South

American port.

Well, this developed into a dialogue. He discussed the feasibility of one of the ports I suggested, and so on, but the purpose of this exercise was to bring into use our radio direction-finders. So when he did open up, we immediately zeroed in on him and after a few readings, why, we were able to pretty well determine what his course was.

Q: He was a little naive about that, was he?

Adm. D.: I think so. I don't know why it didn't occur to him. He went into radio silence in the first place.

In any event, it developed that he was headed for Angola, that's where his course would have taken him. He also told me that if we made any move to interfere with his ship that he would sink it. This was one of the things we didn't want to have happen, obviously. So, while all this dialogue was going on and as time commenced to run, his plight got worse and worse. We did pick him up by air on the 25th, and a Danish merchantman made a sighting about the same time.

Then again we got messages from everybody that you could think of, mostly from people trying to get aboard a search aircraft or something. Then Washington came up with some guidance, mostly negative, but they didn't classify this incident as "piracy."

Q: This was the State Department coming into the picture?

Dennison #9 - 375

Adm. D.: I'm not sure where they got it. I got it through the Chief of Naval Operations.

Then, of course, Commander-in-Chief Naval Forces, Europe, was brought into the picture with a request for air surveillance from the Cape Verde Islands. We continued to shadow him. I had a detachment of destroyers engaged in an exercise off the West Coast of Africa. I ordered them to head west to block the Santa Maria's track toward Angola. I had suggested that Galvao should go to Belem, so I ordered ships to proceed toward Belem to intercept him, in case he did. And we also guaranteed that we would take the passengers off so he didn't have to go into port. One of our main difficulties, of course, was the flood of air traffic, everybody wanting to get in the act. It made handling even such a minor operation quite difficult.

Q: You mean the international aspects of the episode?

Adm. D.: Well, many of the messages came from us, but I did get one - not one but I had an exchange of dispatches with the chief of staff of the Portuguese General Staff, who was a friend of mine, General Beleza Ferraz. He didn't understand what I was up to. The Portuguese were very much concerned, of course, with the people aboard that ship, and also the ship itself represented quite a considerable asset. I don't know exactly what they thought I was up to, but I explained to them what my scheme was and at the end of all of it, why, the Portuguese were satisfied completely that the ship was undamaged. Galvao was given asylum by Brazil. Smith was there when the ship went into port and the passengers all got off all right, nobody was hurt, although one crew member had been killed by Galvao's group.

Q: So it didn't really prove anything from the point of view of the Portuguese revolutionaries, did it?

Adm. D.: No, it didn't. I mean it was an unsuccessful effort. It wasn't a disaster, thank God, but the end of it, to get back to General Ferraz, he said, "I very much appreciate your thoughtfulness in letting me know the reasons which presided over your decisions in the solution of the Santa Maria incident. Please accept my warmest thanks and personal regards for all you have done and accomplished."

So that was it. It didn't prove anything one way or another, but I would like to mention briefly the international law ramifications involved in this.

The definition of "piracy" is contained in the Geneva Convention, and I believe at that time - maybe even now - we were a signatory to it, although it never received enough signatories to become binding. But the United States went along with it and the part of that convention that dealt with piracy was, in fact, drafted by the United States. I believe Arthur Dean was the one who did it. The key to piracy was whether, a ship was seized for conversion. In other words, to sell or to use in trade or profit to whoever seized it. This was claimed by Galvao to be a political act, and indeed it was. Well, that is not covered by the definition of "piracy."

Q: It was mere defiance of the established government?

Adm. D.: Yes, and it couldn't be shown that he was going to or intended to use it for commercial purposes or to sell it. So I suppose, technically, it wasn't the definition contained in the convention, but I don't know that it wasn't piracy.

I happened to be in Washington not long after this incident and spent the night at the Metropolitan Club. The next morning when I had breakfast who should I run into in the dining room but my friend Arthur Dean. So I said:

"I want to retain you as my counsel, without fee, of course, but I understand you drafted this provision of the Geneva Convention concerning piracy, and you're familiar, of course - a lot of people were at this time - with the Santa Maria incident. Was it piracy?"

He said: "I'll be damned if I know." So I said, "Well, how do we ever find out?"

And he said: "Well, if you'd taken that ship into an admiralty court, say at San Juan, that would have been one way to find out. Had you done that, it's conceivable that you might have been sued by somebody, the Portuguese government or I don't know who. It would really hinge on what the court decision would have been, but, of course, that's moot because it never happened."

So I guess we'll never know whether this was truly piracy or whether it wasn't!

Q: The British were very quick to label it as such.

Adm. D.: I think too quick because apparently they didn't read their book. We were more cautious. I think we proceeded at first under the assumption that it was bad and that people were in danger. So we'd put on our white hats and go and save our people, which certainly was the thing to do.

Of course, what a court would have done is strictly academic. We weren't trying to punish anybody. We were just trying to save lives and, if possible, save the ship for the Portuguese government.

Q: You mentioned at one point, Sir, that the media and photographers and so forth were anxious to get aboard the planes and ships. Did this impede your efforts?

Adm. D.: No, it didn't impede them, except it was just a nuisance to try to handle this sort of thing in the kind of an operation we were engaged in. In other words, picking up these people and getting them aboard aircraft and disembarking them and briefing them and all that. And Department of Defense guidance was that we shouldn't put newsmen aboard some of these ships. They couldn't have seen anything anyhow, and the incident was certainly well enough covered when the ship got in and the passengers got off, and everybody was happy.

But this matter of the press, I'll have more to say about that when we get into the Cuban missile crisis.

Q: One other area that you mentioned, the search orperations, the difficulty of the search operations; I recall Admiral Burke when he was talking about this incident saying that we had so little experience in searching with naval vessels in recent years that maybe our techniques got a little bit rusty.

Adm. D.: Well, they weren't rusty. I disagree completely with Burke. In order to conduct a search with minimal facilities, such as I had, you should have an idea of the point of departure, the time of departure, the course, and the speed. We had a large number of unknowns, we were looking at a big sector, and the ship on a course between zero and 90°, say, or zero and 45°, proceeding at an unknown speed, it's a problem over a vast ocean area. And there was a case where the ship was not continuing on a course to Port Everglades or to Cuba, which seemed to me to be the most likely place. So as the hours went on the possibility is expanded because areas where she could have gone based on various speeds and courses were quite large. And my resources were not unlimited, believe me. This was a squadron of planes and two destroyers.

Hell, we knew all about the techniques, but this was a problem where we had a large number of possible solutions which you had to rule out. Of course, once we got him to come up on the air and pinpoint, or nearly so, his location it wasn't any problem at all.

Q: That was a stroke of genius. How did you persuade him to desist from heading for Angola and go to Brazil instead?

Adm. D.: Well, in the first place, he knew that he was completely boxed in and whether we stopped the ship or whether we didn't the jig was up. In other words, where could he go? The Portuguese Navy was alerted by me and the Portuguese government and I requested that they send ships out to meet the Santa Maria. Had the Portuguese forces made contact we would have had no control over their actions. The Portuguese could have sunk the ship or done anything they wanted to with it. We would have just said, well, here he is.

So here he had ships all around him, ships meeting him, including Portuguese ships, and he was in real trouble. In addition to that, he was running short of certain things. We found out later that the passengers were very helpful because they turned on all the fresh-water taps in their bathrooms, so he was running low on fresh water. I suppose he had plenty of provisions because it was a cruise ship. I don't know whether they were planning on replenishing in Port Everglades or not, but his resources were dwindling.

For all these reasons he probably decided that the better part of valor was to put in to Brazil and depend upon what he finally got, and that was asylum. However, what eventually happened I don't know. I've forgotten whether Brazil honored that completely and just what happened to the crew later on I don't know.

Q: Well, it was an extremely interesting event. Admiral, during this period, I can't pinpoint the first event precisely but we began to have the astronauts flying and coming down in the ocean, the search parties for them, the rescue parties. Did this involve your command?

Adm. D.: Indeed it did, and this was a real drain on my naval forces because it involved taking time out from normal training operations, it involved large expenditures for fuel, and if you can put a price tag on lost time we did very, very little training when these ships were deployed along the track. Thousands and thousands of miles of steaming involved. It was a very expensive procedure in terms of lost training time and in terms of actual expenditure for the naval forces. It wasn't that we didn't want to do it. What we did was not done reluctantly, believe me, but when you string ships all the way across the

Dennison #9 - 382

Atlantic in case of a mishap, that takes a lot of ships and a lot of steaming and a lot of time.

Q: This involved you also actively with the Air Force, did it not?

Adm. D.: Not to any great extent. I mean there was no interference or overlap there. Of course, the Air Force could do a lot of the aerial surveillance for whatever that would be worth. Recovery operations, of course, shifted to the Pacific and everybody knows what they involved because if you stop to think what it must mean now in terms of again time and money, not that it's not money well spent but it is subtracted from the Navy budget, which is small enough.

Thank God we never had to call any of these forces into action. We didn't have any mishaps and the capsule didn't land in the middle of the Atlantic.

Q: In July of 1961 President Kennedy addressed the nation with a call to arms because the Berlin situation was heating up again and the Navy got involved in this because there was a certain amount of mobilization and I think elements from the Reserve Fleet were brought out. Do you recall that?

Adm. D.: This is a very interesting point. I'm glad you mentioned it because I think it was quite significant and it had a bearing on some of the things that happened in my command later.

In this Berlin crisis we did call up reserves, unlike the missile crisis where we didn't, the only reserves called up were Air Force pilots for troop transport aircraft. But in the Berlin crisis we did. What I'm about to tell you is just one incident, but it's illustrative of what the situation is when you call up reserves.

One of these reserve destroyers was in port at Norfolk. I had my chief of staff get hold of the captain to tell him that I wanted to be invited down to have lunch with him. He couldn't figure out what this was all about and, of course, it petrified the ship. But I, of course, was invited and as I remember I may have taken one officer with me but that's all. I inspected the ship and chatted with the crew, and I had some fine people there. We had lunch in the wardroom and after lunch we sat around the table talking. By that time they'd stopped being afraid, and I said:

"Tell me what you fellows do in civil life." I believe there was only one regular officer in the ship. I think he was an engineer officer. And the same thing through the crew, there were practically no regular Navy people.

Q: The skipper, was he not regular?

Adm. D.: I don't think so. I think it was the engineer who was. He may have been but I don't believe so. In any event, this was to all intents and purposes a Reserve-manned ship. Well, these young men were so enthusiastic and looked at it as a great adventure. One of them, I remember, had gone into business for himself. He'd had an engineering education. I think he'd started a consulting firm or something, and he had a very young family, and he said:

"Well, Admiral, I love the Navy. This is just wonderful. But I simply cannot afford to be called up again because my business is at a standstill. I don't have any big staff. I don't have any partners. I'm just getting started and I've got to support my wife and children. So, much as I love the Navy, it's just economically infeasible for me to take this again."

Then in the case of another officer there was a slightly different situation. He had gone when he graduated from some college to some large company, and he was assured of getting his job back and all that, but he pointed out something that you're probably well aware of. In spite of these guarantees, the guy who was there while he was gone was the fellow who was probably going to get the first nod for a promotion.

Q: Time marches on, doesn't it!

Adm. D.: Yes. All I'm really saying is that this calling up the Reserves is liable to be a one-shot deal because they can take it only every so often. In time of a really vital emergency, as I'm sure the President felt the Berlin crisis was, well, then it has to be done.

Dennison #9 - 385

Q: Great dislocation.

Adm. D.: It certainly is, and it isn't something - an asset, let's say - that the Navy can depend on in times of emergency. In the Cuban missile crisis, as I mentioned, I don't know, but I feel reasonably sure that one of the reasons we didn't call up the Reserves was because of this experience with the Berlin crisis. Neither did the Army. The Air Force had to because we were talking about an airlift for at least two paratroop divisions - I think it was the 82nd and 101st Airborne - and it takes a lot of airplanes if you're talking about a simultaneous lift. The Air Force quite properly did not have that number of regulars who were aircraft pilots that would be required for any such gigantic operation as that. So that was different.

Q: The reserves then are a bank that you can draw on, but very infrequently.

Adm. D.: Very infrequently, that's quite right.

Q: Was there any noticeable dropoff in the number of Reserves after they were returned to Reserve status?

Adm. D.: I really don't know because I didn't have the facilities at my finger tips to delve into that too deeply. I was really more interested at the moment in the morale of the Reserves that were serving, and believe me I was reassured on that. They were really a gung-ho group of people. This was just one sampling, and I made other, more casual ones. But I really wanted to dig into this one ship because it was typical of all our ships.

Q: There were, what, thirty or forty destroyers brought back into active service?

Adm. D.: Quite a few.

Q: What about the ships themselves? What was their status, their physical condition? How long had they been in mothballs?

Adm. D.: The condition generally wasn't too good. That's one problem about bringing in ships from reserve. The Navy was really eating its seed corn in this reserve program because money was supposed to be provided to keep these Reserve Fleet ships in step with the active fleet as far as their equipment was concerned, fire control, communications, but it wasn't. So as time went on these ships became incompatible for operations with their counterparts in the active fleet.

Q: Ordnance becomes obsolete?

Adm. D.: Yes, not only that but in some ships where communications were so vitally needed - command communications - the older equipment was not compatible with the new equipment. Electronics I think is where this hurts most, anything that has to do with electronics.

Well, you may remember that when they brought the New Jersey back in for gun support in Vietnam, what a terrific amount of money had to be spent on that ship. It wasn't because its paint was peeling and it had to be chipped and repainted and that sort of thing. It was a question of rehabilitating and bringing up to date the equipment.

Q: Off tape, Admiral, I mentioned the fact that Admiral Anderson succeeded Admiral Burke on the 1st of August 1961 as Chief of Naval Operations, and that brought forth from you an account which I thought was very interesting - the several approaches which were made to you, first, to become Chief of Naval Operations after Admiral Burke, and then the other approaches which followed. Do you want to tell me, Sir, about them on tape?

Adm. D.: Yes, if you're interested in them. There were three different occasions when I turned down positions that were offered to me when I was Commander-in-Chief at Norfolk.

The first was after President Kennedy's election when President Truman was coming to Washington. Of course, as you well know, I was his aide for five years -

Q: More than aide! Personal friend, I think.

Adm. D.: Well, I thought I was. He had a suite in the Mayflower and I was invited up there one afternoon, late. I came in and he had several friends there talking, and I sat and had a drink with them. Then he got up and said he'd like to talk to me in the bedroom. So I went in the bedroom and he shut the door, and he sat on one bed and I sat on the bed across from him, facing each other, and he said:

"Bob, Kennedy owes me something and I would like to ask him if he would like to consider appointing you as Chief of Naval Operations." I can remember what I said. I said:

"Please, Mr. Presidnet, don't even mention my name to President Kennedy or anybody else about that because I don't want the job."

He said, "Why not?" and I said:

"Well, I think I'm doing more for my country and the Navy doing what I am doing than being up here in this political environment of Washington. I'm a commander. I command forces, which the Chief of Naval Operations doesn't, and this is the kind of thing I've been training myself for and I think have been reasonably successful at. I simply don't want to leave the jobs that I've got."

So he accepted that and I think he understood it. He said he did at the time, and when he got back to Independence he wrote me a beautiful letter saying that he had thought more and more about our conversation and he thought that I was absolutely right and he approved of it.

Dennison #9 - 389

The next thing was Secretary John Connolly called me from Washington, saying he'd like to talk to me. I offered to come up any time it was convenient for him and he said he'd rather come down.

Q: This must have been right after the new administration came in?

Adm. D.: Yes, it had to be because Connolly was then Secretary of the Navy and MacNamara was Secretary of Defense.

I met him at the field and brought him back to Missouri House for lunch and a talk and so on. We were in the library alone when he opened by saying that he wanted me to become CNO. Again I demurred and gave him the same reasons I'd given the President - that I thought I was reasonably successful in my job and that this was my profession, as I saw it, not to get mixed up with budgets and things like that. I'd let somebody else do that. I don't look on myself as being a sort of father confessor type, the great white father for all the Navy. In any event, Connolly couldn't believe it. He spent the whole day debating it, but there wasn't anything to debate really.

Q: Did you call him Conny?

Adm. D.: I called him Mr. Secretary! Well, he finally said he didn't agree with me but he would certainly respect my views. And that was the end of that.

Dennison #9 - 390

The third time was after the Cuban missile crisis, when I was CinCLant, SACLant, and CinCLandFlt. General Max Taylor was, as I recall it, Chairman of the Joint Chiefs. He called and invited Mildred and me to come up to dinner at his quarters at Fort Meyer. When we got there I found that the dinner was for the Secretary of Defense, the Secretary of the Army, and several former Secretaries, a couple of whom were friends of mine, but I didn't think that Taylor knew that, in advance anyhow. So I couldn't figure out how it happened that I was there, until after dinner when Secretary MacNamara said he'd like to talk to me and he brought up the matter of my staying on in the job that I then held, and that I would be held on beyond normal retirement, I didn't have to worry about that.

I told him that I didn't want the job, didn't want to continue in these jobs, for several reasons. One was that I had opposed the Navy holding Admiral Stump on as CinCPac because I didn't think that was the best thing for the Navy, much as I admired Admiral Stump's ability, because it implied that we didn't have anybody as good as Admiral Stump or, in this case, anybody as good as I, and I don't believe either one. Our whole system is based on training people for successively higher levels of command. Holding one officer on not only gives the wrong implication that this man is the only one who can do the job, but since there are so few four-star admirals, holding one on blocks promotion all the way down the line to more junior command positions.

The Secretary pointed out that we were in tense times, and I said, "Well, we're always going to be in tense times. It may get worse, but right now we've settled the Cuban missile crisis, nothing abnormal seems to be on the horizon, as far as the Navy's concerned. I'll tell you this though, if anybody's making noises against us up to midnight of the day before I retire, you won't have to worry about my staying on. I'll simply tear up my orders. But under the present circumstances and for the reasons I've mentioned to you, I don't wish to be held on."

I think he understood it because he said he was disappointed and he'd come to believe that there wasn't any substitute for experience and for judgment based on experience, which sounded so strange coming from Secretary MacNamara!

Q: He'd been in office a few months, maybe he'd learned something there!

Adm. D.: But he said:

"You know, this is the second time you've turned me down," and I couldn't understand that and I told him that I didn't remember having any other conversation with him on this particular point. He said:

"Who do you think sent John Connolly down?"

I said, "It never occurred to me. I thought it was John Connolly who came down on his own."

He said, "No, he didn't. I sent him down."

"Thank you very much," I said, "but I didn't know that."

Then we got into a very brief discussion about who I thought could relieve me and I suggested Admiral Page Smith who did take over and didn't get along with MacNamara at all. That was a disaster.

One further incident that doesn't bear exactly on this but I thought it rather amusing. After I did retire and was living briefly down at Virginia Beach, I got a call from MacNamara one morning, saying that he wanted my advice and he only intended to call me and Admiral Burke to ask this particular question. He said:

"The question is this. Supposing that Admiral Anderson isn't going to continue on as CNO, who do you think I should appoint? Admiral Sharp or Admiral Dave McDonald?" And I said:

"Well, I don't think you've asked me the right question. Why didn't you ask me who I thought ought to relieve George Anderson? The answer to that is pretty simple. I think it ought to be Claude Ricketts."

Then he said, "I have other plans for Ricketts, but let's get back to the question I asked you. Between the two, which would you think I should get?"

I said, "Well, I know both of them. I think that Sharp is a great deal more intelligent than McDonald, perhaps with a little more background in the kind of things he would need in this job. On the other hand, I think Dave McDonald has a much more attractive personality and probably would have greater appeal to people in the Navy and also to people on the Hill.

So I think, all things considered, maybe McDonald, except that I think you should remember one thing about McDonald. He's an aviator."

And he said, "What do you mean by that?"

I said, "I'm not prejudiced against aviators, but it does seem to me, it has for years, that it's not good for the Navy to set up two different categories of naval officers, aviators non-aviators. It's bad. I've objected to it all through the years. It's just a matter of principle with me, but so long as McDonald doesn't go over backward or doesn't do anything to accentuate the difference between these two categories, he'll get along just fine."

Then he said, "Thanks very much." I hung up the phone and the minute after - not the minute after, I thought for a little while about this and called Burke and he said, "I've just had a talk with Secretary MacNamara." I said, "How long ago?" and he told me about five minutes.

So I said: "Thank God, because MacNamara must have realized that I didn't have time to call you before he called, because I know what the conversation was about. It was about who was going to relieve George Anderson, and I told the Secretary that he had asked me the wrong question. I thought he ought to appoint Claude Ricketts."

Arleigh said, "That's exactly what I told him!"

So that was my participation, whatever it was worth for another fellow being CNO.

Dennison #10 -394-

Interview No. 10 with Admiral Robert Lee Dennison, U.S. Navy
(Retired)

Place: His office in the Davis Building, Washington, D.C.

Date: Tuesday afternoon, 17 July 1973

Subject: Biography

By: John T. Mason, Jr.

Q: Admiral, we come today to one of the truly significant events in American history, almost a watershed, and you played such a major part in it - such a major role - that your story will be of immense value to future historians. I refer, of course, to the Cuban missile crisis.

I think you want to begin the account by talking about the background, the buildup, to this crisis which came to a head in October 1962.

Adm. D.: Well, Mr. Mason, I'd like to start with just a few items of introduction to look into the situation that led to the crisis in Cuba - or rather, the situation in Cuba that led into the crisis.

You will recall, of course, that on the evening of October 22nd 1962 President Kennedy spoke to the nation on radio and television and described the ominous buildup of Russian missiles in Cuba, and announced the establishment of a naval quarantine to be effective at nine o'clock on the 24th of October. The purpose of this quarantine was to prevent the shipment of additional offensive armaments into Cuba. The President also made it clear that he intended to ensure the removal of Soviet missiles from Cuba and, if necessary, the United Staes was prepared to take additional action.

Q: And as you'll make clear that was no idle threat!

Adm. D.: No. Obviously it wasn't because we were prepared to take various courses of action. It came out later as we suspected it at the time the purpose of the deployment of these powerful weapons into Cuba was to change the strategic balance of atomic weapons. In other words, an MRBM or an IRBM in Cuba for the purpose of attacking North and South America was the equivalent of a very long-range missile based in Soviet Russia. So putting lesser-range into Cuba, nearer to us, presented a change in the whole strategic balance of atomic power. The ostensible purpose, according to Dobrynin, was to put atomic weapons in Cuba to defend Cuba against an invasion by the United States.

Before the crisis invasion was farthest from our minds. In other words, there were then no plans to invade Cuba. Everybody familiar with our own history would know that would be farthest from our intention.

Q: But it does imply, does it not, that they misread the Bay of Pigs episode and misunderstood it?

Adm. D.: It quite possibly does, but I think everybody would believe now that that was a complete phony, that the real reason was the one I first mentioned, and that is to change the balance of strategic atomic weapons. And that we couldn't take, and that' why we took drastic actions that I'm about to describe.

Q: There's one element about that position which intrigues me, however. The obvious speed-up that the Russians employed in installing these missile sites. It seemed to be a very hasty operation on their part.

Adm. D.: I think there's a perfectly natural explanation for that. They wanted to face us as rapidly as possible with a fait accompli. Had the buildup been gradual and easy, somewhere along the line we would have commenced to wonder what it was all about and probably would have done something about it. We undoubtedly would. But the chance for the Soviets having this a successful implant of weapons was enhanced by doing it rapidly, as rapidly as they could, so that all these things would be in place. They were quite brazen about it. Sure, there was a lot of subterfuge and trying to conceal things, but our intelligence was good enough so that we knew exactly what was going on and how fast, where, who. The Soviet forces, which I will talk about later, mostly engineering types and so on, put up encampments and in the center of the area they would place a large rock garden, purely decorative, and invariably it was laid out in the form of the unit's military insignia. So with a little low-level reconnaissance, or even high-level, we could read the insignia and determine it was the 185th Engineering Battalion or whatever it might be. We could look in our little catalogue and find out what kind of troops were in that kind of a battalion and what the equipment and what the purpose of it was.

Q: It certainly wasn't their intention to reveal it that readily, was it?

Adm. D.: I don't think so. That would be kind of stupid. But they did. So it wasn't entirely one of these 'do everything at night and hide in the daytime' sort of operations.

But to get back to this brief lead-in.

The President when he made his announcement on the 22nd of October pointed out that this buildup was, in fact, a direct confrontation between the security of the United States and a challenge posed by the Soviet Union. What he was trying to point out, I'm sure, was that the enemy was not Cuba. Castro was just a tool. The enemy all through this operation was Soviet Russia, and he dramatized this fact by asserting that any missile fired from Cuba against a country of the western hemisphere would be considered a direct attack by the Soviet Union.

As we go through this, it's well to bear in mind that the President and we in the military, certainly, and those in the State Department and of course, officials throughout the government didn't lose sight of that fact either. But this was the first warning that the public had had, or the first alarm that was sounded, that there was a serious threat against our own country.

To show you how fast things moved, at the beginning of that month the Atlantic Command was in normal peacetime status. There had been no alert, although we were keeping in very close touch through intelligence with what was going on in Cuba. I recall meeting with McCone in Panama, who was there together with some of his staff, to talk about the scarcity of intelligence on what was going on in Cuba. The C.I.A. was making U-2 flights I think only once every two weeks, which was bad enough, but if cloud cover prevented good pictures on one particular day, then they'd wait for another week or two - I forget whether it was a one-week interval or two weeks - before repeating the sortie Well, this wasn't any good. We didn't know nearly enough about the details of what was going on.

We didn't have very much intelligence coming from on-the-ground or on-site sources. Sure, we had plenty of rumors, but to confirm these was something else again. McCone was very much impressed. He'd just taken over, as I remember, not long before from Allen Dulles. This was a very hush-hush meeting. That's why we met in Panama. So intelligence-gathering activity improved

As time went on, however, the task of high-level aerial reconnaissance was turned over to the Strategic Air Command. They were the ones who did it.

Q: It had been in the hands of the CIA?

Adm. D.: Yes.

Q: And they gave it up reluctantly, I understand.

Adm. D.: I imagine they did. I dont' know just exactly what happened when they were told to cease and desist, but I would certainly expect they would demur. We did have one U-2 plane shot down, as you remember.

In any event, about three weeks before the President's announcement we were just going along pretty much with business as usual, except for planning and taking certain precautionary measures. For example, the Atlantic Command was activated, but not the Army and Air Force components of it.

Perhaps I'd better just stop here and describe what this unified command structure is.

Q: Yes, I think it would be a good thing to put it in here.

Adm. D.: The unified command system was set up as a result of the National Security Act, as amended, and what it did in the way of setting up command was to establish what were called "unified commands." For example, Commander-in-Chief, Atlantic Commander-in-Chief, Pacific, Commander-in-Chief, Europe, and each one of these commands comprised three components: Army Navy, and Air Force. The commander of the unified command, a four star officer, then had under him three elements, as I just mentioned. Each one of these elements was also commanded by a four-star officer. They could be employed separately, the Navy alone or the Army alone, or in any combination of the three. What happened in the Cuban missile crisis, as will come out later in our talk, was that the active element was naval, which meant it was under Commander-in-Chief, Atlantic Fleet. In this particular unified command, I was the unified commander. I was also commander of the naval component, the United States Atlantic Fleet.

The commander of the Army component was General Powell, who was Commander-in-Chief of the Continental Command. His headquarters were in Fort Monroe, which was not far from my own headquarters. The Commander-in-Chief, U.S. Tactical Air Command, who was at Langley Field, also nearby.

So that's essentially what the structure was. Now, there are a number of ways that an operation can be commanded up to the top. You can go through a joint task force or a subordinate unified commander, any number of ways. In this case, I decided that an operation of this magnitude we would discard our original concept, which was to set up a joint task force, and that I would command the operation through my component commanders, including myself. Well, this was command at the top and the magnitude of the operation completely justified it, of course, because we had in this command almost 500,000 men. I'll get into more details later, but it was an operation of very, very large scope. But enough of that.

It might be interesting now to go back a little bit into what were the events that led up to this crisis. What was going on in Cuba. How did the soldiers get there.

Well, when Castro took over in 1959 he openly collaborated with the Communists and allowed them to operate politically. You may recall, too, that for some time he hadn't announced that he himself was a Communist, and many doubted in this country that he was, but that he was a benevolent person who had taken over from Batista. In any event, he was pretty harmless. But the relations of the 26th of July movement with the Communists were strained during the early period of his regime, especially in competition for control of the national labor organization.

Q: These were the regular Communists?

Adm. D.: Yes. And the soviets waited until February 1960 before responding to Castro's growing need for Soviet support. They were sort of watching and waiting to see what was going to happen. Then sugar-purchase agreements were made and followed by a considerable variety of trade and credit agreements. Then bloc technicians and arms began to flow into Cuba, and of course this was an indispensable element toward survival of Castro's regime, and of course aligned Cuba with the bloc.

In early 1962 old-line Communists attempted to gain ascendanc over Castro. Now, whether the move was directed by Moscow or not is not known, but it's evident the Soviets felt uneasy dealing with Castro. In April 1962 Castro won out and the Soviets wound up behind him, endorsing the purge of several leading Communists including Castro's formation of the new Cuban Revolutionary Party, a good step toward a true Marxist-Leninst policy.

In May of 1962 there was a Cuban-Soviet supplementary trade protocol signed, which of course signified Moscow's acceptance of Castro and their belief that he could retain leadership in Cuba. This agreement called for $750,000,000 in trade, an increase of over 40 percent over what had been effective in 1961. It became apparent of course that Castro intended to establish a Communist state in Cuba and was increasing his pro-Communist anti-U.S. actions, which, of course, explains our increased surveillance and intelligence efforts in the Cuban area.

Then Guantanamo came in the picture. Guantanamo is a U.S. naval base, leased from Cuba and as everyone knows, in southern Cuba, about six square miles along the coast, completely exposed. It would be indefensible against any sizeable attack, always in a position to be subjected to harassment. In June 1962 Castro declared a six-mile area around the base a militarized zone, and vacated farms and moved out people, put travel restrictions on the roads to and from the base. Then they commenced to blast us on the radio, claming that our use of the base was for espionage.

They cited 180 or so aircraft violations of Cuban territorial limits, including our ships at sea as well.

Q: Did we read that as a sincere effort on his part to push us out?

Adm. D.: It certainly indicated the desire to get us out. Whether he was going to push us out is another matter. I mean that would be a pretty serious step. It would certainly have brought vigorous reaction from overpowering force which would have showed up as the Cuban missile crisis developed. There never was any attack on the base. I was down there many times in those days myself, and a curious thing went on. A great many Cuban people in the area worked on the base, and they'd go and come daily. All of them were known to us and we didn't make any great effort to search. On the other hand, when they left the base to go back into Cuba the Cubans themselves were the ones who really put them through a wringer, made men and women disrobe to examine their clothing and their persons, and made life miserable for them.

We were getting water from Cuba. The source of our water was outside the base. We were buying electric power from Cuba. All these things were not interrupted, except, as I just mentioned, the flow of people was somewhat impeded. It was just needling. There were very, very few incidents of real friction. For example, I remember on one visit down there during these tense periods- during a tense period--my Marine aide, who was a major, with a couple of Marines went down to the gate that led into the Cuban area on the base - there's one gate. It was late in the evening and the Cuban guardhouse was just, oh, 100 feet beyond where ours was, so my aide and the one or two Marines who were with him walked out into this no man's land and started talking with the sentry, the Cuban sentry. The Cuban sentry provided the men there with coffee, and my Marine aide looked at one of the rifles that one of these sentries had and complimented him on the obvious care he'd given to his weapon. This flattered the sentry tremendously but he handed the gun to my Marine so he could take a good look at it, whereupon the other Cuban sentry became jealous and handed my Marine aide his gun. So here we'd captured -

Q: Disarmed him!

Adm. D.: There were incidents a little more serious than that, but there wasn't any real show of force on the part of the Cubans that presented a real military threat. But the potential was there.

They were trying to get us, of course, scared or unhappy or uneasy so that we would withdraw and wouldn't be able to use that base which was of tremendous value to us during this missile crisis, as it had been before during the Bay of Pigs operation.

Q: This is just a footnote, I suppose, but I noticed in the Abel book that Adlai Stevenson, who was at the United Nations, during the conference in the White House leading up to the President's public announcement urged that we evacuate and give away the Guantanamo base. He said it wasn't of any value to us.

Adm. D.: Well, of course, that exactly what the Cubans were trying to get across, and with all due respect to Mr. Stevenson if he'd examined the history of our use of that base and its tremendously important strategic location, he couldn't possibly have come to such a conclusion.

But we didn't get out and, as I go along here, you'll learn of the steps we took to re-enforce the base and to evacuate people and various other measures.

On 2 July 1962 Raul Castro arrived in Moscow for two weeks of talks with Khrushchev and other high-ranking Soviet officials. We deduced this, which turned out to be correct, as an attempt to secure additional military equipment, and the immediate result of this visit was a complex military buildup in Cuba that was not going to end until the sighting of offensive missiles in Cuba in October. So Raul Castro really sold the Soviets on moving fast and in strength to get in there.

Q: And it was more than just providing Cuba with arms. It was what you said earlier, changing the balance in strategic weapons.

Adm. D.: Yes, but Castro, I would assume, made the case that in order to protect these weapons and to prevent us or scare us into doing anything about them he needed a considerable amount of military strength, which he got in the form of weapons, some of them sophisticated and some not. I'll get into that later and show just what kind of military opposition they were able to present to us.

Then, of course, beginning about that time there was a great increase of Soviet ship movements to Cuba. I mean, for example, in July 30 Soviet merchantmen arrived in Cuban ports, which was a 50 percent increase over a month before. And then in August, 55 Soviet ships arrived in Cuba, four times more than had been there in August the year before. In September, 66 ships arrived. That gave a total of about 150 or 151 ships in three months, which equaled the total of Soviet ship arrivals for the first six months of that year. Obviously there was a buildup going on.

Q: This alerted your command to something unusual, didn't it?

Adm. D.: It certainly did. Remember, as I mentioned earlier, that I'm talking now about the fall of 1962, before the President's proclamation and before they pulled the trigger on our plans.

In addition to the shipping increase, there were large numbers of Soviet-bloc military personnel prior to August and then there was a buildup during August and September when nine passenger ships arrived in Cuba with a total capacity of 20,000 passengers. But at that time we didn't have any way of really confirming how many people were on board these ships because they would disembark at night. So our estimate was about a fourth of the total capacity. In other words, we figured it would be about 5,000 people.

Q: Was it the Navy that was charged with keeping count of the merchant ships and the passenger ships? Was it Navy Intelligence?

Adm. D.: Mainly. We were conducting surveillance as a normal course and we just kept it up. Of course, we had to keep track of all the shipping anywhere near the continental United States and in the Caribbean. Of course, it wasn't limited to just sightings at sea. We had intelligence sources in various parts of Europe and naval attaches all over the place, and the ships that were coming through the Dardanelles and the Bosporus and through Gibraltar or through the Channel, and those that came down past Iceland or off our own coast were sighted and reported and, in most cases, photographed.

We estimated finally that most of the people that the Soviets put in there were split up between the air force and the ground force about equally - the ground forces - and a smaller number for the Cuban Navy. Although we knew that these arms deliveries were beginningin 1960, then the buildup that I just mentioned, during New Year's Day parade in 1962 we got some idea of what Castro's newly acquired ground equipment really was. It turned out to be a sizeable number of medium tanks, a somewhat smaller number of heavy tanks, an assault gun, a certain amount of rocket-launchers, artillery pieces, anti-aircraft weapons, mortars, rifles, carbines, submachine guns -

Q: These were all on display in Havana?

Adm. S.: Yes, a regular parade!

Q: Similar to what the Russians do on May Day!

Adm. D.: Yes. It was a great thing for us. Then, of course, we were able to step up our intelligence and get more and more knowledge of the make-up of the Cuban armed forces. The Cuban Navy, of course, was likewise getting a sizeable buildup in weapons. We'd given them a handful of very small boats - it was not really a navy, but after the beginning of 1962 the Cuban naval forces started to build up. For example, in the first quarter they got a number of PT boats and a patrol boat. Now, these are modern types -

Q: Was that the Kronstadt?

Adm. D.: Yes, the Kronstadt was the patrol boat. These were towed over. The PTs were carried on the decks of ships. So obviously we knew how many they had and what types. We also found out through our sources that a number of Cuban personnel had undergone training in the use of these types.

Q: Training in Russia?

Adm. D.: Yes. Oh yes, in the Soviet Union, of course.

Then we were able through our reconnaissance to detect Soviet merchant ships with crates on deck, which indicated that they were shipping Komar missile-launching boats. These, of course were equipped with missiles, surface-to-surface missiles, homing types, with considerable range and were really quite a powerful weapon against ships, also against shore installations along our coasts.

Q: Coastal type boats, they were?

Adm. D.: Yes. These missiles carried a warhead with about 2,000 pounds of high explosive. They couldn't reload at sea, they had to go back into port in case they fired some of these.

Q: They were among the very newest of the Soviet types, weren't they?

Adm. D.: Yes, they were.

Then in mid-1961, Soviet aircraft commenced to come in, and by January of 1962 the cuban Air Force had about 60 MIG fighters, jet fighters, of several different classes, and again the Soviets had trained about 75 Cuban pilots who were sent back. They had been trained in Czechoslovakia, and that was supposed to be under Soviet supervision. There was another pilot training school near

Havana. And, of course, the airfields had to be improved, longer runways, new airfield construction, revetments built.

In October when the missile crisis was about to break, Castro had 20 airfields going to support these MIG planes. Then in September 1962 we found they had MIG-21s, jet fighters. That was a sophisticated airplane. It's a Mach-2 type, and it was one of the Soviet Union's most modern fighters. It ended up that they had about 42 of these new fighter-interceptors.

Then we found out that these sophisticated planes were being flown by experienced Soviet pilots, not Cubans. The Cubans had been trained in these older fighter-interceptors, subsonic mostly.

In early September we found surface-to-air missiles in Cuba. These were SA-2 which had an altitude capability of about 60,000 feet and some capability up to about 80,000, and a slant range of about 25 miles.

Q: These are familiarly known as the SAMs, aren't they?

Adm. D.: Yes. At that time they hadn't given them highly sophisticated SAMs, so that these had a minimum altitude limitation which worked greatly to our advantage as time went on because we could have planes take off and go down on the deck outside of their range and come in under the minimum altitude, right on the deck. I have many photographs of our fighters going in on a photographing mission at 50 or 100 feet.

Q: Low-level photographing?

Adm. D.: Low-level, yes, and many photographs show the gun crews at these sites running to man their stations, but they couldn't make it because we just appeared out of nowhere at a hell of a speed and were flying at such a low altitude that we were an almost impossible target. As I recall, out of the many, many flights we made over Cuba, I think only once or twice did any plane come back with any bullet holes in it. None of our pilots were hurt nor were our planes seriously damaged. So, fortunately they didn't have SAMs with their radars that could hit anything at real low altitudes.

They had about seven SAM sites. By early September they had about ten of these SAM sites, then in October they had twenty-four. So there was a dramatic buildup, as I've just indicated, of their military power.

Q: Stemming from the decisions that were made in Moscow in July?

Adm. D.: Yes, it was probably Raul's visit that brought most of this on, and it was very rapid. Then, of course, they commenced to get a lot of electronics in there, a number of new radar sites, and they had early-warning systems target-acquisition radars, ground-control intercept radars, fire control, missile control, and all the things that go along with sophisticated aerial warfare.

Q: I think you at one time lumped together all these electronic devices and said such an incredible collection for such a small island -

Adm. D.: Yes, indeed, it was. Then, of course, it was perfectly obvious that these defense were under the supervision and control of Soviet technicians, because it was beyond the Cubans to handle things like that.

Then we commenced to get into Cuba these Il-28s, bombers. These were shipped in pieces and assembled on the Cuban airfields.

Q: They're light bombers, are they not, missile-carrying bombers?

Adm. D.: Yes, they're light bombers. It's a light jet bomber with the usual weapons.

Q: And they became one of the bones of contention, the Il-28s?

Adm. D.: Yes. As time went on and they were assembling them- we could follow the assembling of these bombers and predict when they'd be ready to fly. Then, of course, knowing where they were we could have wiped them out without too much control, if we decided to do that.

There were 42 bombers that were credited and they never got more than 20 of them in various stages of assembly before they took the whole pack of them out when it came to a showdown.

The interesting thing is that the MRBM missiles came into the picture. In early September they started construction of these sites for these MRBMs. We confirmed this on the 14th of October with intelligence that showed that at San Cristobal there was a complex of four sites, each with four launch positions and two additional sites at Sagua la Grande were confirmed on the

Dennison #10 -413-

17th, bringing the total to six sites and a total of twenty-four launch positions. The missile was what was known as the SS-4 with a range capability of about 1,100 nautical miles.

Then on 15 to 17 October we confirmed the construction of the intermediate-range missile sites. Each site contained four launch positions, for a total of three or four sites. These missiles had a range of 2,200 nautical miles, considerably greater then the MRBms, and this meant that they could cover practically all of the United States and, of course, a large part of Central and South American as well.

Q: Admiral, when you had your conference with John A. McCone down in Panama, did he indicate his concern over the possibility of missile installations in Cuba? Because he apparently later on in September kept on talking about this.

Adm. D.: Well, unfortunately I don't have a record of the date. I consulted with people in CIA, one of whom was there. But it wasn't long after he'd taken over and it was quite a while before we had any idea of missiles being put in. It was just that we wanted to know what the hell all this buildup of Cuba was, what was going on. We were then just operating in a dense fog.

No, I don't recall he had anything to say about missiles and I don't think I did either at that time.

Q: You mentioned the overfly of the U-2 on the 14th of October, when we did see missile sites at San Cristobal. The point is made that up until that time the Kennedy administration had been very reluctant to accept the idea that Khrushchev would ever think of putting missiles into Cuba, and after that tangible evidence they changed their minds.

Adm. D.: There was a little more to it than that. All we were doing in the first part of October was flying peripheral missions around Cuba. I forget how far offshore this was, but quite a way. We weren't permitted to go in over Cuba, except with the U-2. But the high-altitude U-2 mission discovered these missile installations, and on the 14th the flight confirmed that offensive missile bases were completed and others were under construction. We were making flights over our own base at Guantanamo, but we were supposed to fly inside the fence line, which was like flying a high-speed airplane around your back yard! I don't know why this extreme caution. It was just the way we were ordered to operate.

Well, we're up now to the quarantine itself or the planning or just whatever it is you want to talk about.

Q: Admiral, I know that the Navy and the other military forces are constantly making plans for all sorts of situations and obviously in the case of the Cuban crisis you had plenty of plans, and you were developing plans as the crisis developed, were you not? Will you talk about that?

Adm. D.: Yes, you're quite right, but remember that as CinCLant my area of responsibility was well defined and well understood. What I didn't have was a fully activated command. In other words, the commander, myself, was, of course, activated and the naval component, and the other two components, the Army and Air Force, were designated. But I was able to perform my responsibilities by developing a family of plans for various contingencies. I received a great deal of help from General Sweeney of the Air Force, whom I designated Air Force component commander, and General Powell, of the Army, whom I designated Army forces commander. And our staff worked together. We were all in the same general area, and this was just great. We were on a very friendly basis, we understood each other and respected each other. So we weren't operating in a vacuum at all, but as the situation developed and the enemy strength became more and more apparent, and the nature of the strength, we finally came to a point where I decided to change the command structure for the Cuban operation from operating under the command of a joint task force, which would be responsible to me, to taking over the command myself, through my component commanders. Then, of course, the Joint Chiefs of Staff finally did activate the command, which resulted in practically no changes in plans, except refinement as time went on.

Just to give you an idea of what I'm talking about in the way of contingency, we had plans, for example, for air strikes in various categories and varying strength. One might be a plan to strike only missile installations, including the control, radar, or it might be a strike to take out Cuban airfields, of which, as I said previously, there was a large number. Or Cuban military installations. And the same thing would apply for the use of Army and Marine Corps forces.

Remember, I had five Army divisions and the 2nd Marine Division, reinforced by elements of the 1st Marine Division. And there were operations planned for the use of these forces against various landing areas in Cuba. All these would require naval and Air Force support. Then, finally, naval plans which would go anywhere from simple surveillance to gunfire support or taking out coastal targets or destroying Cuban shipping or Soviet shipping or any shipping that interfered with us. Or the application of these various components alone or in combination.

So our plans had to be extremely flexible. My plans were approved by the Joint Chiefs of Staff and, of course, were known to the President. The application was of tremendous interest. He had to know what we could do, how we were going to do it. Just consider the seriousness of deciding to invade Cuba, a densely packed area. We were up against some pretty strong ground forces, so some very drastic preparation would have to be made in the way of our bombing, gunfire, a great many people would have been killed. The Cuban beaches are really, by and large, not worth a damn, narrow entry areas, and so on. So it would have been quite a bloody affair.

And then, once having captured Cuba and occupied it, the United States would have had a terrible problem in rehabilitation, establishing a government. We would have been in there for years. All I'm pointing out is that it was a very, very serious decision. Also, the nature and degree of air strikes. You just don't go flying around indiscriminately dropping bombs on Havana, for example. The targets had to be carefully selected. We had to know a great deal about them. The same way with naval operations. What kind of naval operations? Antisubmarine warfare?

But we did have our plans, they were approved, and this put into motion the creation of a large network of communications and a large number of supporting plans from the Strategic Air Command and CinCStrike, and from all commanders who had any conceivable contact with the operations. So the monumental effort of planning had to be very thorough, and there were so many supporting plans.

Every one of these master plans - I'm talking about CinCLant's plans - go to these various subordinate commanders, and they have to create their own supporting plans based on the tasks or missions assigned to them in the master plan. And all the service commands, for example, who are going to supply the food and the gasoline and all the material things, ammunition - they all have to make plans. Just consider what's involved, for example, in the lift of two airborne divisions.

Now, the entire U.S. tactical air force was assigned to me, through General Sweeney, to give you some idea of the magnitude of the air effort. Now this included not only combat aircraft but large numbers of troop transport aircraft. The fleet plans for ships' overhauls had to be alerted. There were a multitude of things that had to be planned for and done.

But these were all done because we had the blueprints.

In this case, we have an example of how a military operation ought to be conducted. I mentioned the various things that we could have done and instead of pulling the trigger and doing everything all at once, that is, invading and conducting air strikes, blockade, and so on, the President made a very wise decision in using naval power, and this fortunately taught Khrushchev a great lesson about what naval power can do, or sea power can do.

The blockade, euphemistically called the quarantine, was directed toward interception of the flow of weapons into Cuba.

Q: Specific weapons?

Adm. D.: Yes, missiles. And of course we also wanted them to get the missiles out that were already in there but not in operating condition yet, at the time I'm talking about.

By using this quarantine system we were able to show the Soviets several things. One was that we weren't going to permit anything more to get in there, we were determined, as the President pointed out, to take whatever steps we needed to protect our own security. And if Castro was going to stand in the way, that was just too bad for Castro.

So, of the various options we had we used the first option, the use of naval forces alone. Whan I say "alone" I don't mean that nobody else was doing anything because the Air Force was doing plenty of reconnaissance work and training and overhauling their own supporting plans and what not. And, of course, the Army. We deployed Army forces forward. For example, we took the 1st Armored Division out of Fort Hood in Texas into Fort Stewart in Georgia.

All this had to be known by Khrushchev.

We combat loaded all the Marines we could lift. They were already to go. So it was perfectly evident. I mean the newspapers had most of it, that we were undertaking a massive preparation for anything that we wanted to do in the way of fighting.

Q: And quarantine was actually the initial step? We could proceed from that point if necessary?

Adm. D.: We certainly could and would. It was perfectly obvious to Khrushchev that we were ready to do it and the will to do it was conveyed to him by the President himself. And he believed the President. He had misread the President some months before this, in that unfortunate meeting in Europe, and I'm sure that he thought we would dilly-dally and write notes and protest and go to the United Nations, but we didn't.

Anyway, to get back to these plans. The plans were under constant revision as the situation developed, but the basic plans were there. I don't think it would be of value to go into the details of the plans. That's much too complicated a matter.

Q: No. Admiral, I would think that it was a considerable relief to you when the decision was made on the 20th to go for the quarantine, or the blockade, rather than one of the other alternatives? I mean something definite was decided.

Adm. D.: Well, it was a relief. In that sense, it was a relief and I certainly believed that this was by far the wisest course of action. But it seemed to me to be perfectly evident that the next priority was air strikes, and that was what we were completely prepared to do, had we had to do it. In other words, if these missiles got operational then we were indeed immediately threatened and we couldn't play around much longer. In the end it came down to a matter of almost hours from the time that we decided that these sites were operational, or would be operational before Khrushchev threw in the sponge.

Now, in those few hours, had the decision not been made by Khrushchev, then we would have had to undertake other provisions in my plans to at least take out those missile sites with air strikes. Don't forget we had tremendous tactical air power there. Not only Air Force forces but the Navy carrier forces. Tremendous power, and Khrushchev and Castro damn well knew it. We were looking right down their throats.

We also had to be ready to undertake amphibious attacks which of course would have required application of Air Force forces and Navy carrier forces in support. I have already discussed some factors concerning this type of operation. I will simply mention here that the landing of assault forces followed by support forces would be an operation of considerable magnitude.

But, yes, I think the decision was wise and I was relieved to get going. The President had given plenty of warning as to when he was going to make this declaration. I had over two days to get my ships in position. When the declaration was made my ships were in position. They were there and ready for business.

Q: Did you, when you went up to Washington on the 21st, see the President?

Adm. D.: Yes.

Q: What kind of a conference did you have with him?

Adm. D.: Oh, it wasn't exactly perfunctory. We both knew what the job was and how we were going to go about it. There wasn't really very much to talk about, except get in there and pitch! But I must say he was perfectly marvelous and I never got a call from the White House during the entire operation. He let me alone. He interfered with my communications sometimes. I don't mean that they changed my messages, but by trying to get through to the commanders who were actually on the line they'd sometimes gum up my command circuits. It happens all the time, I guess. But I had to tell all these Washington stations to get off my circuits and stay off because they were interfering with operations.

Q: Would you tell me at this point the story of the appointment of Admiral Ward to be commander of the Second Fleet?

Adm. D.: Yes. This was an important command, of course, and Ward was the man for it. He was perfectly marvelous.

Q: He'd been in command of the Amphibious Force, Atlantic Fleet.

Adm. D.: Yes. Ordinarily I would have gone to the change-of-command ceremony when he took over the Second Fleet, and I wasn't there because I knew what was coming in the next couple of days. This attracted some attention and speculation in the press because everybody knew that ordinarily I would have been there and, so far as anybody knew, I wasn't in the hospital! Or showing that I didn't like Admiral Ward. He was told by my chief of staff, proba Admiral Beakley, to make the ceremony short and to report to me ir my headquarters after the ceremony's completion, which Ward did. filled him in completely on what the situation at the moment was. He, of course, was familiar with my war plans. Having been commander of the Amphibious Force he knew that part of it anyhow, but he needed a complete briefing and that's what he got.

And I believe it was the next day when he and I went up to Washington together -

Q: It was on the 21st, on Sunday, and this was to meet with the Joint Chiefs.

Adm. D.: Yes, and of course that wasn't anything dramatic either. Everybody knew what the job was, and the Joint Chiefs were completely behind me. They had every confidence that things were going to go all right. They approved the war plans, and we were ready to go, and we did.

Q: Where did Admiral Anderson come in the picture? I mean, with you and your command, or didn't he?

Adm. D.: He was, of course, a member of the Joint Chiefs and, since this was a naval operation, his war room was probably the best informed of any. But he didn't interfere with my operations at all. I ran them through my own staff set-up. Through Admiral Hogle whom I put in charge of my quarantine plot center, and quite an elaborate set-up we had. George was very helpful and I think he was responsible for keeping a lot of people and things off my back, because I had plenty to do without spending time that I could otherwise devote to something more important than talking to people. I didn't see any press during the operation. I moved around quite a bit. We had advance headquarters set up in Florida, Sweeney and Powell and myself.

But everything went smoothly and I think I may have mentioned before that one significant thing about the composition of forces was that they were all seasoned professionals. We had no Reserves called up, except some pilots for the Air Force Air Transport Command. So it was really a joy.

This decision of Khrushchev's, and again had that been delayed more than a few hours after the time he made it, it might have been too late. Not that we were going to resort to atomic weapons, but we would have certainly had to strike Cuba, at least the missile sites and airfields.

Q: Admiral, at one point I believe you said that there were three phases - three actual phases - to the quarantine operation. The first of them, with the inception of the quarantine on 24 October - and this period extended through 4 November and it had to do with the ships that were bound to Cuba - do you want to talk about that?

Adm. D.: Yes, certainly. Let's put this in a little bit of focus.

The quarantine line, so called, could have been established in a number of places. It could be established fairly close inshore, for example, which would have meant economy of forces, or it could have been set up outside of the reasonable range of any land-based aircraft from Cuba. The latter was what was done.

Q: That was the determining factor, was it, that you were out of the range of land-based aircraft?

Adm. D.: Yes. Then, of course, we didn't know at that time exactly how badly off they were for readiness to use these airfields or to use their airplanes, but at any rate the quarantine was set up initially fairly far out, and then the quarantine arc was finally readjusted closer to Cuba, seaward of the Bahamas chain. That was done between 30 and 31 October.

Q: What caused that change?

Adm. D.: Realization that the Cuban ability to do anything about air was so limited, and it meant fewer ships, and a tighter operation. It really didn't have any great significance.

Q: How far out did the line extend?

Adm. D.: Well, I don't have a chart handy, but it wasn't just off the coast of Cuba, it was seaward of the Bahamas. I'll get into it a little later, but of course we did have a quarantine line set up south of Cuba, too. But to get back to these three phases.

We set up a quarantine plot in my OpCon center on the 29th of October, headed again by Rear Admiral R. D. Hogle, who was assigned about 30 officers and men to be on his staff. I'd like to mention the magnitude of this search effort.

About 46 ships, 240 aircraft, and some 30,000 personnel were directly involved in the effort to locate ships inbound for or outbound from Cuba. That's quite a sizable group of people and ships and aircraft. We used naval air patrol squadrons who were flying out of Puerto Rico and Florida and the Azores, principally. We had a very, very complete coverage, visual and also radar. We had reconnaisance planes from the Air Force to help us. They were the ones that operated out of the Azores principally. We were covering something like 4,500,000 square miles of ocean, if you can imagine that.

Q: They operated from their base in Terceira?

Adm. D.: Yes, and the Navy was also flying from Roosevelt Roads, Guantanamo Bay, Bermuda, and the Azores, Argentia, Jacksonville, Key West, Norfolk, Patuxent. Altogether there were about 200 sightings of ships that were of immediate interest, and of course the other ships were by no means of no interest. We just knew where they were headed and what their names were, and had a pretty good idea what their cargo was. Most of the ships were first sighted by aircraft and then were vectored in by my headquarters to ships in the quarantine line. In other words, the line wasn't necessarily static. We just didn't sit there. We knew where these ships were and went out to intercept them.

Q: When the quarantine was first established, what were the orders? To really board the ships?

Adm. D.: No, this was to be done only by direction. Remember this was a selective operation and, again, we weren't looking for POL or for food or for people or anything of that sort. We were looking specifically for warheads and missiles. And the first result of - this operation was a number - I think it was 12 - of Soviet ships sighted in the vicinity of the Azores, or that general part of the Atlantic, in any event, and these ships had sailed from Murmansk mostly. At any rate they hadn't gone through the North Sea or the Channel or the Strait of Gibraltar, unlike most of the other ships which had made ports of call on the way over. Our sightings confirmed the fact that they were configured to handle the IRBM and doubtless that's exactly where the IRBMs were.

And when the President made his announcement within hours these ships had gotten the word because they all hove to and after a few more hours reversed course and went back to wherever they came from. So they never got anywhere near the quarantine line.

Well, we knew this but we didn't just want to assume that all was going to be well and just abandon this quarantine line. We wanted to keep that going, which we did. There could have been warheads or other things that would have been of interest to us.

To get back to these three phases. You might describe them this way: from the 24th of October until the 4th of November, you might call the first one, and many Soviet ships, including the ones that I've mentioned, turned back and never came anywhere near Cuba. Others even with nonsuspicious cargo slowed or stopped, apparently awaiting guidance. Now this demonstrates pretty good control by the Soviets, that they could get through to these merchant ships and with not very much elapsed time either. Most of these ships, the last ones I mentioned were not suspicious cargoes, did resume their course and go in to Cuba. They weren't carrying the kind of cargoes that we were looking for and said we were going to stop.

So, you see, you could say that quarantine was successful without ever having been really tested by facing us with these ships that we damned well knew were going to stop, no matter whether we had to sink them or what.

The second phase you might describe as being from the 5th to the 11th of November, and we established a rapid code to designate suspect ships that we might want to give special attention to.

Eleven such ships that we wanted to pay particular attention to were observed outbound from Cuba. These ships were intercepted, inspected for missiles, without actually being stopped or boarded. It was pretty hard to hide these missiles.

Q: And they were actually carrying missiles out from Cuba?

Adm. D.: Well - yes, that was the case, but the masters of these Soviet ships had been pretty well read into the act too, because even though they were reluctant sometimes to cooperate they all did, we could get an actual count. We knew the number of missiles that were in Cuba. We had an actual head count. We saw them being loaded into ships and we knew what ships. Then we had close aerial reconnaissance ship to ship. We had one amusing experience - I think it was during this stage of the proceedings - where a destroyer closed to speak to this Soviet ship and we had put Russian-speaking officers in each one of these quarantine ships. We did that at the very first. So this Russian-speaking officer in the destroyer hailed this ship in Russian - "Where are you from? Where are you bound?" and all that kind of stuff. And the answer came back from the Soviet ship's bridge in perfect English!

Q: This decision to put Russian-speaking officers on board all of our quarantine ships was your decision, was it not?

Adm. D.: Yes. It was in my plans.

Q: Well, it was known to Admiral Anderson, wasn't it?

Adm. D.: I don't know. I understand later somebody asked him about it and he didn't know.

Q: That's what Abel says in his book.

Adm. D.: I never talked to George, but it's conceivable he didn't. It seemed to me it was a simple routine matter. For God's sake, if you're going to stop Russian ships it would be a good idea to have somebody on board who could speak Russian, one would think.

Q: It was in the second phase that you actually boarded one of the ships, was it?

Adm. D.: I don't think we did. I think the only ship we ever boarded was the Marcula, which was inbound.

Q: Oh, that was in the first phase then?

Adm. D.: Yes, and it carried a nonsuspicious cargo, and really I did it to show that we could and would do it. Of course, they didn't know that we already knew what was in that ship. It was little more than a stunt, a demonstration that we were effective.

Q: Was this called for by Washington, or did you do this on your own?

Adm. D.: I don't remember. I think I did it on my own, but I probably got permission because this was pretty sensitive. I just don't recall. But if I hadn't got an order to do it I would have asked for it because it seemed like a pretty good idea for my own people, as well as the world, because to sit out on a quarantine station and not do a damned thing for a few days gets kind of boring. So I tried out our system.

Well, then from the 11th to the 21st of November you might call the third phase. During this period we trailed some ships and designated six ships that were of special interest.

Q: They were all going out from Cuba?

Adm. D.: No, the ones that I'm now talking about were incoming - some of them were out and some were in. We found no offensive weapons on any of the ships that we intercepted. There were photographs of them, so they obviously had to be the inboard ones.

I remember one interesting point is that during the so-called first phase we held up our operations while U Thant went from the UN down to Cuba. He worked directly with Castro, trying to find some way out of this Cuban crisis. I think that turned out to be a fairly fruitless endeavor because it wasn't Castro we were dealing with, it was Khrushchev.

Q: Admiral, the Latin American nations as a group voted backing of the United States actions. On the 19th, I believe it was, of November the Organization of American States voted 19 to nothing to support us. Would you talk about their support, as it was apparent to your command?

Adm. D.: Yes. You just mentioned that the Organization of American States approved the course of action our President had decided on, but then it turned out that many of them made concrete offers of assistance and we did form a task force under Commander, South Atlantic, one of my subordinate commanders, for the conduct of quarantine surveillance over the southern approaches to Cuba. Actually, we knew that there wasn't any significant block shipping coming from south of Cuba because of the tremendous surveillance effort we had which I've already mentioned. At the beginning we had a U.S. destroyer, and two Dominican Republic destroyers, and while they weren't active for very long they did make a lot of sightings. They were just having the time of their life! They did make some sightings and intercepts, but the major advantage of it, of course, was the valuable demonstration that the United States and South American countries were joined in combating the Communist threat.

Q: It was one of the political aspects.

Adm. D.: Yes. Militarily it didn't mean a damned thing. As a matter of fact, it was more of a headache than it was a help, and they came out of it pretty well because we fueled them and gave them a good repair job. But they were gung-ho, I'll say that, almost embarrassingly so.

An interesting point about command here is that the Latins are very sensitive about having another nation in Latin America command their forces. That's why we setup the Commander, South Atlantic. Not just for this purpose, he'd been in existence for a long time, but to conduct combined operations with these various Latin American navies. They would work together with us under our command and did beautifully, but an Argentinian wouldn't accept a Brazilian task force commander, or vice versa, or any other Latin American wouldn't accept any other. But with us it was different. So we were sort of a catalyst for bringing these people together. I had meetings with the top naval people in these nations from time to time and the CNO used to hold gatherings of Latin American CNos. They were a wonderful social group. They knew each other, they spoke the same sea language, but when it came to submitting forces to the command of some other national, no. So here we had - that accounts for the presence of an American DD in this task group. As I recall, I didn't have them report to Admiral Ward. I had this command report to me so that they had, you know, a little more stature and they were operating an important unit in this over-all effort, and they weren't unimportant. Their importance, as we discussed, was more political than military.

Q: I saw a note, Admiral, to the effect that you recommended to the Joint Chiefs at one point that CinCCarib be given the task of preventing the passage through the Panama Canal of ships carrying prohibited materials destined for Cuba. Was there any

Dennison #10 -433-

action taken on that, or were there any such ships going through?

Adm. D.: I don't remember the circumstances of that at all, but it would seem to be a purely precautionary measure because by the time any bloc ship got anywhere near the Panama Canal we would have known all about it long before, with this gigantic surveillance we had on.

Q: Then there was another minor item. The Turkish government raised the question of the status of three Turkish ships that were in the Cuban trade, and asked that they be exempted from the quarantine. Was this request honored?

Adm. D.: Oh, I'm sure it was because, again, we would have known what was in those ships, and they surely weren't carrying Soviet missiles. It was almost a sure bet that any commercial ship, even though it might be manned by navy people, would be Soviet government. I mean they're not going to put an IRBM in a Polish bottom. It takes a special ship to do it anyhow. And they're certainly not going to put atomic warheads in a Turkish ship.

So if we ever got such a request, which I assume we did, obviously we would never have stopped a Turkish ship unless we knew damned well that they had something on board, which is almost inconceivable. So I assumed and then we made a little hay out of it and said, "Yes, our dear friends, we of course won't include any of your ships."

Dennison #10 -434-

Q: There's one other large aspect of this whole operation, and that pertains to submarines. Do you want to talk about that phase of it?

Adm. D.: Yes.

Q: Perhaps beginning with the 17th of October when we sighted a submarine replenishment ship off of the Azores, the Terek?

Adm. D.: I might mention briefly that Soviet submarine activity in connection with this Cuban missile crisis began with a sightin of a Soviet submarine replenishment ship, the Terek, in the North Atlantic, in the vicinity of the Azores.

Q: Is that a kind of a submarine mother ship?

Adm. D.: Yes, a Navy replenishment ship for fuel and supplies and so on for submarines. We kept this ship under surveillance, and on the 22nd of October the Terek was sighted not far from the Azores refueling the Zulu-type submarine, and the topside condition, and the submarine's requirement for fuel, of course, indicated that she'd been at sea for quite a long period. Considering this together with two possibly valid contact reports she'd been on a covert patrol in the Western Atlantic, near the East Coast of the United States.

Now, we'd had low-level reports for some time that Soviet submarines would be based in Cuba, and the buildup of weapons in Cuba made these reports somewhat significant.

Q: Were they reports from refugees and that sort of thing?

Adm. D.: Some of them, yes. We had nothing really substantial to go on, but it didn't seem beyond the realm of possibility that the Soviets were establishing a submarine base in southern Cuba. A considerable time later we did have hard evidence that they did have tenders and things in Cuban ports that were equipped to handle submarines.

But in any event we did know for a fact that Soviet submarines were in the Western Atlantic, and the first one we brought up was the conventional Foxtrot type, which was picked up on the surface, 300 miles south of Bermuda. After that we picked up more sightings. Altogether there were six sightings of Soviet conventionally-powered submarines in the approaches to the Caribbean, and five of these were photographed. Shortly after we brought them up and put them on their way, our practice was to close these ships that were brought up if they were held down -

Q: Just stood over them till they finally came up?

Adm. D.: Yes, and hail them and ask if we could be of any assistance, then politely tell them to get out of the area and head for home, which they did. One of the submarines that we brought up had a casualty which required it to go back home on the surface. It could have been a casualty to her motors, for example, or it could have been some fault in their tank venting or blowing system. In any event, she couldn't submerge, and had to go back on the surface. Of course, they went back to the Northern Fleet bases in Russia.

There's one interesting point about this submarine deployment of theirs, and that is the fact that we got these submarines so soon after the quarantine was established indicates that they had to leave their Northern Fleet bases in early October. In other words, they probably had to proceed in most daylight hours submerged and then come up at night on the surface, but their speed was so slow that they couldn't possibly have been in the area where we found them without leaving long before we'd established the quarantine line. Nobody knew in early October that we were going to do it or where we would do it, so it's always been a mystery to me as to why these submarines were where they were at the time they were and in that particular area. No, the only explanation, aside from sheer coincidence, is that they were en route to ports in Cuba, the base there. That, as far as I know, has never been confirmed. They were evasive in various ways and wanting to submerge, but I remember one case we brought up one of them with one number painted on the starboard side of her periscope sheers and another number on the opposite side. I suppose the idea was that if she were sighted more than once we might think there were two submarines there when there actually was one. Seems a little far-fetched, but I don't know why you'd paint one identifying number on one side of the ship and a different one on the other.

I hope, one day, to find out why it was that they were in that area at the time they were. Right now I don't know.

Q: Well, Sir, you have some personal observations to make on this whole operation, and on the presence of the submarines in the Western Atlantic?

Adm. D.: Well, I think just the fact that they would deploy submarines so far away from home and so close to our coast was an indication of the seriousness of the Soviet effort in the Western Atlantic. It's quite an important matter when they start deploying that kind of a weapon so close to our shores. They must know that the reaction would have been violent. So it isn't just a minor matter. I think it's a matter of major significance in this whole picture.

Q: And it gives another dimension to the nature of Cuba as a Soviet base.

Adm D.: Indeed it does.

Q: You certainly have some general observations on this operation because you have expressed them to me from time to time. Would you repeat them now?

Adm. D.: I think I certainly made the point about the magnitude of our effort. It turned out that this incident, if you want to describe it as an incident, was the largest, most complicated joint operation since Korea. I told you we had almost 500,000 people involved in it and tremendous power assembled. It proved,

I think, the value of the unified command structure and the workability of it. We have really here in the account of this crisis a blueprint for the application of force.

I think that all of us who were a part of this were greatly educated. We found out a number of things. For example, the ability of our armed forces to react quickly and expertly. But above and beyond all that, it seems to me that in those days, and even more so in these days, when both sides - and I'm talking now about the Soviet Union and the United States, of course - hold weapons capable of accomplishing unimaginable devastation, that we're in a period of nuclear stalemate, and in a condition where each side has an overkill capability.

I further believe that there can't be any acceptable solution to many international problems through the use of these weapons. It just isn't the answer to any situation that can be conceived. There's no such thing as a local application of an atomic weapon. They aren't that kind of a weapon. That doesn't mean that we shouldn't maintain a really effective nuclear force, and I think everybody realizes that, because only by maintaining such a force, or such forces, can we best assure that the enemy will not initiate an atomic exchange. He could wipe us out before we could get up off the deck.

Q: Only is the opposite true, if you do maintain a balance.

Adm. D.: Under these conditions and in this environment the catastrophic results of a missile exchange were fully recognized and I think if that's the case, there's an increasing likelihood of limited probes, incursions, and even extensive hostile action. Just think what has gone on through our recent history. We've had Korea, we've had Vietnam. We're faced with incidents, some small and some large, all over the world. The Middle East is a critical situation now. But none of the situations I mentioned, and others that I haven't, can find a solution by the use of atomic weapons on somebody's part. It just isn't in the cards. What would we do with an atomic weapon in the Middle East situation in case we become involved, or the Soviets?

So, in this kind of a situation, we're going to have more of these sometimes very serious situations where the only solution is the use of force short of atomic exchange. And Cuba is an outstanding example of just what I've said.

In this case, with our background of atomic power and expressed determination to use this power if we had to, we turned back the Soviet adventure into Cuba. It's obvious I think by now how we did it. It was done because we had the power of our military forces, in this case so-called conventional power. That's what did it. It was done by the judicious employment of some of these forces in quarantine, antisubamrine warfare reconnaissance, and the staging of very, very powerful airborne and armored Army forces. I had the whole tactical Air Force under my command. We deployed strong amphibious forces, strong antisubmarine warfare forces, carrier striking forces, and all of this provided tangible evidence of our strength, determination, and ability to apply U.S. power when, where and if required.

Q: None of which can ever be concealed from the enemy, can it?

Adm. D.: No, and it is something which really you don't want to conceal. Obviously, you can't conceal a buildup such as we accomplished, deploy a divison like the 1st Armored Division from Texas to Georgia without everybody knowing about it. It was probably a good thing that Khrushchev did know about it. I think we probably should have published it in all the papers so he would know, let him realize that we were determined to do something and we had the force to do it with, backed up by our atomic weapons.

In any event, we establsihed a necessary atmosphere which gave time for our opponent to consider seriously before resorting to all-out war. And, at the same time, it gave him a way out, an avenue of escape. I concluded, after considerable thought, that this is absolutely the most important lesson to be drawn from the Cuban crisis.

I'm reminded of what President Kennedy had to say as he reviewed part of the Atlantic Command, in this case the 1st Armored divison at Fort Stewart. He inspected the entire command with me, after the missile crisis, and we went all over the various bases. We started out at my headquarters and ended up alongside the dock on the deck of a submarine at Key West just at evening colors. He was, of course, tremendously impressed. At Fort Stewart when he did speak to this massed armored division, and it is a tremendously impressive sight to see one of those armored divisions all in one piece, in one place, he said regard-

Dennison #10 -441-

less of how persistent our diplomacy may be in the final analysis it rests upon the will and courage of our citizens and "upon you here."

Q: It does also indicate the fact that any confrontation involves the whole world now, doesn't it? It immediately involves -

Adm. D.: It does indeed. There's hardly a situation, remote as an area might be, in which a number of powers don't have an interest. Consider Bangladesh. It's a long, long way from there to the United States, but we're involved in it, not actively but our interests certainly are. I can't think of any area in the world where a number of national interests wouldn't be involved in varying degrees, in case of any disturbance in the political structure.

Look at NATO. NATO was founded on the idea that you can't take a square inch of NATO territory. Greece could probably lose Thrace without any great or serious consequence to other nations, except politically. We've signed that we won't permit this to happen, along with our allies. And NATO covers a considerable amount of territory, and we have other treaties almost all over the world, mutual defense pacts, SEATO.

So, at least as far as we're concerned, we're so tied in with treaties, expressed principles, that it's hard to imagine, if not impossible, any situation - the Middle East I've already mentioned - where our interests wouldn't be involved, mostly through some agreement and I think that's true of other nations as well.

Dennison #10 -442-

Q: It has been said that the Cuban crisis taught the Soviets a lesson about sea power. Would you comment on that?

Adm. D.: Well, I think that Khrushchev realized early in the game that, to begin with, our surveillance effort was extremely impressive. He had to know that through the sightings we'd made - he must have known that we knew where his ships were, what they carried, where they were going, and so on. We'd established a line that we said you can't go beyond, and he respected it. I think he wasn't unaware at all of the versatility and the power of carrier-based aircraft. We had a tremendous deployment of those. And above all he must have realized that he was forced to give in because he was facing a manifestation of our over-all power in this simple quarantine line.

This is what threw him. I mean, had we not interfered with his operations and just let him go on, he could have gone through with this buildup and then, surely, we would have had to conduct air strikes or take whatever steps the President wished. But it seems to me that this was militarily, actively at least, a demonstration of how naval forces can be properly employed.

Q: And, to follow through on that idea, that the Russians took this and they have built on it, haven't they?

Adm. D.: Yes, they certainly did, and I think that what's going on in the Mediterranean with the increasing number of Soviet ships there and their strong naval presence, I think that shows that they've taken a leaf out of the book of the Royal Navy and the United States Navy for the political-military uses of sea power. They're reading our text and doing just exactly what they learned from us. They've gone from a purely coastal defense navy, a puny force, to a real blue-water navy. They've got a real seagoing navy and a very good one.

Q: And this is largely since the missile crisis, is it not?

Adm. D.: Yes, I think that was the real kick-off of the whole thing. We taught them too well, perhaps. I mean, for example, they've developed the necessary techniques for a blue-water navy of replenishing and refueling at sea. This was unheard of not too many years ago in the Soviet Navy. They just weren't geared for that kind of an operation.

Q: And now they're coming up with aircraft carriers, too.

Adm. D.: Yes and this is a weapon completely foreign to their strategy all through Russian history. It's no secret, of course, that one of the principal bases of their policy was to search for warm-water ports. Now they've found out that the way to get a warm-water port is to make friends and influence people, through power if you have to. You can't do it by having coastal defense of Soviet Russia.

Dennison #11 - 444

Interview No. 11 with Admiral Robert Lee Dennison, U.S. Navy
(Retired)

Place: His office in the Davis Building, Washington, D.C.

Date: Wednesday afternoon, 25 July 1973

Subject: Biography

By: John T. Mason, Jr.

Q: Admiral, I note that almost immediately after the conclusion of the Bay of Pigs episode you sent a rather remarkable dispatch, I believe, to the CNO, Admiral Burke. Apparently you were drawing on your experience with the Bay of Pigs to say that one lesson we should learn is that we should have adequate land areas in the Puerto Rican area where the fleet could practise at landings, amphibious landings, and what have you. Do you want to talk about this whole area, Sir, which you implemented in September of that year by submitting to Washington an over-all plan?

Adm. D.: Yes, that's essentially correct. I think that the Bay of Pigs didn't really provide anything new in our strategic thinking. It simply underlined what we had believed for a good many years about the importance of adequate bases and training areas in the Caribbean. Guantanamo, of course, we've had under our control for a good many years, but there are other areas in the Caribbean of great potential value for training marine landing operations, shore bombardment, bombing, and all sorts of things.

Guanatanamo has been a sore spot in late years. Sometimes the situation between Cuba and the United States became aggravated and sometimes not, but the Bay of Pigs brought all this back to mind. So in April 1961, I believe, I did send Admiral Burke, who was CNO, a dispatch relating to the general problem of bases in the Caribbean, and pointed out that the recent event, namely the Bay of Pigs, highlighted the fact there was no land area in the Caribbean or elsewhere in the Atlantic which was under our control where we could perform military operations and training in any desired degree of isolation from unwanted observers and the press. And I went on to say that the current Cuban situation might well be reenacted in several places in that general area in the next decade.

Well, Guantanamo had been of tremendous value to us as a base, not as a spearhead for attack against Cuba because as you well know it's completely undefended and indefensible. I mean here it is in a pocket on the coast, with Cuban hills looking down on it. There's really no way to protect it.

Q: It's quite vulnerable in a sense.

Adm. D.: Completely. The great advantage is that it gives us an all-weather training area, and there are no others like it on the East Coast that we're now talking about, where visibility is so good practically every day of the year, and to reach deep water from the anchorage at Guantanamo is a matter of minutes. There's very, very little seaborne traffic passing through the area south of Guantanamo. So it's ideal. Of course, Roosevelt Roads, Puerto Rico, is recognized as being an important strategic point for carriers and larger ships, and that was developed. We had a dry dock there, for example. But these were not enough to satisfy our full needs, as I saw the picture.

So I told Burke some of my views and pointed out that we ought to try to inform key people in the government about the needs that we had and the reasons for the needs so we could get the proper support to help solve some of our real-estate problems.

Q: At that point in time, how important were Culebra and Vieques?

Adm. D.: They were extremely important. Vieques was, and is, an excellent training area for Marine operations, amphibious operations, and together with Culebra, gave us areas for gunfire support exercises, bombing. And our relations with the Puerto Ricans were not bad at all. Lately there's been a great furor about interfering with progress. I think, on the contrary, we've done a great deal to help the Puerto Ricans.

Q: Did we have some sort of arrangements, some sort of treaty arrangement, covering the use of these two islands?

Adm. D.: I don't know exactly what the documentation was, but

Dennison #11 - 447

our relations with Puerto Rico were such that they were a territory, and still are. So it isn't like making a treaty with some foreign nation, like Cuba or any one of thenations who own islands in the Caribbean area. It's more an internal matter for the United States than negotiation between sovereign states.

We didn't at that time, and never did, control all of Culebra and Vieques. This, while highly desirable, was a pretty thorny political problem, relocating people and things of that sort. But as far as U. S. strategic interests were then concerned, and are now, I think that was highly desirable. The Bay of Pigs incident brought out the strategic importance of Swan Island.

Q: That belonged to Honduras, didn't it?

Adm. D.: Yes, it belonged to Honduras, but we had an agreement permitting us to use it for certain purposes, radio broadcasting and radio intercepts and all kinds of related activities. It seemed to me that we ought to formalize in some way our arrangements to use Swan Island. Sovereignty, of course, would have been the ideal, but we could have made some kind of arrangement with Honduras buying out their claim, but I don't know that we ever really recognized the fact - recognized that the claims of Honduras were justified in fact.

Q: Was it populated as an island?

Dennison #11 - 448

Adm. D.: If it was at all, very sparsely. It's not a very big piece of real estate, as you know. I don't believe anything ever really came of that.

I pointed out, too, that the island of Bonnaire, in the Curacao-Aruba group, was fairly large, flat, and sparsely inhabited - about the same area and the same population density as Vieques. I suggested that perhaps we might make arrangements with the Dutch to keep Bonaire in this condition and available to Holland's allies, namely the United States, to ensure its stability in that particular area of the Caribbean. Just our presence there would have been enough to do it.

Q: That, of course, was before it became a tourist mecca?

Adm. D.: That's right. What I was suggesting was that we see if we couldn't stop that from happening. I pointed out also something we've known for a long time, that Trinidad was tremendously important. You may remember in World War II that this came out loud and clear, when we did so many exercises on Trinidad and in the Gulf. A marvelous anchorage.

Q: That's the Gulf of Paria?

Adm. D.: Yes. We were having difficulties then and later with Eric Williams and his government. At that time we were down to a short-term lease, and I went on to suggest that we ought to do all we can to ensure that our relations with Trinidad

Dennison #11 - 449

and Tobago were kept in good repair so that we could eventually extend our lease on the basis of mutual advantage and so on.

Q: Was that one of the bases acquired through the destroyer agreement with Britain?

Adm. D.: I'm sorry, I should know that, but I really don't. I would imagine it was, because I don't think we would just move in there without some sanction.

Well, you're quite right. I did follow this up within a few months - I think in September - with a ten-year strategic plan for the area.

Q: This is something you submitted to the Joint Chiefs, I presume?

Adm. D.: Yes, and as a result of what I sent to Burke I got a concurrence from him, saying that they would see to it that these objectives I mentioned were included in long-range planning. But in September I did formalize my ideas in the submittal of a long-range plan to the Joint Chiefs of Staff for strategic development in the Caribbean area.

One of the reasons in the back of our minds relating to Guantanamo was to provide a base for protection of the approaches to the Panama Canal. As time went on, that became only one of the reasons. The other reasons were those that I have mentioned to you, highlighted by the Bay of Pigs and not long afterwards

Dennison #11 - 450

by the Cuban missile crisis. Would you like me to mention my visit to Haiti?

Q: I would indeed because I think your visit to the President of Haiti and what transpired in your conversation is a part of this whole picture of bases in the Caribbean.

Adm. D.: Well, remember what I just mentioned about this dispatch I sent to Burke in April 1961. In December of that year I made a trip into the Caribbean and visited a number of places. I think Trinidad was one of the places at that time, also Puerto Rico, and Haiti. Ambassador Thurston had just taken over as our ambassador there, a very able man. My wife and I stayed with the Thurstons. They had a dinner party the first night we were there which was a complete disaster - new servants, dishes were crashing all over the galley, tremendously embarrassing but it was so funny that no one could take it seriously! But it was a horror and poor Mrs. Thurston was so embarrassed. I had my political advisor with me and some of my staff.

I met a number of Haitians at the dinner, mainly military people. They seemed to be quite well educated and really delightful people. Colonel Heinl, of the Marine Corps, I forget what his status was, whether he was attache or military advisor or something, but he was a colorful character, and in those days I thought pretty much on the cloak-and-dagger side of the fence.

They had all sorts of radio communications set-up. Not

Dennison #11 - 451

very reliable, as I found out. But during my visit, accompanied by the ambassador and my political advisor and probably one or two of my staff, I paid an official call on President Duvalier in his palace.

It was obvious from the very beginning that Duvalier was trying to be friendly and really lay out the red carpet for me. One of the things he did was to parade his honor guard, which was really a pretty sizeable military contingent, and in the basement of the palace he had really an arsenal and magazines.

Q: We just learned that in the press.

Adm. D.: Well, we'd known it for a good many years but we just had it underlined again when the palace burned down and all the explosives went off! But this was his protection. He had a real sizeable force there, more than an honor guard, a body guard is what it was. These troops were all drawn up to render honors and they gave me a gun salute - it was the wrong number of guns, as I remember. I forget how many they fired, but it was too many or too few. Then they played the National Anthem, which was not really an appropriate honor for an admiral. It was the craziest version of it. Everything was out of tune. It wasn't really the right tune at all. But they were trying. They were some distance away, in the parade ground in front of the palace. Then the commanding officer of the guard came up to the bottom of the steps to escort me for an inspection of the guard. I walked down the steps to meet him and, since I'd been above him and he was some distance away, I didn't realize until I got down on his level that he must have been at least a foot taller than I am, and I'm six feet. A tremendous black man. So I inspected the guard and they were as smart as they possibly could have been, and after the inspection I spoke a few words. I forget what I had to say. Probably complimented them on their smart appearance and so on, thanked them, and then went up to have a talk with Duvalier in his office in the right-hand wing, as you look away from the building, on the second floor.

He had with him some of his staff. The principal one was a Haitian doctor - I believe he was Haitian - who quite obviously was the man Duvalier really depended on. After exchanging the usual pleasantries, he said that he wanted to make the offer to the United States for the use of some Haitian territory and would like to ask me if I would transmit the offer to President Eisenhower. Then he went on to say that he was willing to permit the United States the use - I've forgotten on just what terms, whether it was a lease, or treaty, or just what the form of agreement would be - but anyway the use of the area of northwestern Haiti, around the area of Cap Haitien. This was a tremendous piece of real estate and Duvalier's idea was that this could be developed into a training ground for Marines and with the few small ports up there that need a little bit of improvement, good anchorages -

Q: It's in what's known as the Windward Passage, isn't it?

Adm. D.: Yes, it's on the eastern side of the Passage, and of course it is a tremendously important strategic location. This would be, in his mind, in lieu of Guantanamo, because he realized as well as we did that we were having our troubles with Cuba, and what he would get out of it was money coming in to the Haitain economy and a tangible demonstration of ties to the United States. He would get probably some improvement in communications, including roads and port facilities.

We explored this offer briefly. I wanted to be sure I understood exactly what it was. That was the only really significant thing that happened during the visit.

Q: You did ask him if he'd made this offer before, didn't you?

Adm. D.: Yes, I did ask him, and he said yes he had, he'd made it to the previous ambassador, U. S. ambassador, and also some congressman whose name I've forgotten. But he never knew whether the President ever heard about it, so I assured him I'd do what I could and, when we left, my political advisor, Lansing Collins, and I sat down with Ray Thruston to discuss this offer. Neither one of us, of course, had ever heard of it till Duvalier made it to me. My conversation with Duvalier was transmitted to the State Department. Quite obviously, it would have been completely out of order for me to transmit it directly to the President. It should go through our usual diplomatic channels. So I assume that, one way or another, it did come to the President's attention, but, of course, as everyone knows, nothing was ever done about it, probably for several reasons, one of the most important ones being that we didn't really trust Duvalier. We disapproved of his oppressive measures to rule Haiti, and this, of course, would be a rather implicit recognition that we were backing the Duvalier government. There were probably other reasons beside what I've just mentioned. The amount of money it would take to develop that particular area and the fact that we had no intention of withdrawing from Guantanamo.

Q: That being so, it would have been a duplication?

Adm. D.: It would have been a duplication. Of course, if we'd been really up against it with no alternative, then the offer would have been a great deal more attractive. But nothing ever came of it.

Q: What came of your submission of the ten-year plan for the bases in the area?

Adm. D.: I've really forgotten. I should imagine that the Joint Chiefs of Staff had it stamped and it probably was approved for planning purposes. That's what it was. It was a plan, and I see no reason why it shouldn't be approved for planning so that the various services involved in these plans for the area would be able to come up with their individual plans. The Navy, of course, were the ones most involved. That's why Burke would have been the leader in the Joint Chiefs to see to it that these plans were

Dennison #11 - 455

in everybody's file and that they were making supporting plans. This would, indeed, be guidance for our dealings with these various countries. The latter thing, of course, had to be done through the Department of State. Although I wasn't in Washington at the time, I'm reasonably certain that the State Department was informed of my views and the actions of the Joint Chiefs of Staff on them.

It's fairly obvious, of course, that the United States does have a tremendous stake in that area, and here was one way to ensure that we were in a position to act to maintain the security of that area. It's in our interest. That's what it's all about.

Q: As a matter of fact, our hold on the use of the two islands, Culebra and Vieques, has become increasingly difficult?

Adm. D.: Yes, it has, and mostly through exploitation for domestic political purposes.

Q: Is it related to the rise in nationalistic feeling in Puerto Rico?

Adm. D.: Oh, I think that's perhaps a part of it, and maybe through the years it's become more and more of an important part, but I think that there was then, and I think still is, a lack of appreciation throughout our government of our real need for this particular area. We have no place else to train, no place else to establish a U. S. direct presence in that area. It's a benevolent presence, surely, Nobody in his right mind would think we were down there for purposes of conquering somebody or taking over countries.

Q: As a matter of fact, it seems to me that there have been public pronouncements, or at least one public pronouncement, to the effect that we could dispense with our use of these islands.

Adm. D.: Oh, yes.

Q: Just as Adlai Stevenson said we could get along without Guantanamo.

Adm. D.: Yes, I remember that. Such remarks are based on a complete lack of understanding of strategy or how you further U. S. interests by peaceful means.

Q: There's another subject which is very closely related to this and to the actions and policy of the Navy in the Caribbean, and that is, with the development of difficulties in these various countries, the Navy has always been obliged to get involved or to stand by, with the thought that we might be involved. I'm thinking of in 1961, in June of 1961, for instance, in the Dominican Rupublic, the president, the dictator, was assassinated. The Navy immediately got involved. Do you remember that incident?

Dennison #11 - 457

Adm. D.: Yes, I certainly do. Our policies toward the Dominican Republic seem to me to have never been really firmed up or understood. Again, we have a tremendous stake in that area, but we were so hamstrung really as to what exactly to do about it. Later, of course, we did land there.

Q: In 1965.

Adm. D.: Yes, sort of a fiasco. I remember one of the things that I was supposed to do and did do was a show of force. Well, now, that's all right to show force. I hate to keep disagreeing with some of the things the State Department has done, or did, but this is typical. A show of force was supposed to include naval forces plus air power, but my ships were supposed to stay so far offshore that they couldn't even be seen. My idea of a show of force was to steam right along the coast where you could throw a baseball on the beach if you wanted to, and if we were going to do any air demonstrations to do them where everybody could see them.

Q: A visible show!

Adm. D.: That's it. What good is a show of force if nobody except dolphins are going to look at it?

But, here again, we had all kinds of plans, we made thorough studies of the various ports in the area, we had information efforts going on for years, communications within the Dominican Republic, and the relationship between the Dominican Republic and Haiti, and communications on who the bad guys were, and all the rest of it. Finally, things got out of hand, as you mentioned, in 1965 and I don't think that would have ever happened if we'd taken a firmer stand in 1961 and really got things calmed down and under control.

One of the lessons that we learned, and it was a good lesson, in Nicaragua. It's one thing to move into a country but it's quite another thing to ever get out of it. If you're really going in to stabilize a situation, it may mean that you have to take over certain control of government activities. And once you do that, then the problem becomes how do you establish a sufficient degree of stability in local governments for domestic purposes so that you can withdraw without everything going to hell all over again.

I think I brought this out when we were discussing Cuba. Sure, we could have gone in and we could have established a military government, but who could we install to replace Castro? As I remember, at the time there were at least seven identifiable Cuban parties in the Florida area. Groups of people who claimed to represent the people in Cuba. Well, of course, no one group —

Q: They certainly weren't united in any sense.

Adm. D.: I was about to say that. There was no way that the U. S. government, through CIA or through the State Department or through anybody, could bring these elements together to agree on a man - I mean there was talk at the time, I remember, about setting up a government in exile. But when you tried to find out who would be accepted - you can't just pick a man and say here's the president of Cuba in exile, the Cuban people had to support him, even only those in exile. I just mention this in passing of the diffic-lty that we're talking about of taking over - in this case, Santo Domingo - even briefly. There isn't any such thing as taking over a country briefly. This is a great deterrent and it's a lesson that we've learned too well, I think. We go from taking over a government to going back to a show of force over the horizon.

Q: There were two other instances during your time as CinCLant which occurred in the year 1962 of similar nature. In August of 1962 there was a potential disorder brewing in Haiti itself, and the Navy again was called upon and a Marine Landing Force was actually put aboard a ship to stand by. Do you remember that incident?

Adm. D.: Yes, vaguely. This was one of a number of incidents in our whole general area, and again this was really, from my point of view, a means to demonstrate our interest and hopefully to indicate that we would consider using force to intervene if we felt the situation was serious enough. Now that latter part of my statement, we just hoped to indicate that this was the case. I don't think we ever would. We can't afford to advertise that, but this business of landing Marines, or loading Marines, is something that you can't very well conceal and shouldn't want to conceal, for the reasons that I have mentioned.

Q: The later one was in November of that year and it involved the perennial Guatemala.

Adm. D.: Yes, I know, and this shows that there are smoldering fires all over that area.

Q: Well, is there any over-all policy of the United States government, as expressed by the State Department, which governs all these incidents?

Adm. D.: Yes, of course. The United States does indeed have an over-all policy. For example, we believe in self determination, security and stability in the Caribbean area and such things as that. The basics of our policy, of course, are involved in any contingency plan or any country plan which we may develop. In practice, however, many instances are and probably must be treated on an ad hoc basis.

Q: There's the Monroe Doctrine standing back of it all, but that's fairly general.

Adm. D.: Well, it's the same with a good many policies of ours but that is completely understandable, of course. Any plans we developed for specific action must be examined, of course, so that we may be sure they are completely compatible with our general policies.

Q: Well, Admiral, does this whole situation tie in with the question of the Organization of American States and the defense of all of the states? I notice that on 24 May of 1960 you attended a meeting in Key West with representatives from a number of the Latin American countries to discuss common problems for the two hemispheres.

Adm. D.: Yes. This was only one of several that I attended. One, I remember, was in Puerto Rico. This involved almost entirely military personnel - navies were really the ones we were talking to. Military cooperation between the Latin American states has always been a very great problem area. They're natural enemies, as they see it. I mean the idea of cooperation and military coordination of any kind is not in their thinking. There's basic enmity between so many of those states. Argentina and Brizil are one example. They're not natural friends. And it's only been in the area of naval operations that we've been able to establish cooperation, friendship, and exchange of ideas. But between naval officials of the latin American countries we've been the catalyst. That's why we set up our South Atlantic Force, which is based in Trinidad, and it accomplished two purposes. One was to bring the Latin American navies together, also to give us an opportunity to get a foothold in Trinidad and establish a benevolent presence there. We didn't have any great number of people there. There were some Air Force installations and missile-tracking stations. But the larger problem about the Organization of American States was really outside the scope of my military responsibilities. But you remember, I think i've already commented on it in connection with the Cuban missile cirsis. The Organization itself approved President Kennedy's action, which was a great thing, just the same as it was a great thing for the Security Council of the United Nations to pick up the Korean situation and underwrite that.

However, in the case of the missile crisis, the OAS did not appear in the role that the United Nations did in Korea, obviously. But some individual nations, as I've already mentioned to you, did contribute forces which actually were employed in our operations.

Q: In dealing with the military representatives of these various nations, did you find any latent hostility toward the Big Brother to the north?

Adm. D.: Quite the contrary, because the Latin American navies looked on us as one of their great boosters. They were getting ships from us, they were getting training from us, a lot of publicity about the importance of sea power, and the relation between sea power and the defense of their own countries. No, we were their saviors, and among themselves there was camaraderie

Dennison #11 - 463

and exchange of ideas. It was really quite refreshing. I mean it was just like a group of United States officers discussing matters with each other. But when it comes to the national interest, or as they see national interest, for example the Latin American navies agreeing to operate under the command of any one of them, it's just unthinkable. They just wouldn't do it. So, again, we were the catlyst. They'd operate under our command gladly, in groups, all these navies together in a task group. But, no, we were the great booster of sea power in Latin America.

Q: How valuable were the - I think they're called the amity cruises?

Adm. D.: Oh, amity.

Q: Yes, it's a yearly event, isn't it?

Adm. D.: We call them SoLantAmity, South Atlantic Amity. I dug that name out of the back of my head some place. These are marvelous things. The idea was that we should have a periodic cruise down the coast of West Africa, and the composition of the force varied from time to time, but basically it was a Marine Landing Team. We had one or two LSTs and some destroyers. I had a man on my staff - I wish I could remember his name because he was marvelous, he was a helping hand fellow - and he was able to get contributions of medicines, books, and all kinds of things from various commercial concerns that we could distribute

Dennison #11 - 464

in the various ports we went to. And we had a band so we could have a band concert, put on a landing team demonstration, which is quite colorful, you know, the way the Marines do it, and entertain all the people aboard ships, give the kids ice cream, and give them sets of encyclopedias, and all kinds of things. Amity really was a good word for it.

Q: And it was for the benefit of the Latin Americans?

Adm. S.: In South America we scheduled naval exercises all around South America involving forces of the various South American navies. These met with considerable success. We would provide the task force commander and elements from the other navies would serve under our command.

Q: How did these conferences you had with Latin American representatives tie in with the InterAmerican Defense Board, which was exclusively military, too, wasn't it?

Adm. D.: Yes, but this was sort of passive organization. I don't remember much, if any, contact with it. This was more of a planning agency or something up here in Washington, as I remember it, and this college they've got - I don't know what they teach. But this is typical of anything to do with Latin America. The first thing you do is set up a hell of a lot of organizations, committees, and colleges, and all kinds of structures. This seems to be just the natural way that the countries operate. Then many

Dennison #11 - 465

of them just fall into disuse, if they ever had any use, and most of them - and I don't want to appear to be too cynical about it, most of them are really public relations or hands-across-the-sea sort of thing.

It seems to me that the way to do something correctly is like this SoLantAmity. You get out in the field, you see people and talk to them, and do things for them, and exchange ideas.

Q: Admiral, CinCLant was involved in education, too. You were constantly receiving delegations and groups of people. I noticed at one point over 100 - well, 164 students came down from the Naval War College to your headquarters. On another occasion, 25 or 30 faculty and students came from the State Department senior seminar. Do you want to talk about that area of your activities?

Adm. D.: Not only what you've mentioned but we had many groups of foreigners, mostly from NATO nations, and not only groups but individuals. Norfolk was almost a must for people visiting the United States, if they were interested in military affairs, because it's not far from Washington. It's a great deal handier than going to Hawaii, for example.

I looked on these visits not as a burden but as a great opportunity for us to really talk to people who were interested in military business or military strategy, and be as open as we could with them about what we were thinking and how we did things and why.

Q: Did this include demonstrations?

Adm. D.: Yes, we did everything. Whenever we could we took these groups to sea. We had a carrier available or a suitable ship, and the amphibious base, you see, is right next to the naval base. LeJeune is not all that far away. We could get down there to put on a typically gung-ho Marine demonstration. So we spent a lot of time on these activities, which I thought was far from wasted. As a matter of fact, I welcomed and generated some of these meetings myself.

And another thing we did through my wonderful fleet surgeon, Real Admiral John Cowan, was to have a meeting of international surgeons. The first time it's ever been done, and these noted men came from all over Europe, and our chief of the Bureau of Medicine and Surgery was down there and a group of our own doctors. They met as a group of medical men, speaking a common medical language. It was a great opportunity for them to associate with their peers and to learn something about, in this case, military medicine from others.

Q: Cross fertilization of ideas.

Adm. D.: Indeed it was. I hate to bring myself into it, but I remember this occasion because I wanted to recognize it and I just had my doctor run it, so I told him that I would open up the meeting. He sort of gulped, I think, but said politely that that would be just fine! So I did, and as I started out I could see that Ed Kenny, the chief of the Bureau of Medicine and Surgery, was practically asleep and my own surgeon looked kind of bored. So I sort of broke in to what I had started to say and said, "My real problem is that I don't really know how to address you. If I addressed you as 'fellow doctors' that would seem a little presumptuous because your field and mine are not quite the same, and I can't just say 'Welcome aboard,' so I decided the only suitable way for me to address you is as fellow practitioners of the art of psychological warfare." That sort of loosened things up!

But, anyway, to get back to the real point. This visit and other similar visits with different kinds of groups was of tremendous value, I think.

We had congressional groups come down, and a good many skeptics would come down. Maybe they left being skeptics, but we had a chance to try to convert them. A great many foreign visitors came, not only from Europe but from all over the place. I remember one experience I had with one of the newspapers. It seems rather incredible now that I'm sort of tied in with the newspaper business. But we went through sort of a routine. A foreign visitor would come, he'd pay a call, and then we'd ask him if he wished to have a press conference. Usually they said yes. Then we would have reporters there from the wire services as well as papers and anybody who wanted to come.

And one time we had a visit from the Minister of Defense of the Philippines - or Secretary or whatever his title was. He was a very nice gentleman but obviously not too well read into that business. So I decided that I'd better go to this conference with him. I sat at the table and introduced him, and then I moved to one side so that I wouldn't be in camera range with him, unless they wanted me to. The reporters started in on him. It was just God awful. I remember one reporter asked him a question that would draw a parallel between the Philippines and Japan in terms of culture, for example, philosophy. Well, if you can think of a more insulting question to ask a Filipino, I don't know what it could possibly be. So I immediately got up and said:

"I'm so sorry, gentlemen, but I've just remembered that my guest and I have a very important engagement, so if you'll excuse us." I stood up and everybody else had to stand up, so all we had to do was turn around and walk out.

Then I got hold of my public relations people and I said:

"This is going to stop. We're not going to have any more press conferences, and furthermore we're not going to have any press interviews with any of my guests." I could make this stick, because we controlled the whole area, the landing field and everything. Nobody could come in or approach, any of these people, without our allowing them to do so, and ordinarily we would. We were not trying to cut everybody off.

When this word got to the Norfolk papers - the publisher was a man named Frank Batten, who was and is a dear friend of ours - his two papers - one editor was a man named Mason and the other a man named Fitzpatrick, both very able men and both friends of mine. After this had gone on for a week or so, we did have one or two guests in the meantime, Batten called and wanted to know if he could come up and see me, and I said sure, bring Mason and

Fitzpatrick, and have lunch with me.

So they came to my office and Batten said:

"OK, we give up. What do you want?" And I said:

"What I want is very simple, something that will benefit you just as much as it will me, maybe more. You're looking for news, worthwhile stories, and I'm looking to protect my guests. And if you will brief your reporters to come up here and ask questions, give them the questions, if you have to, to ask to draw out the stories that you're looking for. If you need any help on that my PIO or even I myself will help you, brief you on who these people really are, what they've done, what their field is, and so on."

He said, "OK, that's a deal."

I forget who it was that came next. Maybe it was Dirk Stikker, the Secretary General of NATO. He came over quite frequently. I attended the conference and, my God, you'd have thought it was a State Department seminar. The questions that he was asked were really penetrating, intelligent, and, of course, drew out from him answers, because he felt he was talking to people who were intelligent and understanding. They were understanding enough to write down what he had to say, but the questions came from these marvelous editors. So it was great. I don't know what happened to the First Amendment!

Q: So there was some frame work to the questions?

Adm. D.: Well, it was some pretty radical treatment of the press

Dennison #11 - 470

and it didn't accuse me of hiding things because Batten understood exactly what the problem was. I had to bring it home to them by just establishing the blockade long enough to make my point.

Q: When you spoke to foreign visotors I noticed that one of your visitors who turned up several times and others from his navy turned up, and that was Admiral Ruge, of the German Navy. Was he interested at that point in building up a German Navy and was he coming for advice and help?

Adm. D.: Ruge was essentially, I believe, at least as far as I saw him, a great naval student, a naval historian, a writer, a very intellectual type. Of course, he was interested in the German Navy.

Q: He was more or less charged with building it up again, wasn't he?

Adm. D.: Yes, but there are two things to remember about that German Navy in those times. One is that the British principally and other European nations after World War II wanted never to see a blue-water navy in the hands of Germany, and the German Navy, such as it was, was put under Supreme Allied Commander, Europe, rather than Supreme Allied Command, Atlantic, because they really were a sort of coastal force, and still are. So the idea of building up the German Navy, if you mean a blue-water navy, was absolutely out of the question. Ruge would have been

Dennison #11 - 471

the first to understand that. But I enjoyed him. He was a gentleman and, I think, a good friend.

Mountbatten was another visitor who appeared quite frequently. I've already mentioned Stikker. We had quite a few guests from Norway and many other European countries.

Q: This must have made great demands on your own personal time, especially these groups of students that you had to address, didn't it?

Adm. D.: It wasn't all that bad because we developed a pattern of how these visitors would be handled. We were extremely well organized for them. We knew what we had to offer in the way of demonstrations and lectures and visits and so on, so personally I was only a symbol of our interest. I didn't have to do much except welcome these groups, which I did every time I possibly could, just to indicate that from the top of the command on down we were damned well interested and honored to have them visit. So it really wasn't all that much of a problem.

What was sort of a problem was that these visits of various kinds came so quickly and so frequently and we had to do a great deal of entertaining, which meant dinners and receptions, lucheons, and so on. This was boring sometimes and sometimes it wasn't. We usually made it as much fun as we possibly could.

Q: You had SacLant Bar to help out, didn't you?

Dennison #11 - 472

Adm. D.: Well, yes, SacLant Bar down in the mess but of course there were no restrictions on wines or cocktails in my own home. It was really no strain. You could make it an ordeal, I suppose, if you wanted to.

I had a perfectly marvelous band, which was a help at ceremonies. We had a number of colorful ceremonies. We had a colors ceremony daily at SacLant headquarters where we had all the NATO flags displayed. There are many showmanship things that you can do to lighten things. Of course, at sea it's another matter. You can put on quite a spectacular.

Q: Now, if we might turn to different areas. About this time, I think, the Navy was active in terms of hurricanes, hurricane hunters. Do you remember any of that?

Adm. D.: Only in general.

Q: This must have involved cooperation with the Weather Bureau.

Adm. D.: Oh, indeed, yes, and our own hydrographic office and various agencies. The whole idea was to track hurricanes, which usually originate in theCaribbean area, measure their intensity, and provide the basis for predicting where they're going. At that time we weren't engaged in seeding operations to try to break up the storm. It was really a storm surveillance system. The planes would go out but I never was aboard one, and fly right into the eye of the hurricane.

Dennison #11 - 473

Q: To measure the volocity!

Adm. D.: Yes, and to measure the speed of advance and so on. It was quite a useful thing. It didn't prevent any storm, of course, That wasn't the purpose of it. It did give a basis for prediction as to whether the storm was going to recurve early or whether it was going to take the usual path, heading toward the coast and going up the coast, and then out eastward. But it was just a usual operation. I don't think there was anything too dramatic about it, except the bravery of these people who would fly these planes into the terrific turbulence that they experienced.

Q: And it was something of tremendous potential benefit to the Navy itself?

Adm. D.: Oh, indeed, yes, we're interested in storms.

I remember in theWestern Pacific, in the Philippine area, typhoons are almost unpredictable. I mean you just knew that they were coming, but where they were going to hit and what the intensity was was something nobody knew.

Q: Admiral, in 1960, of course, the Polaris submarines began to come into operation, and in September of that year you as CinCLant personally took operational control of the submarines. This was in accordance with a Joint Chiefs' directive. Do you want to talk about that? You told me about the meeting with Secretary Gates and how Polaris came under the wing of the Navy.

Dennison #11 - 474

Now this was actually the operational aspect of it that you assumed personally.

Amd. D.: I think I mentioned at the time what that meant. When I said I took it over personally it was patterned generally after the Strategic Air Command system for bombers. It simply meant that the usual administrative chain of command wasn't used in commanding Polaris, that the firing signal came from me, or it could be sent direct by the Joint Chiefs or the President, if they wanted to.

I don't think there's anything particularly significant about that September date, except that was the date that we were in business. And, of course, it worked. We had drills very, very frequently to be sure that not only our primary communications but these various subsidiary communications systems also worked. The messages were repeated by relays from various stations all over the United States and also from ships at sea. So there was a tremendous diplication of messages just to be sure that something would get through.

Remember that this is very-low-frequency transmission, basically, to permit reception by submerged antennae. The submarine didn't have to show anything above the surface to receive a message. Furthermore, we kept a constant flow of messages going so that an enemy couldn't gauge our activities by the volume of our radio traffic. It was the same volume all the time, and if nothing of an operational nature was going through we used to send what we called "familygrams." In other words,

Dennison #11 - 475

a wife could get in touch with our headquarters and send a message to her husband aboard one of these submarines that little Tommy had fallen and broken his arm, or maybe she had some good news to send along.

Q: You became a mailman!

Adm. D.: Well, it was only one way because the people aboard the submarines were observing radio silence and couldn't talk back. But it was a tremendous help in morale.

Q: I would think so, considering the long tours of duty.

Adm. D.: It was a great help, as you point out, to morale and a great comfort to the men out at sea to know that if anything was important, or even unimportant, that happened to their families they'd know about it.

Furthermore, they well knew that if there were an emergency or any way that anybody could be of help, these messages to them had gone through my headquarters and we would do what we could to alleviate whatever the condition might be or to help in any way we could.

Q: I noted with great interest that in March of 1963 the Atlantic Fleet adopted something quite in keeping with the times. The Atlantic Fleet Computer Programming Center was set up at Dam Neck in Virginia.

Adm. D.: Even before that I had a computer center in my headquarters. Computers got to be more and more important in naval operations. The one I had in my headquarters was for the principal purpose of maintaining intelligence displays. We had various screens around my headquarters, including one - a very large one - in my operational control center, and you could call up a display of any given ocean area. Let's say north of Puerto Rico, that part of the Atlantic, or in the Caribbean, and you'd see a display that showed you where ships were and where airplanes were, and then the computer would update the positions very frequently - I think every twelve minutes, or sonething like that. And, of course, the updating was based on the prediction through sightings or radio tracking or whatever means of the course and speed of these ships. So you had to remember that when you were watching these displays, and realize that it was conceivable that it was erroneous to a certain extent because you might have her course and speed wrong. If you had some question about it, you'd have to send out some reconnaissance planes or do something to verify it. But it was a very useful tool.

I remember a visit I had from Lord Carrington, a friend of mine, who was at that time First Lord of the Admiralty - he now is in the British government as Minister of Defense, and one of the things I did was take him on a tour of my headquarters and into this computer room. There were computers all around and it was really quite a large installation, various screens and people doing various things, and the man I had in charge of

Dennison #11 - 477

the computer room was a very enthusiastic young naval officer, a lieutenant, I think, deeply immersed in his work and the importance of it. He showed Carrington all around the place and explained things to him, and then when he got all through he asked Lord Carrington:

"Sir, do you have any questions?" and Carrington put on a very solemn look, thought for a moment, then said:

"No, Lieutenant, your explanations have been so lucid, so thorough, that you've answered all the questions I might otherwise have had. Thank you very much."

When we got outside the room, I said:

"Peter, you certainly let that young man down because he's so immersed in the job he's got. Why in the world couldn't you dream up something to ask him?"

He said: "Well, you know I was thinking there. I realized I didn't understand a damned word he said, and the only thing I could think of to say was "gee, it's big, isn't it?"."

Q: That's one way of covering up!

Adm. D.: He was a master at it! I must say I've often felt that way myself.

Q: Did the advent of the center on shore contribute so much more to the operations of the fleet?

Adm. D.: Yes. I mean there were many other applications besides tracking to use computers for. You see, the Atlantic Fleet

Dennison #11 - 478

headquarters is a tremendous business organization. I don't have any figures now about the number of dispatches that came in and out of that headquarters every day having to do with logistic matters, fuel oil supplies, invoices, inventories, food, pay schedules, keeping track of the location of personnel, and all kinds of administrative matters. And one of the problems that came to light very early in the game - I think I may have mentioned to you that I felt that a fleet headquarters was not properly organized if it was tied down in operational control to any given location, particularly ashore -

So I decided that I would go to sea periodically in whatever suitable ship might be available and exercise command of the fleet from a ship. Beside the feeling of a sailor for environmental reasons, it makes a great deal of sense tactically as well.

So I had my chief of staff organize an operating staff. It had to be a small one because we couldn't move several hundred people aboard any ship. We had to have operations, communications, intelligence, and plans. We had to have the right files to take with us, not only codes and cyphers, but contingency plans. We had to have our Polaris control. Anyway, it was a relatively small group, and these men were told to pack a suitcase and leave it at headquarters, and periodically I was going to sound a general alarm and on a few hours' notice we were going to get aboard ship and to to sea.

Well, it sounds fairly simple but one of the greatest problems was in winnowing out of the tremendous volume of dispatches those messages that were of operational importance to the fleet commander, which was only a small proportion of this total tremendous inflow. We pretty well disregarded written correspondence because there's usually no great time element involved in that kind of communication. We had our voice radios, if we had to use them, but to find a dividing plan between purely administrative traffic and operational traffic was difficult. But what I started out to say was that fleet headquarters was much, much more than just a command post, and this experiment of mine demonstrated very quickly what was needed and to see that everybody had got into the habit of reporting to an office every morning, instead of aboard ship. It was my idea to bring to everybody's attention that they were basically sailors and the sea was the place to be.

Q: Sort of refreshing!

Adm. D.: Yes, but it was a shock when I first did it. But it worked and it worked not only there but in the Cuban missile crisis, for example, where we had to establish command facilities at our advanced command post in Florida. That was just one example of shifting the right people and the right documents, the right communications. Or when I went to sea with an exercise I couldn't just go to sea, as I did many times - I went with President Kennedy one time, maybe more than once - I couldn't just be isolated, I had to be there as a commander, so it was essential to have a ready means, not just on an ad hoc basis, prime-time basis, to have your plans made and the

Dennison #11 - 480

right people available and the right documents. It just makes sense.

Q: Yes. Toward the end of your tour of duty we had the loss of the Thresher.

Amd. D.: Yes, that was a tragic thing.

Q: That happened on 10 April of 1963.

Adm. D.: Yes, I remember it well. I had a submarine background, as you know, and I think I told you sometime ago about my early experience in connection with several of these submarine disasters. I could pretty well put together in my own mind what happened, and the chances were slim of ever doing anything except salavaging that ship at the depth that she was in. You see, there's a very severe limitation on the depth at which you can conduct diving operations by normal means.

Q: And this was beyond that depth? This was 8,400 feet.

Adm. D.: Yes. As I recall, I believe I grabbed onto Count Austin - I may be mistaken in that, but I needed an on-scene commander, somebody to get out there, some senior officer. I do remember I think it was Count Austin who was the president of the board of investigation and court of inquiry - if it wasn't Austin it was some responsible senior officer that I got to sea and got out there, realizing that the chance that they'd be able to do anything was almost nil. But you just can't sit on shore and wring your hands. You've got to do something.

I don't know whether Admiral Austin mentioned this in his oral history to you or not, or whether he even had one.

Q: He did mention the fact that he served on the court of inquiry, yes.

Adm. D.: Yes, he was the president of it, so perhaps he wasn't the one that I sent out there. In any event, whoever did go out there was able to keep our communications open and advise me what the situation was, which of course was pretty damned grim.

Q: The report of the court has never been actually made public, has it?

Adm. D.: That I don't know. I'm not certain, but I would think the chances were that the report was never issued while I was in command because I retired the 1st of May, I think it was, 1963. But Admiral Austin is a natural choice because he's an experienced officer and a very, very thorough one. If anybody could ever get to the bottom of it, it would be Austin.

INDEX

for

Series of Interviews with

Admiral Robert L. Dennison,

U. S. Navy (Retired)

ACHESON, The Hon. Dean: as Assistant Secretary of State, p. 105-6, p. 180.

ALASKAN CAMPAIGN: p. 62-3; the landings, p. 64-6; see also entries under COMAMPHIBFORPACFLT.

ANDERSON, Admiral George: p. 392-3; p423, p 429.

USS ARKANSAS: Dennison's first tour of duty, P. 1

ARMED FORCES STAFF COLLEGE: Dennison stresses the importance of, p. 287-8.

ARMY-NAVY ATTITUDES: in pre-World War II, p. 36-7; King and Nimitz begin to develop an appreciation of need for cooperation, p. 37; MacArthur treatment of a navy representative as different from his staff, p.38.

ASIATIC FLEET: Dennison assigned there - 1940-41, p. 17 ff. Dennison becomes skipper of the DD John D. Ford, flagship of Division 12, p. 21; Dennison detached by Hart to become senior patrol officer in Manila, p.23; after outbreak of war Dennison becomes only contact between Hart and MacArthur, p.23-24; declaration of Manila as open city played havoc with navy plans, p.27; SSs attempt to operate out of Subic Bay, p. 28; Hart gives Adm. Rockwell the operational command of units remaining in the Manila area, p. 28-29; Dennison's description of the nature of the Asiatic fleet, p. 34; complete lack of air cover for the fleet, p. 35; Dennison's comments on reasons for little liaison between Army-Navy, p. 36.

ASTRONAUTS: rescue operations in the Atlantic p. 381-2.

ATTU: P. 56; p. 63-4.

AUSTIN, Vice Admiral B.L. (Count): p. 480-1.

AUSTIN, The Hon. Warren: U. S. Delegate to the United Nations, p. 102-3; his handling of the Mandated Islands debate, p. 103.

AUSTRALIA - in the war, p. 45 ff.

AUSTRALIAN LABOR: their early attitudes towards the war - incident involving a U. S. submarine, p. 46-7; an incident on the West Coast of Australia after the Battle of the Coral Sea, p. 47-8.

AZORES: Importance of, p. 308-9; use of base in the QUARANTINE OPERATION of Cuba, p. 425.

BALLENTINE, Admiral John J.: p. 127-8.

BATTEN, Frank: Norfolk, Virginia publisher - his encounter with Adm. Dennison and the question of reporters and foreign guests of the Naval Command, p. 468-470.

BAY OF PIGS (BUMPY ROAD-code Name): p. 330-360; Dennison's general observations on the operation, p. 360-369. Dennison called to testify before the special committee headed by General Max Taylor, p. 368.

BEGLEY, Paul: Photographer's mate who went with President Truman everywhere, p. 170-1; on the fishing boat, the "Big Wheel", p. 172.

BERLIN CRISIS (July, 1961), p. 382 ff;.

BISSELL, Richard M. Jr.: p. 333-5; p. 339; p. 361.

BONAIRE: p. 448.

BRADLEY, General Omar: his views on General MacArthur, p. 37-8. becomes Chairman of the JCS - briefs the President, p. 176-9; p. 181; Truman consults him about relieving Gen. MacArthur of his command, p. 214.

BRISBANE, Australia: base for Comdr. U. S. Naval Forces, West Australia - and for General MacArthur, p. 53.

BROWN, Admiral Charles R. (Cat.): Carrier Division Commander in the 6th Fleet, (1953), p. 242-3.

BUMPY ROAD: code name for Bay of Pigs, p. 330. Other entries on the subject of this military episode will appear under the more familiar name - BAY OF PIGS

BUNCHE, The Hon. Ralph: p. 102.

BURKE, Admiral Arleigh: Dennison's story of the efforts of Secretaries Johnson and Matthews to strike the name of Burke from the Selection Board List, p. 194-200; his injection of self into a NATO war game under the command of Dennison - the show down, p. 290-3.; on the search process for the Portuguese steamer SANTA MARIA, p. 379; McNamara consults him on a successor to Admiral Anderson, P. 392-3; p. 444; p. 454.

USS CANOPUS: Submarine tender - based at Manila - prepared to operate submarines until the MacArthur order on the open city - p. 27; hit by Japanese bomb, forcing U. S. subs to abandon the area, p. 28.

CARIBBEAN BASES: Dennison's action to underscore U. S. need for them - p. 444 ff; suggestions on Culebra, Vieques, Swan Island, Bonaire, Trinidad - long range plan as submitted to the JCS, p. 449- 454; Dennison's trip to the Caribbean in December, 1961, p. 450 ff; p. 455-6.

CARIBBEAN POLICY - of the U. S.: p. 460.

CARNEY, Admiral Robert B.: p. 241; calls Dennison back to take Op 60 (Director of the Strategic Plans Division), p. 241.

CARRINGTON, Lord: First Lord of the Admiralty visits CincLant, p. 476-7.

CASSIDY, Admiral John: Commander of the 6th Fleet (1953), p. 242-3.

CASTRO, Fidel: p. 333-4.; see entries under CUBAN MISSILE CRISIS.

CASTRO, Raul: brother of Fidel - his role in selling concept of a rapid build up of missiles in Cuba, p. 405; p. 411.

CATES, General C.B. (USMC): Commandant of the Marine Corps - his role in Truman's confrontation with the Corps, p.208.

CHIANG kai-Chek his headquarters in Chungking, p. 121; discussions with Gates, Pauley and Dennison, p. 121-2; Dennison's feeling that the U. S. let the Generalissimo down in actions on the Chinese mainland, p. 126; p. 265-7.

CHIANG, Madame: her part in the reparations discussions, p. 121-2.

CHINESE POST WAR POLICY: Dennison's views on the post
	war mistakes of the U. S., p. 126-7.

CHRISTIE, Vice Admiral Ralph Waldo: p. 53.

CHUNGKING: visit of the Reparations Team to Chiang kai-
	chek p. 121.

CHURCHILL, The Rt. Hon. Winston: p. 73-4; his voice heard
	in Combined Chiefs of Staff, p. 77; P. 80; his off-
	beat ideas, p. 89-91; his visit to President Truman
	on the WILLIAMSBURG, p. 171-2.

CIA: The intentions of President Truman for the CIA- and
	developments, p. 314-5. See various references under
	BAY OF PIGS.

CINC LANT - CINC LANT FLEET - SAC LANT: Dennison assumes
	command of these several commands in February, 1960;
	p. 317 ff; how command control of POLARIS came under
	CINC LANT, p. 319-321; the program for visiting
	dignitaries, p. 328-9; McNamara offers to keep Dennison
	on the job after the retirement age, p. 391; Dennison
	suggests Adm. Page Smith as his relief, p. 392.

CINC LANT COMMAND: Visiting delegations and VIP's p. 465-
	472; European medical men, p. 466; press conferences
	for foreign visitors, p. 467; and incident involving the
	Norfolk, Va. press and a foreign visitor, p. 467-9.
	Dennison decides to take his command to sea on occasion -
	arrangements, for, p. 478-9.

CINCLANTFLEET: see entries under CINC LANT.

CINC NELM: Dennison becomes commander on April 1, 1959; p. 300; his story of a joint operation with the British off the coast of Libya, p. 300-301; ever present problems such as Cyprus, p. 303-4.

CLIFFORD, The Hon. Clark: served as an aide to President Truman, p. 146.

COCHRANE, Vice Admiral Edward Lull: (Ned) Truman names him as first head of the new Maritime Administration, p. 159-161.

COLCLOUGH, Vice Admiral O.S.: his part in writing the Denfeld speech for presentation to Congress, p. 200-201.

COLWELL, Vice Admiral J. B.: Executive officer on BB MISSOURI - takes temporary command when Dennison is detached and called to Washington, p. 145.

COM AMPHIBFOR, PACFLEET: Admiral Rockwell takes over - asks Dennison to be his chief of staff - based in San Diego, p. 53-4; problems in personnel and equipment - training for the Alaskan campaign, p. 54-7; problem with 14 inch shells for shore bombardment, p. 57-9; p.65.

COMBINED CHIEFS OF STAFF: Dennison serves on their War Plans Committee, p. 76; the British method of negotiating, p. 76-8; some of the problems they had to contend with, p. 79; the sticky question of landing craft allocations, p. 80-1.

COMPUTER PROGRAMMING CENTER: set up at Dam Neck, Virginia, March, 1963, p. 475; visit of Lord Carrington, First Lord of the Admiralty, p. 476-7.

CONNOLLY, The Hon. John: p. 389; offers Dennison appointment as CNO - at the behest of Secretary McNamara, p. 391.

COOKE, Admiral Chas. M.: askes Dennison to join the sub-committee of the Far East under State Department chairmanship and get things arranged for Admiral Nimitz to sign Japanese surrender along with Gen. MacArthur, p. 91-2.

COWAN, RADM John: Atlantic fleet surgeon, p. 466.

CRAIG, Mae (Elizabeth) Mrs.: White House correspondent for various papers in state of Maine - Dennison's refusal to have her quartered on board the MISSOURI, p. 138-40.

CUBA: discussion of it and the Monroe Doctrine - and some strategic thinking that developed because of the missile crisis, p. 259-60; quotation from a letter of President Teddy Roosevelt written to Secretary of War Taft, p. 261.

CUBAN MISSILE CRISIS: p. 383, p. 391; the story of the Cuban Missile Crisis as told by the Cinc Atlantic, p. 394-443; the Soviet deployment of submarines, p. 434-7; Dennison's general observations on the subject of the crisis, p. 437-443; need to establish command facilities at the advanced command post in Florida, p. 479.

USS CUTTLEFISH: Dennison assigned command, p. 15; the first of the fleet submarines, p. 16.

DEAN, Arthur: the question of piracy in the case of the SS SANTA MARIA, p. 376-8.

DENFELD, Admiral Louis E.: the story of his dismissal as CNO, p. 200-203.

DENNISON, ADMIRAL Robert Lee: his concept of his career as a naval officer - emphasis on command - the reason for choosing service in submarines., p. 2, 17; he studies for a doctorate while on duty at the Experimental station in Annapolis (1934), p. 5-8; the oral examination, p. 8-11; serves as Chief of Staff to Admiral Glassford, p. 32; calls on Mr. Forrestal with President Truman two days before Forrestal's death, p. 114; his narrow escape in automobile accident in Japan, p. 128-130; his orders to become naval aide to President Truman, p. 144-5; President reminds him that he is a professional officer and not a politician, p. 152-3; his role in the reconciliation of Presidents Eisenhower and Truman, p. 220 ff; promotion to Rear Admiral, p. 239; his assignment to Command CruDiv 4 (Feb. 1953), p. 240-1; an account of the three times offers were made for his advancement - the Truman offer, p. 387-8; the offer from John Connolly (SecNav) for appointment as CNO, p. 389; the offer of Sec. Def. McNamara for extension of his appointment as CincLant, p. 390-1.

DEPARTMENT OF DEFENSE: Truman's concept for the new department, p. 294-5.

DEUTERMANN, Vice Admiral Harold T.: Command of the 2nd Fleet, p. 292-3.

DOBRYNIN, His Excellency Anatoliv F.: Russian Ambassador
to the United States - p. 395.

DOMINICAN REPUBLIC: Assassination of the President (June, 1961), p. 456.

DULLES, The Hon. John Foster: p. 110; p. 258-9; p. 268; p. 270; p. 333.

DUTRA, Major General Eurico Gaspar: President of Brazil - makes a visit to BB MISSOURI, p. 134-5.

DUVALIER, Dr. Francois: puts out the red carpet for Admiral Dennison (1961), p. 451; offers to President Eisenhower (through Dennison) use of area around Cap Hatien as a base, p. 452; Duvalier had made the offer before through the U. S. Ambassador but had no reply, p. 453-4.

EARLY, The Hon. Steve: Dennison suggests him to Louis Johnson as a Deputy SecDef, p. 191-2.

EISENHOWER, The Hon. Dwight D.: President of the U. S.

Truman convinces him to leave Columbia University for the NATO job, p. 149-50; he calls on President Truman and the President gives him a DSM, p. 150-1; the falling out with Truman, p. 152; p. 218-20; story of the reconciliation with Truman, p. 220-1; his efforts at smooth transition for President Kennedy, p. 225-6; his staff system in the White House contrasted with Truman's system, p. 225-7; p. 265. p. 333-5.

Dennison

ELECTRIC BOAT COMPANY: Dennison serves as Assistant Naval
  Inspector of machinery, 1938-9, p. 15-16.
ENDS OF THE EARTH CLUB: p. 247-8.
FAR EAST SUBCOMMITTEE- State Department: Dennison sits
  in on sessions to get provision made for Admiral Nimitz
  to sign surrender document along with Gen. Mac Arthur, P. 91-2
FECHTELER, Admiral Wm. M.: Chief of BuPers, p. 67-8. p. 144;
  Truman calls him to the White House for meeting, p. 239-40.
FEDERAL MARITIME ADMINISTRATOR: Truman reorganizes maritime
  affairs - sets up a Maritime Administrator and goes after
  Admiral Cochrane for the job, p. 159-161.
FERRAZ, General Beleza: Chief of Staff to the Portugese
  General Staff - messages relative to the SS **SANTA MARIA**
  p. 375-6.
FIRST FLEET: Dennison succeeds Admiral Hopwood in June, 1956,
  p. 273-285; the Fleet Review in San Francisco Harbor,
  p. 278-9; Dennison builds an image of the 2nd Fleet as an
  operating force, p. 278-281; the golf team and the matches,
  p. 281-4; p. 285.
FISHER, Adrian: counsel at the State Department - his role
  in clearance of the Forrestal papers (diaries), p. 116-7.
FOLEY, Kate: Secretary to Mr. Forrestal, p. 113-4; Secretary
  to Mr. John Sullivan, p. 187.
FORRESTAL, The Hon. James: Secretary of the Navy, approves of
  plan to create office of Asst. CNO for Political and

Military Affairs, p. 96-7; Dennison becomes political-military advisor to Forrestal, p. 98; p. 101; p. 107; an illustration of Dennison's job, p. 108-9. Truman asks for his resignation, p. 111-13; Dennison's story of the taking of the Forrestal papers from the Pentagon to the White House, p. 113 ff; Truman and Dennison visit him in Bethesda hospital two days before his death, p. 114-5; Dennison advises Forrestal on several occasions about keeping marines on the Shantung Peninsula, p. 124 p. 127; p. 184; p. 190-1; p. 193. (SEE ALSO- entry under FORRESTAL PAPERS).

FORRESTAL LIBRARY- Princeton University: repository of the Forrestal Papers, p. 117-8.

FORRESTAL PAPERS (DIARIES): the story of the Forrestal papers, p. 113-118.

FOSKETT, Captain James: served briefly as a naval aide to President Truman, p. 146.

GALVAO, Enrique: Portuguese "bandit" who had seized the SS SANTA MARIA, p. 372-3; p. 376-7.

GATES, The Hon. Artemis: goes to Far East on reparations mission in place of Secretary Forrestal, p. 119 ff.

GATES, The Hon. Thomas: Secretary of Defense - his decision to assign the POLARIS subs to CINC LANT, p. 322.

"GENERAL MOTORS" PICNIC - at Quantico, p. 320.

GERMAN Post-War NAVY: p. 470-1.

GLASSFORD, Vice Admiral W.A. Jr.: Adm Hart turns over his command in Java to Glassford, p. 31; Glassford, p. 31; Glassford names Dennison as his chief of staff, p.32; leaves by plane for Freemantle when the Japanese invaded the island, p.33; p. 42-3; Glassford in Freemantle, p 51-2.

GUANTANAMO, Cuba: Dennison's concern over a possible Cuban attack on, p. 330 ff; Castro's efforts at harrassment, p. 402-4; Adlai Stevenson's suggestion that we return the base to the Cubans, p. 405; p. 444-6; p. 449; p. 454.

HAITI: story of Dennison's visit there in Dec. 1961, p. 458 ff; a stand-by force of Navy units and Marines ordered there because of disorders (1962), p. 459.

HARDY, Porter: p. 156.

HART, Admiral Thomas C.: Commander of Asiatic Fleet - thought Japanese war would break out in September, 1941, p. 18; consultation with Adm. Tom Phillips, p.20 detaches Dennison from the DD John D. Ford for duty on his staff and as senior patrol officer in Manila, p. 23; his reaction to the news that Gen. MacArthur was declaring Manila an open city, p. 26-27; his departure from Manila, p.27; his concern for personnel left behind, p. 29; his parting gift to Dennison of his binoculars, p. 29; sends for Dennison in Java but by time Dennison arrives he had turned over command to Adm. Glassford, p. 31; Dennison on Adm. Hart, p. 39; p. 90; p. 189.

HEINL, Col. Robert D. Jr. (USMC): attached to the
    diplomatic mission in Haiti (1961), p. 450.

HELFRICH, Admiral (Dutch): takes over from Admiral Hart
    in command of naval forces - ABDAcommand), p. 31, p. 33.

HOGLE, RADM R.D.: p. 423, p. 425.

HOLLOWAY, Admiral James L. Jr.: in command of the relief
    operation into Lebanon, p. 296-7.

USS HOUSTON: flagship of Admiral Hart, p. 34.

IBERLANT: p. 310-11; p. 313.

USS INDEPENDENCE: p. 354p. 357.

INTER-AMERICAN DEFENSE BOARD: p. 464-5.

INTER-AMERICAN TREATY OF RECIPROCAL ASSISTANCE: (1947)
    reception for the delegates on board the BB MISSOURI,
    p. 134-5.

JAPAN: U. S. plans for invasion of the homeland, p. 83-6.
    post war attitude of her people, p. 120.

JAPANESE EXPECTATIONS: p. 18-19 ff.

USS JOHN D. FORD: Dennison ordered to command her with the
    Asiatic Fleet, p. 12, p. 21.

JOHNSON, The Hon. Louis: Relieves Forrestal as Secretary of
    Defense, p. 112. his cancellation of the contract for the
    CV UNITED STATES - resulting resignation of Secretary
    John Sullivan, p. 186-7; felt need for a Deputy SecDef,
    p. 191-2; his budget cutting proclivities, p. 192-3;
    Dennison discounts a current story about Johnson's

appointment to succeed Forrestal, p. 193; his attempt to strike Adm. Burke's name from the selection list, p. 194; p. 200; his naming of Matthews to succeed Sullivan as SecNav, p. 195; his role in the resignation of CNO Denfeld, p. 200-203.

JOHNS HOPKINS UNIVERSITY: Dennison begins his studies there (1934) for doctorate in engineering, p. 6 ff.

JOINT CHIEFS OF STAFF: Dennison comes back from Alaskan campaign to serve on Joint War Plans Committee of JCS, p. 68-75; the plan for the invasion of Japan, p. 70-1; MacArthur and island hopping, p. 71-2; method of procedure in planning, p. 71-2; question of need to invade Japan, p. 84 ff; question of Russian entry into Pacific War, p. 86 ff; manner in which chiefs dealt with some of offbeat ideas presented by FDR and Churchill, p. 89-91. General Bradley becomes the first Chairman of the JCS - Adm. Leahy whom he succeeded had carried the title of Chief of Staff to the Commander-in Chief, p. 175-6. roll of JCS in BAY OF PIGS Operation - see entries under BAY OF PIGS and General LEMNITZER: see also entries under CUBAN MISSILE CRISIS.

KENNEDY, The Hon. John F.: an incident involving former Presidents Truman and Eisenhower who attended his funeral, p. 220-3; p 334; p. 357; p. 359-60; p. 368; p. 387-8; speaks to the Nation on the build up of Russian missiles in Cuba, p. 394-5; his role in the crisis, p. 397 ff; p. 413-414p. Dennison's meeting with, Oct.21, 1962, p. 421; the President's remarks at Fort Stewart after the crisis was over, p. 440-1.

KENNEDY, Robert: serves on the Taylor committee to investigate BUMPY ROAD, p. 368-9.

KEY WEST QUARTERS for President Truman (Little White House): p. 167 ff; Dennison sees to its redocoration, p. 168-9; life at Key West, p. 168-174.

KING, Fleet Admiral Ernest: p. 67-8; on the JCS, p. 69; characterization of, p. 72-3; his responsibility for shifting war emphasis to Pacific, p. 73-4; an incident from his retirement, p. 74.5.

KINKAID, Admiral Thomas C.: p.67.

KISKA: p. 62.3.

KOREA: see entries under GENERAL MAC ARTHUR and PRESIDENT TRUMAN.

KRUSHCHEV, Nikita S.: Russian Premier: see entries under CUBAN MISSILE CRISIS.

LaGUARDIA, The Hon. Fiorello: p. 14. his interest in the S-4 and the SS service, p. 14; pressea a bill in Congress for extra pay, P. 15.

LANDRY, Major General Robert B.: Air Force aide to President Truman, p. 146-7.

LEAHY, Fleet Admiral Wm.: p.69; his way of dealing with members of the Joint Chiefs, p. 70; p. 72-3; his view of the proposed invasion of Japanese mainland, P. 83-4;

on board the BB MISSOURI with President Truman - he is the Senior Shellback, p. 140; he leaves the White House staff, p. 175-7; serves as continuity at time Truman assumes the presidency, p. 224; p. 227; once told Forrestal that the Joint Chiefs would have nothing to do with budget matters for the services, p. 253; p. 267.

LEBANON CRISIS: p. 296-7.

LEMNITZER, General Lyman L.: p. 291. p. 332, p. 337; p. 346; p. 351; p. 369.

LITTLE WHITE HOUSE - see entry under KEY WEST QUARTERS - PRESIDENT TRUMAN.

LONG BEACH PARAPLEGICS HOSPITAL: p. 161; Truman names Dennison to head a committee for investigation of proposed closing of the hospital, p. 161-2.

MAC ARTHUR, General Douglas: Dennison (on Hart's staff) is designated as contact with MacArthur, p. 23-4; MacArthur's cooperation with Dennison as the liaison, p. 25; MacArthur and the air raid on Cavite, p. 25-26; announces that he is declaring Manila an open city - Hart's consternation, p. 26; details to Dennison on his plans for the army, p. 30-31; his mistake in leaving bombers on Clark Field, p. 35; p. 36; Gen. Bradley on MacArthur, p. 37-8; p. 40-41; p.71; p.91-92; the story of the President (Truman) and the General - their meeting on Wake Island, p. 211 ff; MacArthur returns to the U. S., p. 215 ff.

MAGIC CARPET: attitude of the U. S. Army on the Chinese mainland, p. 125.

MALTA: p. 244, p.249; desire to belong to NATO, p. 249-50.

MANDATED ISLANDS - Pacific: struggle of the U.S. in United Nations to get a Trusteeship, p. 100-4.

USS MARBLEHEAD: p. 43.

MARINE CORPS: story of President Truman and the Marine Corps, p. 203-211.

MARITIME AFFAIRS: Truman names his naval aide to coordinate matters for the Executive Branch, p. 154 ff; practice discontinued when the Truman Administration went out, p. 225; p. 236-7.

MARSHALL, General George C.: the cause of a falling out between Eisenhower and Truman, p. 152; Truman consults him about the relieving of MacArthur, p. 124; Truman names him as SecDef after Louis Johnson, p. 232-3.

SS MARUCLA: the only merchant ship actually boarded by the U. S. in the Missile Crisis, p. 429-30.

MASSIVE RETALIATION: Doctrine of, p. 258-9; p. 268-270.

MATTHEWS, The Hon. Francis P. - Secretary of the Navy: successor to John Sullivan, p. 194-5; his role in attempting to prevent selection of Arleigh Burke, p. 194-200; his part in the dismissal of Louis Denfeld, p. 200-203; asks Dennison to sit in on preparation of the Denfeld speech to Congressional Committee, p. 200-1.

McCONE, John: Director of the C.I.A. at time of the Missile Crisis, p. 398; his role in intelligence gathering in Cuba, p. 388-9; p. 413.

McDonald, The Hon. David: McNamara considers his appointment
    as CNO - asks advice of Dennison and Burke, p. 392-3.

MCDONOUGH, The Hon. Gordon, M.C.: Congressman to whom
    Truman write about the Marine Corps p. 204.

McNAMARA, The Hon. Robert: Secretary of Defense - invites
    Dennison to stay on as CincLant, p. 390-1; asks
    Dennison's advice on a successor to Admiral George
    Anderson, p. 392-3.

USS MISSOURI- BB: Nimitz gives Dennison command, p. 108;
    the story of his command period, p. 131 ff; the mission
    of the MISSOURI to Rio de Janeiro to pick up President
    Truman and his party, p. 133-6; good conduct on the part
    of the crew in Rio, p. 136-7; the ceremony in crossing
    the Equator, p. 140-1; the presidential party, p. 141-
    3; p. 234-5.

MONROE DOCTRINE: p. 259p. 264.; p. 460.

MOUNTBATTEN, Admiral (Lord) Louis: p. 244; the Task Force of
    the 6th Fleet fires a salute to Mountbatten in the Sea of
    Marmora, p. 246.

NATIONALIST CHINA: Discussion of our policy towards, p. 265-8.

NATIONAL SECURITY ACT - 1958 amendments, p. 289-290.

NATIONAL SECURITY AGENCY: outgrowth of the Committee of Three -
    eventually becomes statutory agency -- the CIA, p. 100.

NATO: p. 307-311; De Gaulle and NATO, p. 311-312.

USS NAUTILUS: Dennison offered command after duty at
    Electric Boat - asks instead for DD command, p. 16-17.

NAVAL AIDE TO PRESIDENT TRUMAN: p. 144-5; p. 152-3;
Truman names Dennison to coordinate maritime affairs for
the Executive Branch, p. 156; the investigation of the
Veteran's Administration, p. 161-2; the WILLIAMSBURG, p. 163-
164; emergency plans for the Executive, p. 164-5-6; the
"Little White House" at Key West, p. 167 ff; takes over
briefing the President as a task once performed by Admiral
Leahy, p. 175 ff; briefs the President on Joint Chiefs
of Staff material, AEC matters, etc.. p. 176 ff; Dennison
is careful about giving his reactions to the President
on various subjects, p. 180-1;

NAVAL EXPERIMENTAL STATION - Annapolis: Dennison there
(1933-35) as Superintendent of the mechanical engineering
laboratory, p.6

U. S. NAVAL FORCES - WEST AUSTRALIA: a new command set up
in 1942 with Adm. Rockwell in command, p. 52-3.

NICARAGUA: p. 356; one lesson learned by U. S. in Nicaragua -
easier to establish a military government than to extricate
ourselves from responsibility afterwards, p. 458-9.

NIMITZ, Fleet Admiral C. W.: his response to BuOrd on 14
inch shore bombardment shells, p. 58; anger over communication from Adm. Rockwell, p. 60-2; p. 64; struggle
in subcommittee on the Far East (JCS) to get permission
for Nimitz to sign surrender document, p. 91-2; p. 94;
Nimitz approves of charter and spade work of Dennison
to set up a job as Asst. CNO for Political and Military

Affairs, p. 96-7; p. 107-8; Nimitz wants to assign negro for duty on BB MISSOURI, p. 234-6. reviews the 2nd Fleet in San Francisco Harbor when Dennison is in command, p. 279-80.

ORGANIZATION OF AMERICAN STATES: Their backing of the U. S. in the Cuban Missile Crisis, p. 430-2. Dennison attends several meetings while serving as CincLant - his comments, p. 461-2; attitude of the several navies towards each other and the U. S., p. 462-3; the Amity cruises, p. 463-4.

PANAMA CANAL: p. 432-3.

USS PAULDING: fueling incident that came to the attention of Admiral Hart, p. 21.

PAULEY, The Hon. Ed.: p. 115; his trip to the Far East in the interests of post war reparations, p. 119 ff; p. 193.

PENNSYLVANIA STATE UNIVERSITY: Dennison as an engineering student goes from P.G. school to Penn State, p.5, p.8 p. 11.

PHILIPPINES: p. 18 ff.

USS PILLSBURY: rejects proposed course outlined for her from Java to Australia - is sunk by Japanese force, p. 42-3.

PLANS AND POLICY - Deputy CNO: Dennison relieves Adm. Libby in 1958 and serves until end of March, 1959, p. 286; Dennison's views on essentiality of dealing with opposite numbers in other services, p. 286-8; comments on contingency plans, p. 296-7.

POLARIS: p. 268-270; p. 272; story of how POLARIS submarines were put under the command of CONC LANT, p. 319 ff; the nature of the command, p. 323-5; Dennison's use of the command procedure for the benefit of President Kennedy and his party, p. 325-7; Dennison takes operational control of POLARIS in September, 1960, p. 473-5.

POLITICAL AND MILITARY AFFAIRS: establishment of the office of Assistant CNO for, p. 94 ff; some of the immediate problems the navy had to deal with, p. 95-6.

PROTUGAL: p. 308-310.

POST GRADUATE SCHOOL: Dennison goes (1928) - his thesis deals with a determination of a laboratory method to predict engine knocking tendencies in gasoline, p. 4-5.

POWELL, General Herbert B.: Cinc. Continental Command (1962)- army component under unified command of CincLant, p. 400; p. 415; p. 423.

PUERTO RICAN NAVAL BASES: (Culebra and Vieques), p. 446-7.

QUARANTINE: See entries under CUBAN MISSILE CRISIS.

QUEMOY AND MATSU- Offshore Islands: our position there - the opinion of Dennison and of the Taiwanese Defense Minister, p. 265-6; p. 299-300.

RACIAL ISSUES: Adm. Nimitz raises question of a negro officer for the BB MISSOURI, p. 234-5.

RADFORD, Admiral Arthur: his role in B-36 controversy, p. 200 ff; p. 212.

RAINBOW Five: a US-British war plan for the Far East, p. 20; plan was killed with the loss of the PRINCE OF WALES and the REPULSE, p. 34.

REID, Mrs. Helen Ogden: her purchase of the Forrestal papers, p. 115-8.

REPARATIONS COMMISSION ON JAPAN: discussion of question with the Chinese, p. 119-123.

RESERVES- Mobilization of: President Kennedy calls for mobilization because of the Berlin crisis (July, 1961), p. 382-6; Dennison visits a reserve DD and talks with the officers, p. 383-4; mobilization works a hardship on young reserves, p. 384.

RICKETTS, VADM Claude V.: Dennison and Burke both propose him to McNamara as successor to Adm. George Anderson, p. 392-3.

ROBERTSON, The Hon. Walter: U. S. Ambassador to Chiang in Chungking, p. 121.

ROCKEFELLER, John D. III p. 132.

ROCKWELL, Rear Admiral F.W.: Commander of the Naval District - given command by Hart of remaining fleet units in Manila area, p. 28-9; p. 30; comes to Australia with Gen. MacArthur - in command of Naval Forces, West Australia, p. 52-3; takes over as Comdr. Amphibious Force, Pacific Fleet, based at San Diego with Dennison as Chief of Staff, p. 53-4; sends Dennison to Pearl Harbor with letter for Admiral Nimitz, p. 60-1.

ROOSEVELT, The Hon. F.D. - President of the United States: p. 69-70, p. 80, p. 83; his desire for Russian entry into Pacific War, p. 89; off beat ideas, p. 89-91.

ROOSEVELT ROADS - see entries under Caribbean Bases.

ROSS, Charles: White House Press Secretary (1947), p. 138-9; p. 187-8; corrects error General Vaughan created with his announcement on the presidential aides, p. 197; Truman asks him for help with the Marines, p. 205; p. 206-7.

RUSK, Dr. Howard: serves on Dennison's committee to investigate the paraplegic hospital and the Veterans Administration, p. 162.

S-4: the story of her sinking off Provincetown, Mass, p. 12-15.

S-8: Dennison assigned as engineer officer, p. 2; p. 12.

SAC LANT: see entries under CONC LANT.

ST. FRANCIS HOTEL- San Francisco: p. 270, p. 281.

SANDYS, the Rt. Hon. Duncan: British Minister of Defense, p. 301-2.

SS SANTA MARIA: Portuguese cruise ship - story of her seizure by rebels - role U. S. Navy played in her recapture, p. 370-381; British and U. S. interpretation of this seizure as an Act of Piracy, p. 372, p. 376.

SHANTUNG PENINSULA: Dennison visits Gen. Lemuel Shepherd there for briefing on Washington attitudes in respect to the marines stationed in Shantung Peninsula, p. 127.

SHEPHERD, General Lemuel - U. S. Marine Corps: in command of marine contingent on the Shantung Peninsula, p. 124. P.210.

SMITH, RADM Alan Jr.: Comdr. CarSeaFrontier (Jan. 1961) involved in search for SS SANTA MARIA, p. 371-2; p. 376.

SO LANT AMITY: p. 463-4.

STATE-WAR-NAVY COORDINATING COMMITTEE: p. 97; early stage - committee of three (Secretaries of State, War Navy) - difficulties, p. 97-8; addition of Adm. Leahy this becomes National Security Agency, p. 99-100; Dennison serves on a number of subcommittees - accompanies Secretary John Sullivan to most of the meetings, p. 100; question of the Mandated Islands and the United Nations, p. 100-4; post war question of U. S. property in the Philippines, p. 104-5; other issues, p. 106-7.

STORM SURVEILLANCE SYSTEM: U. S. Navy participation, p. 472-3.

STRATEGIC PLANS DIVISION (Op. 60): Dennison takes over as Director in Jan. 1954, p. 251; purpose of Op. 60, p. 251-3; Dennison's remarks on the complexity of plans and their evolvement, p. 253-5; effort to get established a service identity for each of the unified commanders, p. 255-8; need to go back to broad government policy when engaged in service planning, p. 259-60; strategic planning and consistency in national policy, p. 261-4; the doctrine of massive retaliation and strategic planning, p. 268.

STUMP, Admiral Felix B.: p. 275-8; p. 281; p. 390.

SUBMARINES: Dennison requests training in Submarines - an early approach to command, p. 1-2; sinking of S-51 brings awareness of hazards of SS duty, p.3; sinking of the S-4, p. 12-13 ff;

SULLIVAN, The Hon. John: Secretary of the Navy, p. 110-111, p. 186; resigns his office over cancellation of the contract for the UNITED STATES, p. 187-8.

SUTHERLAND, Lt. Gen. R.K.: Chief of Staff to Gen. MacArthur, p. 31, p. 38.

SWAN ISLAND: episode, April, 1960, p. 330. its importance to the U. S. Navy as emphasized by BAY OF PIGS operation p. 447.

SWEENEY, General Walter G. Jr.: Cinc U. S. Tactical Air Command (1962) - under unified command of CincLant in the Missile Crisis, p. 400; p. 415; p. 417; p. 423.

TAYLOR, General Maxwell: President Kennedy calls him from his job in Mexico to chair a committee to investigate BUMPY ROAD, p. 368 ff; invites Dennison and his wife to dinner at Fort Meyer in order that McNamara might speak to him privately, p. 390-1.

TEREK - Soviet Sub-replenishment Ship: sighting of her off the Azores - significance, p. 434.

USS THRESHER: loss of, p. 480-1.

THURSTON, the Hon. Ray: new U. S. Ambassador to Haiti (Dec. 1961) - host to the Dennisons, p. 450; p. 453.

TITO: p. 142-3.

TJILATJAP: Dennison's account of his last hours there before escape to Australia - provision for wounded sailors from the USS MARBLEHEAD, p. 43; Dennison departs in SS, p. 44-5.

TORPEDOES: Dennison's experience in Australia, p. 59.

TOWNER, VADM George C.: Commander, Amphibious Forces, Atlantic Fleet, p. 332.

TRIESTE: Truman and his reaction to Tito's threat against Trieste, p. 142-3.

TRINIDAD: p. 448; p. 461-2.

TRUMAN, The Hon. Harry S.: his decision that Admiral King should stay at Bethesda hospital if he desired, p. 74-5; as senator, his concern for construction of ships, p. 82. orders Forrestal and Pauley on trip to Far East in the interests of reparations, p. 119 ff; p. 127. often reminded Dennison that he (Dennison) was a professional officer and not a politician, p. 152-3; his attitude towards emergency plans involving the White House p. 165-6; acquiesces in Gen. Bradley's wish to brief him on military matters, p. 177; on two occasions reads about matters in the press first - calls Bradley for explanation, p. 178-9; his description of how he arrived at a decision, p. 181-2; his delineation of the several roles he was called upon to play as President, p. 182-4; his background of knowledge, p. 184-5; his attitude towards unification, p. 189-190; on budget cutting in the Dept. of Defense, p. 192-3; his role in retaining Arleigh Burke's name on the selection list, p. 194-200; his role in the resignation of CNO Denfeld, p. 200-203; Truman and the marine corps incident, p. 203-209; asks for help with the Marines, p. 205; his trip to Wake Island the story of MacArthur and the President, p. 212ff; tells Dennison that he could have advised MacArthur about political niceties of his return to the States, p. 215-6; Truman and Eisenhower - the falling out, p. 218-220; the reconciliation, p. 220 ff; Truman's account of his take over as President after death of FDR, p. 223-4; Truman invites Eisenhower to come to the White House before assuming office, p. 224-5; Truman meetings with his staff every day, p. 226-7; his rehearsal with staff for news conferences, p. 227-9; the news conferences, p. 229-31; the end of the Truman Administration, p. 238; reassures himself that Dennison's duty with him has no adverse effect on career, p. 239-40; offers to push naming of Dennison for office of CNO with President Kennedy, p. 387-8.

TURKEY, p. 433

TYPE COMMANDS AND FLEET COMMANDS: discussion of, p. 274-6.

UNCONDITIONAL SURRENDER - as a national policy: Dennison's comments, p. 270-2.

UNIFICATION OF THE SERVICES: p. 188-9; Louis Johnson's attitude, p. 188; Truman's ideas, p. 189-190; Burke's role, p. 199-200. Dennison's description as it pertained especially to the CincLant, p. 399 ff.

UNIFIED COMMANDS: discussion of wisdom for having a service identity established for these commands, p. 255-8.

UNITED NATIONS: does not figure often in military matters, p. 304-6.

USSR - her role in the Missile Crisis, p. 394 ff.

USSR - SUBMARINES: deployment in the Cuban Missile Crisis, p. 434 ff; Deductions on the presence of Soviet Submarines in the Atlantic, p. 437.

U THANT: Secretary-General of the United Nations - his participation in the Cuban Missile Crisis, p. 430.

VARDAMAN, Commodore James K., Jr.: p. 146.

VAUGHAN, General Harry: Military aide to President Truman, p. 146; announces to press that Dennison is to be his assistant, p. 146-7; his background, p. 148-9.

U. S. VETERANS ADMINISTRATION: becomes a subject for investigation by the special committee set up by Truman and headed by Dennison, p. 162.3.

VIEQUES: a training exercise scheduled for April 15-18, 1962, p. 349; p. 446.

WARD, Admiral Alfred G.: his appointment as Commander, Second Fleet, p. 421-2; p. 432.

WARREN, The Hon. Lindsey: Comptroller General of the U. S. (1947), p. 155-6; his attitude on the maritime subsidy question, p. 155-6; p. 158-9.

WEDEMEYER, Lt. Gen. Albert: his headquarters in Shanghai, P. 126.

USS WILLIAMSBURG: Presidental yacht, p. 157; p. 163-4, p. 210

WINKLER, Bernace L.: Chief Yeoman who worked thirteen years for Adm. Dennison - worked for President Truman when he was at Key West, p. 170.

www.ingramcontent.com/pod-product-compliance
Lightning Source LLC
Chambersburg PA
CBHW082148070526
44585CB00020B/2132